NEW DIRECTIONS IN ENGLISH TEACHING

This book provides through the blending of selected published articles and specially commissioned work a perspective on the teaching of English in the 1980s. It starts by summing up the work in curriculum development in English from the mid-60s onwards — an especially formative period. It seeks to place the achievements of this period in an historical perspective and to suggest how they may be built upon to provide a focus for further developments in the future.

It examines the essential challenges to English teachers at the present time: those presented by the media; those of microtechnology; the need to reshape the examination system; the demands of helping pupils to cope with developing their own ability; and to make use of the sources of information available to them. Within this context it continues to argue the place for the central role of literature and affective education, and suggests an approach to initial and in-service education for teaching that will equip teachers to meet the needs of pupils in a rapidly changing society.

ANTHONY ADAMS is University Lecturer in Education and Director of Studies in Education, Trinity Hall, University of Cambridge. He is Chairman of the National Association for the Teaching of English. He is a prolific author and editor, writing equally for the teacher and the taught. His most recent publications include *The Humanities Jungle, English Language Teaching and Learning Across the Curriculum* and *Sixth Sense: The Teaching of English 16-19*.

NEW DIRECTIONS IN ENGLISH TEACHING

Edited & Introduced by
Anthony Adams
(University of Cambridge)

 **The Falmer Press**

A member of the Taylor and Francis Group

First published 1982

ISBN limp   0 905273 36 2
       cased 0 905273 37 0

Jacket design by Leonard Williams

Printed and bound by Taylor and Francis (Printers) Ltd
Basingstoke for

The Falmer Press
(*A member of the Taylor and Francis Group*)
Falmer House
Barcombe, Lewes
Sussex BN8 5DL
England

Contents

v

General Editor's Preface

The teaching of English is a major concern of all our schools, both primary and secondary, but in what shape is it and how is it poised, if at all, to take on new tasks critical to the development of awareness and understanding in the young in an age of rapidly evolving information technology?

It is to these key questions that this volume of collected articles, some of which have been specially written to confront emerging issues in the teaching of English, addresses itself.

With concern for the practical as well as the theoretical, Anthony Adams introduces and comments upon the trends in English teaching as they are and might become; and in so doing, he has created a reader which is as relevant to the experienced teacher as it is to the beginning teacher of English and as relevant to the primary school teacher as it is to the secondary school teacher. It is also of particular relevance to students intending to teach English at any level of schooling, especially as it is they who will carry English teaching into the next century and give to it new meaning and direction.

Philip H. Taylor
Birmingham
October 1981

Acknowledgements

The Publishers are grateful to the following for permission to reproduce copyright material:

Times Newspapers Limited for FOX, G. and MERRICK, B. Thirty-six things to do with a poem, and TAYLOR, M. and DELLER, W. Twenty-two ideas for variety in comprehension work

The Editor, *Children's Literature in Education* for FOX, G. Twenty-four things to do with a book

The Editor, *Westminster Studies in Education* for ADAMS, A. and HADLEY, E. A study in method: Some aspects of the Postgraduate Certificate in Education

The Editor, *English in Education* (NATE Publications) for WILKINSON, A. *et al* The development of writing

The Publications and Publicity Committee, Department of Education, University of Southampton for BENTON, M.G. How authors write, How Children Write: Towards a rationale for creative writing

The Editor, *Aspects of Education* for MITTENS, W.H. Modern views of English language

The Editor, *The English Magazine* for JACKSON, D. Controlling the word

Introduction: New Directions in English Teaching

The original intention of this collection of essays was to have gathered together a number of articles which had already received periodical publication. However, when I came to select the material it was quickly apparent that there was not really available much of the kind that I was seeking. A book written at the beginning of the 1980s looking towards *new* approaches to English teaching should surely concern itself with the challenges to the English curriculum presented by contemporary society. Yet, one looks in vain in the journals devoted to English teaching for any real attempt to remodel teaching to prepare our students for the final twenty years of the century and beyond. Too many of them seem still to be fighting the battles and controversies of the sixties, to be arguing, at one level, the rival claims of 'literature' and 'communication studies' to be the centre of the English programme, or, at another, the rival claims of the disciplines of 'literary criticism' or 'structuralism'. It does not seem to me that the classroom teacher of English will find much here at either a practical or theoretical level to help him remodel his curriculum for the future. We look in vain in the curriculum development of the sixties and seventies for any serious treatment of media studies in the English classroom. Film, through the efforts of a small and dedicated band, attained a certain respectability but the state of television studies in schools is still at a very low ebb. Where it is undertaken at all it is all too often still seen (as is the study of advertizing) as a matter of inoculating the students against the wickedness of the media manipulators. Yet this is, for the vast majority of our students and their parents, the major source of information and entertainment and the most immediate means they have of access to culture of any kind. Can we afford to go on in our classrooms either ignoring or scorning so potent a medium of communication? Yet, within the last six months, the Schools Council has consistently turned down the urging of its own English Committee to include something on television studies in school as part of its programmes of work, and, when I attended a recent meeting of specialists in English education in university Departments of Education specifically to discuss Len Masterman's book, *Teaching about Television*, about a third of those present were actually proud of the fact that they neither had a television set nor watched television at all regularly.

The same is true of the implications of the microprocessor and the new technology for English teaching. We are on the verge of the greatest revolution in communications since Gutenberg; we are also about to enter a period when information from data-banks is going to be readily available on a grand scale to all. Yet, schools for the most part in the United Kingdom are still very limited in the teaching of study skills and have not begun to think about the implications of the knowledge explosion for enabling students to handle the information that will become available to them.

One looks in vain in most of the periodical literature for any treatment of these and related topics. In compiling the present volume, therefore, I have found it necessary to commission especially a number of essays, such as those by Masterman and Chandler, and, through them, to suggest some of the new approaches and the expansion of the English curriculum that will be necessary if we are to continue to do a worthwhile job in English teaching in the closing years of the century. Unless we do this I would predict that by the year 2000 English teaching in our schools will be in the same position of decline as the teaching of classical studies today. The world will have passed it by and what we have traditionally thought of as English studies, the subject of the battles of the sixties that we are still fighting and that are ably chronicled in Allen's *English Teaching since 1965: How Much Growth?*[1], will become the preserve of an eccentric few.

As this introduction is being written we are engaged in the consultation stage which is to lead to the new single examination system at 16 +, the General Certificate of Secondary Education. The report from the English working party of the Joint Council of GCE and CSE Boards is disappointing in its almost total failure to do anything to break the mould of the past. We are to have two optional alternatives: *English* and *English Language*, alongside each of which students may also take a subject called *English Literature*. What kind of single examination system is this? Clearly the present O-level entry will now be entered for *English Language* and *English Literature* while the current CSE entry will be entered for *English* alone, and this will inevitably become a more low status examination in the eyes of employers, selectors for higher and further education and the like. But the problem is more serious than this: it lies at the heart of the proposed contents of the new examination. We look in vain for the inclusion of considerations such as those advanced in the opening of this introduction, the 'assessment objectives' are defined in such terms as to mark no real departure from the English curriculum of the past. Candidates will be expected:

In a subject carrying the title 'ENGLISH' or 'ENGLISH LANGUAGE'
(a) To demonstrate the following receptive skills in speech and writing:
   (i)   understanding of information;
   (ii) selection and evaluation, where appropriate, of relevant material;

     (iii) recognition of underlying meaning and perception of tone, mood and style.

  (b) to produce appropriate speech and writing which—

     (i) conveys information;

     (ii) presents ideas and opinions;

     (iii) expresses experience and feelings.

In a subject carrying the title 'ENGLISH LITERATURE' to demonstrate:

     (i) close reading and first-hand knowledge of texts;

     (ii) the ability to communicate sensitive and informed personal response;

     (iii) understanding and appreciation of authors' use of characterisation, narrative, plot, setting, description and language.

Clearly these objectives are very wide ranging and they *might* be interpreted in such a way as to make possible within the English curriculum the incorporation of the kind of considerations mentioned above, but, so far, the discussions to which I have been party suggest that they are to be interpreted in a very narrow and traditional way as is indicated especially in the definition of the objectives for *English Literature* which seem like the present O-level Literature paper all over again. In particular, the GCE Boards have shown themselves to be very lukewarm about the inclusion of spoken English as part of the new examination procedure in spite of the known fact that spoken English skills are those most needed by the average 16 + school leaver on entering employment.

It is not that these proposals are particularly pernicious; rather, they, like so much of the current writing in periodicals and so much of the curriculum development programmes of the Schools Council, are disappointingly tame; there is no vision of preparing students in school for the work and the world they are likely to be living in at the end of the century. It is symptomatic of yet another opportunity that has been missed. We should never forget that those students whom we shall be training to teach English in the year 2000 are already in the infant schools today. How far are we remaking the curriculum to meet their needs?

In selecting and commissioning the material for this book, therefore, I have tried to point the way towards the necessary rethinking of what we are doing in the English classroom. Because of the different curriculum structures of primary and secondary schools the bulk of the contents seems to have a secondary orientation though this is not through intention or design. In fact, many of the ideas promoted in the articles have as much relevance to junior school teaching as to secondary although there (perhaps more happily) they may flourish in an interdisciplinary context. But the first time I actually saw a microprocessor being used in a school and the first time I saw children making television for themselves was, in both instances, in an infant school. There may be lessons for us here. It may be easier to break the mould of the curriculum in such a context and further away from the constraints of the 'reformed' 16 + examination.

In looking towards the end of the century I would identify the following challenges to the teacher of English.

1 *The Challenge of New Content*

Some of the implications regarding content have already been outlined above. But the new content will also have to be related to changing conditions in society, especially the likelihood of continuing unemployment. We are likely to see a further movement away from manufacturing industries in this country (for which our present curriculum was explicitly designed) towards an economy which places much more emphasis upon caring and service industries, and for this very different kinds of skill will be needed such as adaptability, articulacy, the ability to work in groups and the ability to select, retrieve and use information. We should ask whether the content of our present curriculum goes anywhere near enough to providing our school-leavers with these skills and attitudes. Above all it is still based primarily upon an epistemological model that thinks of knowledge in terms of transmission rather than in terms of something that each generation has to make for itself. Yet the latter is necessary if we are to generate as products from our schools young people who are adaptable and, above all, capable of being re-educated throughout their lives. In the past we have been able to assume that the world would remain more or less the same as the one in which we had ourselves grown up; we could thus legitimately see the task of education as passing on to the next generation the inherited wisdom of the elders of the tribe. This is no longer the case. The one thing that we must educate the next generation for is a world of uncertainty and change. This will mean in our English teaching a much greater stress on those things that call for working together in groups, that challenge our thinking, that require divergent rather than convergent approaches, that refuse to take anything for granted. The real importance of the new technology for the English teacher is the opportunity it offers to open up new areas of experience, to break with a traditional curriculum that is being taught for no other reason than that it has always been taught.

2 *The Challenge of Developing Study Skills*

Six years after the publication of the Bullock Report,[2] we are still woefully inadequate in our schools in giving pupils the ability to learn. This is, perhaps, especially true in secondary schools. Too few have heeded the words of Bullock that 'we are all of us learning to read all of the time' and, in spite of the important theoretical work on the reading process that has been done by Lunzer and Gardner and by the Open University. it is still too little known and too little applied in our schools. Many of our pupils leave school unable to make effective use of a library, much less more

modern and complex methods of information retrieval. A recent Schools
Council publication emphasizes this point:[3]

> Never before has so much information been available to so many,
> and never before have our lives depended so much on our ability
> to handle information successfully. We need to be able to search
> out what we require, to assess critically the ideas and facts offered
> to us, and to make use of our findings . . . . And yet schools, which
> are concerned with learning above all else, find great difficulty in
> teaching pupils *how* to learn. Although some pupils are able to use
> the full range of learning resources which the school can offer,
> most are not, and it is a central responsibility of the school to help
> its pupils cope with learning.

Anyone who spends any length of time in North American classrooms is
struck by the much greater attention given there to helping students
acquire the tools of learning so that they can find out and process information for themselves.

Of course there are some (amongst them some of my own students,
English teachers in training) who would affirm that, important though this
may be, it is not part of the responsibility of the English teacher. But it has
to be *someone's* responsibility and, in present circumstances, if it is not
taken on board by the English department it is unlikely to be dealt with by
anyone else. Helping students to become competent learners for themselves
seems to me an inescapable part of the English curriculum for the eighties.

3 *The Challenge of Education for Leisure*

One of the consequences of the economic changes in society is certainly
going to be greater leisure for many people. We may be wise enough to
replace *unemployment* with a measure of *underemployment*, but, in any case,
we shall certainly see further developments in the direction of early retire-
ment schemes and shorter working weeks. In this context helping people
to have the interests and skills to fill their leisure time constructively
becomes of fundamental importance. Work, for many, serves a variety of
functions, one of the most important being association with others, the
engagement together in common pursuits. This means that in the English
curriculum we need to place more emphasis on educating students in the
social and cultural skills that enable them to work creatively with and
alongside others. It should place drama and the related arts firmly in the
centre of both what we teach and the way we go about the teaching. In a
time of increased voluntary or enforced leisure the affective and the creative
should be at the very heart of curriculum planning. (And there is not, as
some have from time to time sought to suggest, any necessary dichotomy
between this and the need for cognitive and study skills such as have been
discussed above.) But in recent pronouncements on curriculum planning
we look in vain for any central place being ascribed to the arts in education.

5

The Government's own publication from the Department of Education and Science puts them very firmly in their (subordinate) place:

> ... there should be substantial common elements. These should include English and mathematics, whose vital importance schools already recognise in the time and attention they devote to them. To these should be added science, religious education and physical education; in addition, pupils should undertake *some study of the humanities* designed to yield lasting benefit *and should retain opportunities* for *some* practical and *some* aesthetic activity.[4]

It is, at least, some improvement on its predecessor, the now notorious *A Framework for the School Curriculum*,[5] recognizing some place for the arts and aesthetic education, but it is a grudging and meagre mention nonetheless.

I have written elsewhere about what I have called a 'celebratory' approach to English teaching in which I have advanced the idea that it is through making and doing with others that much of the students' most valuable experience with literature will be found. That to produce a play, to mount a poetry and song ensemble, to present a carefully chosen set of slides to accompany a sequence of poetry readings, to dramatize a short story or present a rehearsed studio reading is the best way to motivate and to enable pupils to engage with the text. Recently Lorac and Weiss have shown some of the further advantages of this approach across a wide range of subjects and, most importantly, have demonstrated that the learning that takes place in such cases is a learning about relationships with others as much as about the ostensible subject matter with which the students engage.[6] If we are to take seriously the implications of education for leisure in the English curriculum it is this kind of learning that will have to take precedence in the schools of the future. In this case we shall also have to think about necessary reforms in teacher training so that students preparing to become teachers learn to develop themselves and their own awarenesses in similar ways. We shall have to move away from an over instrumental and mechanical view of what it means to learn to teach. In this collection of articles my colleague, Eric Hadley, in a specially written contribution indicates some of the implications for the educator of the English teacher and takes further in a more specific direction some of the ideas we explore together in *A Study in Method*.[7]

4 *The Challenge of Institutional Change*

The one thing that is certain about the schools of the year 2000 is that they will have to be very different places from the institutions we have now. We have much to learn from the alternative school movement, both in this country and abroad. Dale Shuttleworth, who was responsible for ten years for the development of a system of alternative schools under the Toronto

Board of Education, is quoted in *The Times Educational Supplement* (2 October 1981) on the paramount need for change:

> Unless we change our schools, we shall soon be bypassed. IBM and Westinghouse have plenty of programs coming along to 'educate' kids. The 'content' side of education can be provided on videotape and education can be provided on videotape and by computer. If the schools don't change, less and less money will be voted to the state school system—and commercial interests—possibly through the vouchure system—will dominate the education of the future. Until teachers realise that they have to become masters of process—how you learn, how you relate to others—and are seen to be expert in this, a takeover of education by big business will remain a danger.

Interestingly enough these words are almost an exact echo of a talk I heard given last summer by an HMI considering the future of schools as institutions and its implications for the English teacher. This will mean the need for fundamental change in the relationship between the school and its immediately local community—'City as School' in the heart of New York City takes the whole of the city as its campus and resource, following on from the pioneer work of the Parkway School (the 'School without Walls') in Philadelphia. This, too, is the pattern on which many of the Toronto alternative schools have been based. We have already, in this country, a number of schools which have begun to explore these ways of working in the British context, schools like Stantonbury Campus and Countesthorpe College which have taken the first faltering steps towards exploring what schools of the future might look like. The alternative is the stark one presented in the opening quotation from Asimov's short story, *The Fun They Had*, with which Daniel Chandler begins his article in this collection. For English teaching this means more involvement with the local community both as a resource (libraries, museums, people with skills or interesting stories to tape record or write up) and as a collaborator in community based projects such as access television, community newspapers, local bookshops, and community drama.

If schools are to survive as institutions they will have to become more 'open' institutions, forging a new set of relationships with the communities they serve, educating retired and prematurely retired adults alongside the school-pupil so that 'éducation permanente' becomes a reality, and placing much more responsibility for their learning in the hands of the students themselves. Ted Hopkin and I have recently argued the case for the tertiary college at 16 + and our arguments for 'collegiality', a contractual relationship between learner and teaching institution, have numerous implications for schooling up to the age of 16 also.[8]

All of this is going to demand great reserves of resiliance and willingness to adapt from the teachers. It means, too, that in teacher training we have to train teachers to be ready to accept and to accelerate change rather than to accept the situation in the schools as they find it. The hope behind this collection of articles is that it will point some of the ways forward. None of the contributors would claim to be especially gifted in the art of predicting the future; their brief was to write about things that were of importance to them in the English curriculum now. But, in assembling these contributions into a volume, I have been struck by how much they point the way towards beginning to meet some of the challenges I have identified above, something I try to point up in some of the introductory sections to the essays themselves. The collection is largely one that illustrates the best of current thought and practice in 1980 and 1981; the hope is that it may give us some insights that will prepare us for the practice of 1990 and the year 2000.

Notes

1 ALLEN, DAVID (1980) *English Teaching since 1965: How Much Growth?*, Heinemann.

2 BULLOCK REPORT (1975) *A Language for Life*, DES.

3 SCHOOLS COUNCIL (1981) *Information Skills in the Secondary Curriculum*, Methuen Educational.

4 DEPARTMENT OF EDUCATION AND SCIENCE (1981) *The School Curriculum*, HMSO, p. 13 (author's emphasis).

5 DEPARTMENT OF EDUCATION AND SCIENCE (1980) *A Framework for the School Curriculum*, HMSO.

6 LORAC, C., and WEISS, M. (1981) *Communication and Social Skills*, Wheaton.

7 ADAMS, ANTHONY, and HADLEY, ERIC (1980) *A Study in Method*, Westminster Studies in Education.

8 HOPKIN, TED, and ADAMS, ANTHONY (1981) *Sixth Sense*, Blackie.

1
Language

Introduction

One of the permanently valuable developments of the sixties and seventies has been the growing awareness amongst English teachers of the theoretical work that has been done on language and the development, in consequence, of much greater understanding of the value of the language which the pupils themselves bring to school. Books like Wilkinson's *The Foundations of Language*[1] and Halliday's *Explorations in the Functions of Language*[2] have enabled a new generation of English teachers to be more aware of linguistic complexity and less prescriptive than in the past.

But, in spite of this, there are still many myths about language that persist in the minds of many teachers. Our judgement of language is as much a matter of attitude as anything else. In *Attitudes to English Usage*,[3] Bill Mittins describes a revealing piece of research which explored the attitudes of a number of respondents to disputed items of English usage. Each of the fifty or so items is discussed in detail and Dr Mittins brings to bear on the issues a unique blend of linguistic knowledge and sturdy common sense. It seems appropriate, therefore, to begin with an article written as long ago as 1966 by Bill Mittins in which he sought to provide for teachers some account of modern views of the English language. He has been kind enough to add a specially written addendum in which he looks back at his article from the standpoint of 1981. David Jackson's article explores from a practical classroom standpoint some of the implications of our discovery of 'the sheer energy of the vernacular voice' and 'the developing awareness that comes with controlling your own experience through your own language'. The two together represent a position that would hardly have been possible in the classrooms of 1960 and also point towards the kind of language work in schools that we might hope to see in the 1980s and beyond.

Notes

1 WILKINSON (1971) *The Foundations of Language*, Oxford.
2 HALLIDAY (1973) *Explorations in the Functions of Language*, Oxford.
3 MITTINS, BILL (1970) *Attitudes to English Usage*, Oxford.

Modern Views of English Language[*]

Bill Mittins
Formerly Lecturer in Education,
University of Newcastle upon Tyne

No one expects or wants all teachers of English to teach the same things in the same way. But the area of reasonable tolerance seems quite insufficient to contain the many differences that tend to split the subject into fragments. The catalogue of unanswered basic questions is far too long for comfort: In what sense, if any, is it a 'subject' at all? Is it one subject or two? What are the relationships between language and literature, language-study and language-use, speech and writing, 'standard English' and dialect? Is there such a thing as correct English?—and so on. We do not need final answers to these questions, but we do need enough agreement to provide a framework within which theory and practice can co-operate systematically and purposefully.

Some teachers, failing to find an internal unifying principle, seek an external one by orienting themselves towards examinations. At worst, such an orientation extends a baleful influence from testing to teaching and from limited candidate-groups to whole school-populations; at best, it is dubiously preferable to no orientation at all. Other teachers organize their work round the study of grammar or literature. Neither of these last two can be expected to unify the English programme as a whole. Each occupies only part of the territory. Grammar is partial in the sense that, though it concerns all language, it is essentially a study of it rather than an activity in it, and as a study is perhaps proper only to older and abler minorities. Literature is partial in that, though relevant (and most valuably so) to all pupils, it is but one of a range of language activities. It is 'only literature against the background of the language as a whole'.[1]

Any unifying conception must embrace not only grammar and literature, but also many other linguistic or partially linguistic operations, such as— to name only a few of the more familiar ones—creative writing, conversation, newspaper-reading, analysis of advertizements, drama. It must be based, in fact, on a definition of 'English' as broad as 'any piece of human

[*]This article was first published in (1966) *Aspects of Education 4—The New Look in English Teaching*, Institute of Education, University of Hull.

behaviour that is clearly meaningful language, whether spoken or written, and which is not any language *other* than English'.[2] This definition comes from a writer on linguistics (a 'linguistician', though the less cumbersome 'linguist' is preferable where—as in this article—it is clear that fluency in foreign languages is not the topic). Since all 'English' is language activity, it is reasonable to ask whether linguistics, the study of language, can offer teachers of English a view of language conducive to unity and direction in their total work.

Before venturing an affirmative answer, one needs—at the risk of seeming over-cautious—to make several reservations. The first is that, as a comprehensive rigorous science, linguistics is very young. Its youth, however, has not protected it from vigorous attack; Barzun, for example, has blamed 'modern linguists' (i.e., linguisticians) for developments by which 'in one generation grammar has been uprooted and pedantic fantasies about teaching the mother tongue have been made to seem liberal and advanced'.[3] There would be no point in countering this denunciation with an equally dogmatic affirmation. I would merely suggest that there is a prima facie case for taking modern linguistics seriously enough to see whether it can contribute towards the comprehensive rationale that English teaching needs but lacks. Taking it seriously involves concessions to youth, to differences reflected in rival schools and rival terminologies. One of the most intractable problems—the role of 'meaning'—seems to be reaching resolution, with those who tried to insist on the complete exclusion of semantic factors yielding to those who allow meaning a respectable if restricted part in methods of analysis. But there remain other areas of variation; for instance, hardly have we got used to the 'new' structural grammar when we are confronted with a 'newer' transformational-generative grammar.

A second caveat is that linguistics exists, of course, in its own right. Any help that teachers of English (or for that matter teachers of foreign languages, communication theorists, or machine translators) may get from it is secondary to its main purpose. It is possible to arrange the various branches of linguistics in a sequence leading towards teaching—from general linguistics through applied linguistics (the study of particular languages) to comparative or contrastive linguistics (the analysis of resemblances and differences between languages). But it remains the educationist's job (sometimes called 'methodics') to work out the actual teaching implications. It does not follow, however, that, because linguistics is more or less distant from actual lessons or because it has relevancies to other operations than the teaching of English, it cannot provide 'English' with a unifying principle. It may well do that from a position '*behind* the classroom teacher, in the training that he received for his job as a teacher, in the preparation of the syllabus according to which his teaching programme is organised, and in the preparation of the teaching materials of all kinds that he makes use of in class'.[4]

A third—and last—cautionary point is that knowledge of linguistics no more guarantees success in language teaching than ignorance ensures failure. As in all teaching, theory does not always or necessarily correlate with practice. Nevertheless, at a time when better English teaching is both demanded and in some ways impeded by social and technological developments, we ignore at our peril the possibility that language theory can help.

By providing a new description of language, linguistic studies have a direct and explicit bearing on the teaching of grammar. But since grammar of any kind is not taught to all and in any case is only one aspect of language, it is appropriate to examine first the less obvious but broader and probably more important bearing of linguistics on general conceptions and attitudes. Traditionally teachers have tended to treat language as if it were a set of facts more or less separable from experience. The newer view regards it as form rather than substance, as 'patterned social behaviour'[5] operating meaningfully in social situations. The great variety of possible situations is matched by a great variety of kinds of language. There are many Englishes, and to disentangle them requires more and better sets of distinctions than the familiar old ones. Much linguistic thought is devoted to the working out of such distinctions. A simple example is the replacement of the rather crude prose/verse classification by a threefold prose/verse/conversation division, recognizing that 'writing is a device for recording prose, not conversation'.[6] The popular contrast between dialect and standard English is refined similarly, by subdividing speakers of the latter according to whether they have an 'accent' or speak in Received Pronunciation (RP).

Differentiation by dialect and accent focuses primarily on the speaker or *user*—his living-place, social and educational status, etc. Another scale can be devised in terms of *use*, or area of discourse; this scale identifies, for instance, the 'registers' of scientific English, legal English, advertizing English, English for addressing babies and foreigners, and so on. To some extent the criteria here are occupational. By contrast, a third variable is largely social. Other things (semantic purpose, users, register) being equal, utterances can vary in style; for this, Martin Joos[7] proposes a categorization into five modes—frozen, formal, consultative, casual, intimate (e.g., from 'Visitors should make their way to the upper floor' to 'Up you go, chaps!'). At the intra-linguistic level, grammar is usefully separated from lexis, with related separation of 'closed' from 'open' word-classes, and of syntagmatic from paradigmatic word-groupings. Within grammar itself, various strata have been identified—for instance, the academic study of language in general, the description of a single language, 'teaching grammar', 'linguistic etiquette', and even 'disguised grammar' (the unformulated 'rules' underlying much teaching).

Perhaps there are teachers who intuitively recognize the realities underlying these distinctions; to them, this kind of analysis must seem unnecessary, even pretentious. But the evidence of some teaching and many text-books seems to reveal naive over-simplifications which need the corrective of a more delicate appreciation of the extraordinary complexity of language. Some teachers still insist on a spoken 'May I . . . ?' instead of the normal 'Can I . . . ?' (an American questionnaire in 1949 found an 'acceptance ratio' among teachers of only 40 per cent for the latter usage); red ink has been used in amending 'last night' to 'yesterday evening'; text-books still set exercises in eliminating 'get' and in 'correcting' sentences so short that context and co-text are quite inadequate for judgement of appropriateness. These and similar practices, by implying that language is single and simple, neglect real English in favour of a dangerously unreal 'school-mastered' English.

Reluctance to accept that language is manifold is commonly accompanied by reluctance to accept that it is constantly changing, and that change is not deterioration. Over the ages contemporary usage has always been accused of falling short of some ideal. For centuries, Latin and Greek of the classical period afforded such a model. With the triumph of the vernacular, standards came to be variously located—for example (in eighteenth-century England) in universal reason, in logic, in the authority of grammarians or literary writers, or in etymology and linguistic history. The heterogeneous and conficting nature of these criteria (not even the best writers escaped censure for being ungrammatical; and language serves many purposes besides those of logic), the vain attempts—by Swift, among others—to establish an Academy, and the failure of the pronouncements of grammarians to win acceptance not only from the public but even from their colleagues and successors, ought to have put an end to vain notions of 'fixing' English once and for all. (It is ironic that Swift's very word for fixing —'ascertaining', i.e., making certain or stable—has changed out of recognition.) Nevertheless the 'ipsedixitisms' have continued Canute-like to defy the currents of natural change. Johnson's dismissal of 'low' words such as 'budge', 'fun' and 'clever' can be paralleled a century later with insistence on '*Down* (not *up*) to this time the Turks had done nothing'[8] and today with arbitrary legislation in current manuals of 'correct' English (e.g., 'very interesting' is correct, but 'very interested' is a mistake for 'much interested';[9] 'When they were first married . . . ' must be changed to 'Just after . . . '[10]). Even where the appeal is to a real as distinct from a fictitious past, it has no authority in itself. Earlier usage may illuminate but cannot regulate current usage. Contemp'ry language (William Cooper has suggested elision to mark the 'modern' sense of 'contemporary') exists in its own right and should be judged by its own purposes. To this end the linguists' uncompromising separation of 'diachronic' or time-bound historical facts from 'synchronic' facts abstracted out of the time-dimension is invaluable.

Past attempts to defeat *time* by establishing an Academy were matched by attempts—equally futile—to defeat *place* by creating a universal language. The latter, it was hoped, would represent the thought-categories that were assumed to exist pre-verbally and therefore everywhere. The fallacy of this assumption has been thoroughly exposed by modern examinations of the relationship between thought and language. Whatever the truth in this abstruse field, notions that ideas are 'clothed' or 'labelled' with words are seriously misleading; in some sense words are an integral part of thinking. (How do I know what I think till I hear what I say?) Without necessarily accepting the full implications of the so-called Whorf-Sapir hypothesis—briefly, that the 'real world' is unconsciously built up on the language habits of a community—one must concede that different languages apply different 'grids' to the same experiences. Structural analysis of a wide range of languages reveals that not even predication is universal, though it is common to all Indo-European and some other languages. More specifically, the colour spectrum (a favourite example) has national variants. Speakers of English, Welsh, French, Japanese and Navaho apparently not only use different numbers of terms but site the boundaries between colours differently, even where there are equivalent terms. So strong is the pull towards assuming that words have essential or 'real' meanings that we need this sort of reminder that language is an arbitrary man-made convention.

Undesirable conservatism in matters of language is sometimes reinforced by an excessive emphasis on literature as the realization of linguistic excellence. Obviously, over and above its unquestionable humanistic value, literature is a most valuable exponent of the art of writing. But language activity is more than an art, and more than writing and reading. It includes the practical business of speaking and of understanding speech. To stress the primacy of the oral skills—as linguistics does—is not to claim for them a superior absolute value, but to recognize that they have their own special importance. Speech comes first in the processes of personal and cultural growth. Furthermore, whereas writing is a wholly linguistic activity, speaking includes extra-linguistic elements (voice, gesture, 'presence', etc.) which help to give it a more nearly total expressiveness (at the price, of course, of being more ephemeral). Ordinary speech is the basis of all language, including the prestige-bearing language of literature.

The prestige which literature properly enjoys, while intrinsically unobjectionable, can be harmful if it leads—as it sometimes does—to depreciation of other language uses. The descriptive emphasis in modern linguistics is not wholly suitable for teaching purposes, but it at least has the merit of discouraging the divisive tendency, peculiarly strong in England, to equate language variations with social-class ratings. On educational grounds we must welcome the insistence that no one language is intrinsically better than another, that literacy is not superior to articulacy, that 'standard English' is not preferable as such to local dialect, nor 'RP' to regional accent, and that modern sophisticated languages are no more efficient than so-called primitive ones.

Linguists doubtless have private tastes in these matters, but their refusal as professionals to evaluate languages deserves some degree of emulation by teachers. The example is not, however, one to be followed utterly, since the teacher has responsibilities to pupils as well as subject-matter. He may himself speak and write a socially-preferred English, just as he may read an academically-preferred literature; and he is entitled to personal opinions about the aesthetic and functional values of different dialects, registers and styles. Further, he has a right, perhaps a duty, to share these opinions with his pupils and to help them to appreciate the social and aesthetic valuations placed upon different modes of language. But—and this is where linguistics can help—he must beware of crossing an invisible line separating legitimate advice (e.g., to speak RP when acting in serious plays, or to write standard English when applying for jobs) from illegitimate authoritarianism (e.g., deprecation of local dialect or of use of slang in familiar letter-writing).

This line is extremely difficult to draw. The teacher on the one hand needs to reject the role of language-policeman, but on the other hand cannot reasonably adopt a totally descriptive 'anything-goes' position. To some extent he must prescribe to educate. His most appropriate position is that of Bloomfield's 'wise and moderate prescriptivism'. To be 'moderate' his injunctions should be few in number and liberal in tone; to be 'wise' they should recognize the facts—as distinct from the folklore—of language. R.A. Hall[11] looks forward to a distant future when claims to dispense 'correct' English will (like quack medicine) be indictable offences. We readily concede that the courts would have been kept busy in the past— with all those offenders who condemned split infinitives and final prepositions, and insisted on 'not *so* . . . as' and '*his* (not *him*) agreeing'. We too readily assume, often without taking the elementary precaution of consulting the records, that our own prescriptions are more soundly based. An interesting example, from lexicon, of a prescription that misrepresents inconvenient facts is disapproval of the current tendency to make 'disinterested' mean 'uninterested'. As distinguished a scholar as I.A. Richards[12] quotes this to exemplify 'degradation of language' through the destruction of 'a noble distinction'. (That such misleading emotive terms as 'degradation' and 'noble' can be provoked from a campaigner against the confusion of emotional and referential language testifies to the surprising power of arguments about language to shorten tempers.) Admittedly the distinction is a useful one; it is a pity it is disappearing. But a glance at the OED makes the charge of 'degradation' look very odd. The awkward facts seem to be that 'disinterested' began (before 1612) with the meaning 'not interested', while 'uninterested' was introduced later (before 1646) to mean 'impartial'. By about 1660 each had acquired the other's meaning in addition to its own. Subsequently, of course, the second meanings superseded the first. Now we may be experiencing a kind of reversion. It may be that this particular usage is one on which (if it is not too late) we should at least fight a retreating action. If so, at least we should take a stand on firm ground rationally chosen.

Knowledge of linguistic history helps in choosing a position between the extremes of authoritarianism and permissiveness by providing the facts both about shifts of meaning and usage and about the efficacy or otherwise of past attempts to control the shifting. It suggests, for instance, that 'the expressions about which puristic objections center are not so much neologisms as they are old forms and usages of the language which are struggling to survive'.[13] It reveals the futility of demanding conformity to etymology, to logic or to grammatical 'rules'. No amount of etymological history will make people 'averse *from*' rather than 'averse *to*', or will prevent 'contemporary' meaning 'modern'. No amount of logic will make two negatives mean a positive, or will outlaw 'from hence' or 'the reason is ... because' (any more than it would succeed if it advocated, as in principle it should, that 'hisself' and 'theirselves' are more logical than 'himself' and 'themselves'). As for grammar, linguistic history is punctuated with fascinating attempts to regiment a recalcitrant English. Two or three generations ago, for example, dispute raged over the admissibility of certain passive constructions. 'I am paid regular wages' was a 'preposterous locution'[14] because only the Direct Object could become Subject of a passive verb; and, 'the house is being built' was 'an incongruous and ridiculous form of speech'. Paradoxically, the former was faulted for having no parallel in Latin, the latter for providing one—a classical education caused some 'precise and feeble-minded souls' to feel 'conscientious scruples at saying, The house is building ... '.[15] At the same period Nesfield was rejecting 'The play had *quite* a run' because 'quite' is an Adverb and 'if we are to say that Adverbs qualify Nouns, then what distinction between Adjective and Adverb will remain?'[16] A similar attitude was adopted by H.E. Palmer[17] who, in 1930, thought that the use of the subjunctive, though obsolescent, still distinguished the best writers from the slipshod; he complained, too, that most people misused prepositions, saying, for instance, 'rolled about *with* (instead of *from*) laughter'. Many of the prescriptions still persist. Nesfield's grammar was re-issued as recently as 1952, and today usage handbooks, which proliferate,[18] promulgate complicated shall/will paradigms, and fictions about 'It is *I* (not *me*), and '*among* (not *between*) three or four'. Even the technically advanced programmed text-book is not immune; a recent American one[19] insists that 'I forgot that there *were* eight quarts in a peck' is unacceptable in formal use—such a perennial truth needs '*are*'.

Rulings like these are not merely wrong and futile; they are harmful. They focus grossly disproportionate attention on a comparatively small selection of items, and they foster a censorious, negative attitude in which the *pre*scriptive readily slips into the *pro*scriptive. This attitude can even acquire a moral flavour, extending a tradition which stretches from the ancient scholar (Smaragdus, *c*.800) who assumed divine authority for the eightfold parts-of-speech classification, through the 'doctrine of original sin in grammar' characteristic of the eighteenth century, to the situation parodied by a modern humorist:

> Unless I have been intolerably misinformed from my childhood up, the English language, its vocabulary, syntax, and spelling, was given us by God in their present form as an uplifting discipline. Mis-spellings, split infinitives, and neologisms I take as calculated affronts to my moral code.

Since the childhood of Michael Frayn, emphasis has doubtless moved to more positive, productive processes. Of these 'creative writing' is the most conspicuous. Its growth in popularity reflects, as well as psychological enlightenment, the linguistic enlightenment which sees language activity as a range of practical skills, with close connections between oral and written, and with recognition that children's writing differs in degree rather than kind from adult writing and literature. The concept of productivity in language may even come to be extended from composition to grammar. It is not impossible that Chomsky's so-called generative grammar,[20] identifying a limited range of 'simple, active, declarative' sentences ('kernel' sentences) from which all other sentences may be derived by 'transformation', may, among mature students, stimulate thinking about language and fuller exploitation of its grammatical resources.

It is too early to assess the teaching-value of generative or any other 'new' grammar. But it is probably true to say that the old grammar, already undermined by its failure to produce measurable practical results in composition, has lost what theoretical status it had. The main objections to it are twofold: it attempts to establish categories largely by notional criteria, and it uses these categories in a description more suited to a synthetic, inflexional language (like Latin) than to an analytic, positional language (like English). Consequently its definitions are often almost meaningless (e.g., a verb names an action), its abstractions bogus (e.g., gender, dative case), and its emphasis misplaced (on paradigmatic features such as declensions and conjugations rather than on syntax, word order and collocation).

Modern grammar is more concerned with word groups and less with single words than traditional grammar. Even so, where the latter allocates words to a number (usually eight) of categories of more or less equal status, the modern grammarian presents a more complicated, hierarchical scheme. He distinguishes, for example, between open classes of 'form-words' and closed classes of 'function-words'. The former (conventionally nouns, verbs, adjectives, adverbs) are unrestricted and can admit new members; the latter (e.g., prepositions, pronouns, conjunctions) can be catalogued in quite short, finite lists. Broadly, meaning is carried lexically by the open, grammatically by the closed, classes (as well as contextually by extra-linguistic factors). The contributions of lexis and grammar are not precisely separable, but that of grammar seems the more fundamental. Tampering with lexis reduces meaning; tampering with grammar destroys it, as experiments with nonsense words show. Not much of Henley's sense survives in 'I am the tongle of my huck', but even less in 'Wu faz dom master ti ag fate'. And Colin Cherry[21] has pointed out that, when grammatical clues are retained, nonsense sentences can not only be analyzed (The ventious crapets pounted raditally = adjective + noun + verb + adverb) but even translated (Les crapêts ventieux pontaient raditallement). Though it is hardly to be expected—or desired—that grammar will ever regain its proud medieval position as the door to all knowledge, such limited grammar teaching as does go on can expect to be based on much sounder descriptions than those of the old 'recipe-books'.

The modern view of language is, then, a distinctively scientific one. As such, it tries to provide an exhaustive, consistent, and economical account of language in general and languages in particular. In so far as its descriptions are relevant to the teaching of English, it does not exclude any of the recognized activities, but it does expose weaknesses of content and attitude. It provides the facts for replacing bogus Latin-oriented grammar by a realistic grammar of the vernacular as actually spoken and written, for eliminating much of the folklore and fallacy from usage theory, and for developing a more reasonable, encouraging attitude to language activities of all kinds than the legislative and often prohibitive methods all too common in the past. Above all, at the same time that it breaks down over-simple 'monolithic' views of language, it offers a much-needed theoretical framework for the integration of the varied skills, topics and experiences that make up the total of 'English'.

Notes

1 HALLIDAY *et al.* (1964) p. 244.
2 STREVENS (1965) p. 74.
3 BARZUN, J. (1959) *The House of Intellect*, Secker and Warburg, p. 240.
4 HALLIDAY *et al.* (1964) p. 187.
5 STREVENS (1965) p. 2.
6 ABERCROMBIE (1965) p. 6.
7 JOOS, M. (1962) *The Five Clocks*, Mouton, p. 13.
8 Letter in *Notes and Queries*, 5th Series, Vol. VII, 1877, p. 137.
9 COLLINS (1960) *Everyday English Usage*.
10 WEST AND KIMBER (1964) *Desk-book of Correct English Usage*, Owen.
11 HALL (1960) pp. 247–8.
12 RICHARDS, I.A. (1955) *Speculative Instruments*, Routledge and Kegan Paul, p. 10.
13 MARCKWARDT, A.H., and WALCOTT, F. (1938) *Facts about Current English Usage*, Appleton-Century-Crofts, p. 51.
14 PROFESSOR PECK, quoted in *Notes and Queries*, 11th Series, Vol. IV, 1911, p. 287.
15 WHITE, R.G. (1899) *Words and Their Uses*, p. 315.
16 Quoted in SHEFFIELD, A.D. (1912) *Grammar and Thinking*, Putnam, p. 90.
17 PALMER, H.E. (1930) *The Teaching of English*, Murray, pp. 28, 25.

18 See 9 and 10 above, also BERRY, T.E. (1963) *The Most Common Mistakes in English Usage*, Pitman; WOOD, F.T. (1962) *Current English Usage*, Macmillan.
19 BLOWENTHAL, J.C. (1962) *English 3200*, Harcourt, Brace, item 2205.
20 CHOMSKY, N. (1957) *Syntactic Structures*, The Hague.
21 CHERRY, C. (1957) *On Human Communication*, Wiley, p. 118.

Postscript 1981

A week may be a long time in politics; it certainly isn't in education. Re-reading 'Modern Views of English Language', I am persuaded that, at least in the teaching of English, even fifteen years isn't very long. 'Subject English', now as in 1966, conspicuously lacks a rationale that commands moderate agreement among its teachers. Differences about what should be included in English and in what order of priority are to some extent tolerable, even desirable; but the persistence of old, deep, often fundamental cleavages cannot but be harmful. It is time that common interests and common concern with the totality of English reduced the opposition between those dedicated to an almost exclusive concentration on literature and those preoccupied with language 'skills', accuracies of convention and grammar, correctness of usage and the like. It is time that the comparative (even if now rather less marked) neglect of the spoken language— a neglect characteristic of teachers of both the above persuasions and many in between—gave way to a more balanced recognition of the wide range of activities legitimately involved in English and of the very diverse needs of the multifarious population of learners of English.

Sixteen years ago I wondered whether, 'since all "English" is language activity, it is reasonable to ask whether linguistics, the study of language, can offer teachers of English a view of language conducive to unity and direction in their total work.' I thought then, and think still, that it is reasonable both to ask that question and to answer 'yes' to it. In hindsight I am glad I phrased the question with some caution: could the results of systematic language study at least *offer* (not necessarily *give* and certainly not *impose*) a view of language useful to teachers? Might such a view be *conducive to* (not necessarily *productive of*) a better sense of unity and direction? I am glad, too, that I made those reservations about linguistics: that it was a youthful study, that it was pursued as an academic discipline in its own right and not to serve pedagogy, and that in any case a theory of language, no more than any other theory, could not guarantee success in practical teaching. All the same, I wish I had avoided the term 'linguistics' altogether. It seems to rouse such strong and hostile feelings in some teachers as to paralyze normal thought processes. I.A. Richards long ago commented on the deadly effect of the word 'grammar':

> The word has been pronounced, its influence descends upon the scene, and with it a strange and deadly cramp seems to spread over the intellectual faculties, afflicting them with squint, making them unable to observe all sorts of things they are perfectly conversant with in normal life.[1]

With the virtual disappearance of grammar teaching from our schools, the word 'grammar' has lost much of its debilitating power. But 'linguistics' seems to have taken over as the chief bugaboo of many teachers of English. I suppose it is the quasi-scientific sound of the term that alarms and antagonizes many who—quite reasonably—see English as the curricular centre of the humanities and—much less reasonably—see an essential incompatibility between the humanities and the sciences. My question might then be rephrased to ask whether the study of language—meaning, of course, those aspects of language study with pedagogic relevance—could contribute to greater unity and direction in the totality of English teaching.

Of the three reservations originally made, the first has lapsed with the passing of time; linguistics, including that part of it relevant to education, has by now firmly established itself as an independent discipline. Moreover, language study has made important contributions to other disciplines, such as psychology, sociology and anthropology. The considerable attention given in recent decades to language acquisition and development, to language interaction in classrooms, and to communication processes makes it likely that the potential contribution to education and to the teaching of English has also greatly increased.

My second reservation—that linguistics does not exist primarily to serve educational purposes—follows on from the first. Even a perfunctory glance at the linguistic section of an academic library will reveal that most of the books and articles have nothing to say to teachers, indeed sometimes nothing to say to anyone other than academic linguists. But recognition that, say, research in the fascinating area of 'The History of Raising and Relativization in Polynesian' or 'The Nonexistence of the Trace-Binding Algorithm' (actual recent articles) falls well outside the professional concern of teachers does not, of course, reduce the educational usefulness of work in, for example, dialectology or usage acceptability or the theory of register. The problem, in the absence of journals of English educational linguistics, is to keep abreast of developments in linguistics and, above all, to select from the vast mass of publications those topics and those aspects of topics which bear on the language learning process.

The third of my reservations is so obvious as to need nothing more than reiteration. Linguists provide facts and theories about facts. Mere familiarity with such facts and theories as have an educational relevance is necessary but by no means sufficient to the making of an effective teacher.

The enormous expansion of language studies in recent decades—the 'explosion in linguistics', as it is sometimes called—has included, along with a great deal of no value to teachers, one major development that greatly increases its possible bearing on language teaching. That development is the abandonment of the attempt, characteristic of structural grammatical theory, to exclude considerations of meaning from descriptions of languages. This attempt may have been a phase which language study, if it were to be taken with scientific seriousness, had to pass through. In retrospect, it was surely doomed to failure. However that may be, the recognition of semantics as an essential (though intractable) feature of language greatly increases the possible area of contact with education. The curriculum can fairly be seen as a classified arrangement of sets of meanings. Similarly, the school can be seen as an agency for the communication of these meanings; to that extent the development in linguistics of the notion of 'communicative competence' as a central criterion of language use reinforces the bonds between language study and teaching.

If the direction of linguistic studies has favoured a closer relationship between language theory and education, so too have recent developments in 'language in education'. Two of these deserve mention. One is the multi-lingual character of an increasing number of school classes. More and more teachers of English—and that includes all teachers using English—are in effect teachers of a foreign or second language. The pedagogic problems raised by this situation are inseparable from linguistic problems which demand some knowledge of the languages involved and consideration of the nature of language in general.

The other—and closely related—development is the so-called 'language across the curriculum' or (better) 'language for learning' theory enshrined in, though not of course initiated by, the Bullock Report of 1975. This 'movement' disturbs many teachers. On the one hand, it looks like a significant recognition of a crucial truth about the learning process, and therefore has far-reaching implications for curriculum design and teaching method. On the other hand, it can be regarded as a threat: it threatens teachers of subjects other than English with an invasion of their territory by English-language 'experts', a take-over bid for the whole language-mediated curriculum; it threatens teachers of English, in so far as they teach language, with destruction of their specialism by dispersing it throughout the timetable. Examples of these two 'threat' reactions are not hard to find. Opposition by non-English teachers to alleged expansionism by Englishers is exemplified in the school where 'an influential group of senior members of staff resisted the English department's efforts to focus attention on language, and particularly rejected attempts to encourage pupils' talk as a means of learning.'[2] On the other side, the loss of status by specialist English teachers is succinctly expressed by Peter Abbs, who identifies a 'current socio-linguistic movement' in English teaching which

> tended to ignore the previous traditions and made language and
> learning its essential theme. In doing this, it broadened English

(language across the curriculum!), engendered a concern for the process of learning, widened the perspective of the specialist but tended to dissolve English as a specific discipline. The English teacher became concerned with the whole of the curriculum but at the expense of having no place in it.[3]

Both these negative reactions seem to me unjustifiable. The former is irrational and—if I dare say it—unscientific. When a new planet is discovered, astronomy revises its planetary system to accommodate the newcomer. Similarly, if it is discovered that learning depends more heavily than was assumed on language, then the arrangements of schools, being places of learning, must be adjusted to take account of the fact, even at the cost of departing from hallowed tradition and the vested interests of entrenched specialization. The other objection—the one put by Peter Abbs—is equally reactionary but more complicated. Whatever may be said against what he calls a 'current socio-linguistic movement' in English teaching, it is distinctly odd to blame it for engendering such an admirable thing as 'a concern for the process of learning'. Perhaps his objection is specifically to emphasizing the *process* of learning; if so, it is hard to see how that can be separated from the *achievement* of learning, at least in the mind of the teacher. The other criticism—that the same movement so broadens English as to dissolve it—is only valid if 'language across the curriculum' is taken to be incompatible with 'subject English'. Admittedly the relationship between these two can be awkward and complex, as some schools seeking to follow Bullock Report recommendations and formulate language policies have found. But co-existence is surely feasible as well as desirable. Underlying Abbs' contrary thesis seems to be an identification of 'subject English' with English literature and with the notion that language and literature are in some way antithetical. This seems to me a retreat to the barricades rather than the 'way forwards' he claims it to be. The exclusivity and consequently the divisiveness of the demand for 'the proper practical and conceptual definition of our subject in a literary-expressive discipline' allied to drama, art, music and dance[4] in effect reaffirms the polarized antagonism between language and literature that has bedevilled English ever since it became a separate 'subject'.

To reject Abbs' general case is not, of course, to reject his re-assertion of the value of literature. No one, I imagine, would deny 'the appalling neglect of the aesthetic and expressive in our schools'.[5] No one, I hope, would refuse English literature a place within the community of the arts— a large, important and, in that literature is the most readily accessible of the arts, a rather special place. But this very quality of accessibility derives from the ubiquitous nature of literature's medium—language. Abbs' use of 'expressive' is much narrower than that in James Britton's triadic model of expressive/transactional/poetic language. In fact, it seems to correspond much more closely with Britton's 'poetic' than with his 'expressive', the latter being the mode in which the two continua of expressive-transactional and expressive-poetic are rooted. The Abbs argument also in effect denies the association made by Britton of poetic mode with spectator role. In doing so, it reinforces the false division in schools between language and literature. This division has turned a basic truth into a seeming paradox, namely that it is in the poetic mode/spectator role activity (characteristically the study of literature) that language demands and deserves special attention, by contrast with the transactional mode/participant role (e.g. 'utility' English), where the less attention that language attracts, the better.

The broad view of language as the medium of all verbal expression, including literature, supports a synoptic notion of 'unitary' English, embracing all language skills and uses, non-literary as well as literary. It still allows of considerable variation in the distribution of time and emphasis between the more aesthetic and the more practical. It can take into account the diverse needs, for example, of potential university students of English literature and of learners of English as a foreign language, for whom literature must remain literally a closed book until they have achieved some competence in the language. It recognizes the very special cultural value of literature, but without elevating its use of language above other uses and without, therefore, according invidious prestige in non-literary contexts to standard English by contrast with non-standard or to the printed word at the expense of the spoken one.

The curricular question of whether English should be treated as unitary or dual (language/literature) cannot be isolated from the question of how it is to be examined at the school-leaving stage. For the public examination boards these are severely practical issues of organization and accreditation: should English language and English literature be regarded as one subject or two? should success in a single-subject (unitary) examination be rewarded with one 'pass' or two? These matters are complicated by the development of new examining techniques (notably teacher assessment of course work), by the introduction of new examinations (such as the proposed I-level test), by the extension of the candidature (e.g. for the new GCSE examinations) further down the ability range than has traditionally been the case. Despite the serious shortage of English-teaching specialists— both the Bullock Report and *Aspects of Secondary Education* documented this shortage—many English teachers are willing, even eager, to devote much of their time to examination classes. One price paid for this dedication is the excessive allocation of the most able teachers of English to examination groups. It could be argued that their teaching time might be better spread over a wider range of pupils and their non-teaching time better devoted to reading and thinking about the nature and content of their subject, and in particular to improving their knowledge of the facts of language.

Notes

1 RICHARDS, I.A. (1938) *Interpretation in Teaching*, Routledge and Kegan Paul, p. 182.
2 DEPARTMENT OF EDUCATION AND SCIENCE (1979) *Aspects of Secondary Education*, HMSO, p. 105.
3 ABBS, P. (1981) 'English within the Arts: A Pattern for the Eighties', *English in Education*, Vol. 15, No. 1, Spring, p. 42.
4 *ibid.*, pp. 45–6.
5 *ibid.*, p. 39.

Controlling the Word*

David Jackson
Toot Hill School, Bingham, Nottinghamshire

The Blockage

Almost everywhere in Britain a culture of acquiescence seems to be spreading. Generals tell us that cruise missiles are our friends. And the people of Thetford and Brandon agree even though Lakenheath, the USAF air base in East Anglia that might have been one of the major centres for the missiles, 'came within a hair's breadth of radioactive disaster in July 1956'.[1] The Coroner tells us that the Special Patrol Group's method of crushing Blair Peach's skull was a 'reasonable' way of coping with a 'riot situation' and we accept, almost without a ripple of dissent. The media, although still a potentially constructive force, suggest, hint, persuade, inform us that trade union protest is an evil, disruptive force, and we become—many of us members of unions ourselves—professional moaners about the latest strike. Supposed experts, the media, established authority, working for the interests of the ruling groups in Britain, create habits of dependence and passivity.

The sense of baffled impotence experienced by many working people today is deepened by the language of established authority. Often people's sense of their own lives, their lived experience is appropriated by an official version of that reality. So, William Whitelaw speaking in the House of Commons on immigration can say:

> The White Paper is the result of a comprehensive review. The new rules will be clearer, easier to operate and firmer in a number of critical areas .... . Obscurities have been cleared up, anomalies have been removed, and the scope for abuse and evasion of the control has been reduced. The Government believe that firm immigration control is essential in order to achieve good community relations.

*This article was first published in *The English Magazine No. 7*, ILEA English Centre, London.

The brisk, administrative efficiency of Whitelaw's tone, supported by the high status of a government report (' . . . a comprehensive review'), almost persuades the reader to believe that these are necessary tidying up measures until s/he realizes what is hidden beneath the surface of ordered decisiveness. What is being masked is quite simply the reality of being black and living in Britain today, of being, for example, an Asian woman in a white land without a voice:

> Yesterday when I was alone in the house, there was a knock at the door. There were two policemen standing there. I couldn't really understand what they wanted, but they kept asking me for my passport. Their voices were very hard. I was worried because I was not sure where my son kept it. The policemen pushed their way into the house. At last I managed to find it and they went away. This sort of thing has been happening a lot in this area, usually at night. People have been taken away without being told what they have done wrong.[2]

Whitelaw's series of faceless generalities can't disguise what is missing in his account: some particular and specific recognition of what people like this are having to put up with in their daily living.

In schools there are similarities; children are nearly always the ones who are being acted upon and rarely see themselves as the ones who act. Most classrooms, despite popular fictions about sloppy informal teaching, are severely regulated places arranged to help teachers transmit their understandings about what they're teaching to quiet, submissive receivers. School knowledge is seen to be owned by the teacher alone, and appears remote and external to the child; most of the children's perceptions about themselves and their own experiences are shut firmly out of most classrooms by a regime of exercises, tests and copied notes. And even when the teacher's intention is to let the children say what they know about something important to them, the way the activity is arranged so often prevents the work from becoming anything more than a series of servile jumps through the teacher's hoop. The children are instructed to write, without any preliminary stages of talking and drafting having been gone through. They are asked blank questions, to which they give blank answers. Response shrinks to dutifulness: you can keep the teacher quiet, you go through the motions; and you don't ever seriously investigate, weigh up, make sense of your out-of-school experience through a confident use of your own language. And, as a result, so many children, like many people in the community today, undervalue their ability to make their own mark upon the world through reading, writing and talking.

Wilson and Wailey

With a new economic and political harshness apparent everywhere and with a related demoralization in the schools the limitations of such tight restrictions are becoming more obvious. Inside the walls of a school, with its own organizational order, atmosphere and complex web of relationships, it's sometimes easy to assume that outside forces have nothing to do with what's going on there everyday. In fact schools respond closely and quickly to external pressures and, however much some teachers want to ignore this, the ground is shifting uneasily beneath our feet. It's not just the emerging insight that the possibilities in the English classroom are dependent on external forces apparently beyond our control, but that with the dole queue extending towards three millions there is a vital need for youngsters to be able to stick up for themselves and others in the way they handle language in an increasingly tough world.

Some possible ways out of this blockage are suggested by fresh impulses that have been stirring in the outside world in social history, local publishing and adult literacy schemes over the last ten years. Movements and projects like the Oral History group centred on Paul Thompson at the University of Essex, the History Workshop movement that came out of Ruskin College, community-organized adult literacy groups—and especially the many local publishing projects (like Bristol Broadsides, Hackney Centerprise, and Newcastle's 'Strong Words') co-ordinated by the Federation of Worker Writers and Community Publishers.[3] All these movements are united by their attempt to challenge and question the official, supposedly authoritative description of reality offered by those groups that are in the driving seat in Britain. Take two perspectives on the 1966 seamen's strike for example: Harold Wilson's from his *The Labour Government, 1964–1970: A Personal Record* and Tony Wailey's from *History Workshop* (Issue 5, Spring 1978).

Harold Wilson's first:

> On 13th May I met the forty-eight seamen's leaders at noon in the State dining-room at No. 10, laid out as a conference room. I urged on them the damage they would do to Britain and to their own industry and emphasised the benefits of Ray Gunter's proposed inquiry. Their reaction was militant and bitter and with many offensive comments on the shipowners' methods, and their excessive profits, and with political attacks on us for backing the bosses against the workers. We argued through and through the subject. But the gap was too wide. The employers, who had granted a thirteen per cent increase in March 1965, had offered five per cent, with four per cent to follow in each of the next two years. The seamen were demanding that all work over forty hours a week should be paid at overtime rates; this would be equivalent to a seventeen per cent increase in earnings averaging £20 per week. The employers pointed out that the thirteen per cent of the previous year had included a payment of £8 per month over and above the basic rate, to compensate for working more than forty hours a week at sea. The executive withdrew to a room in the Cabinet

Office where once again they took just forty-five minutes to reject our appeal.

As a contrast, this is how Tony Wailey (a) saw the problem of overtime and (b) received Wilson's radio broadcast to the seamen homeward bound to Liverpool:

(a) The big hours started the trouble. Bloody Sunday in Durban harbour where you can look over and see the waves crashing on the bluffs and people out on the beach surfing and having a good time and there's a shout from the far end of the companionway and you can see the mate and the skipper grabbing hold of Sid. Poor Sid with his shoulders giving that little twitch and a vacant look in his eyes you sometimes see in people that are deaf. And Paddy Hayes comes running from out of the galley and tells you he's just given the chief engineer a clout. And the firemen come up in their clean clothes saying the second had knocked them off for the afternoon but the chief had changed his mind. They were all off to the beach when he calls them back and tells them there's a job below. It was after that that Sid went up to see him and the engineer starts shouting about him being in the officers' mess and Sid starts twitching and it was all over in a couple of seconds.

(b) ... and the next thing you know Wilson's slow Yorkshire accent comes filtering out over the room in such a tone that you think the sea is going to turn back or something. And it goes on and on telling you what good fellows you all are and how the nation is in debt to you and at this time of crisis you are more than valuable. You can see some of the lads nodding and others just sitting there quiet and then the voice tells of the harm a strike could do and the margin of the balance of payments and that the seamen of this country don't want to hold the nation and a Labour Government to ransom by their action; and the voice trails on and on until it fills the room and seems to come out of every stitch of wood on the bulwarks and has everyone rooted until its presence slowly fades and there is a silence in the mess.

Many ordinary people are still nodding too readily, 'just sitting there quiet' being intimidated by voices, like Wilson's, that boom around them with status and authority. But in these radical projects there is a new sceptical tone growing. There are beginning to be more people like Tony Wailey who are asking questions about the ownership of experiences like the seamen's strike, about the means to shape, interpret and learn from that experience and about opening it up to broader audiences than had previously been the case.

Harold Wilson's account is offered as a distanced, definitive version of that strike experience with the unruffled assurance of somebody who's in the know. The impression is that he's had a uniquely privileged access to information from all sides to be able to take a calm overview. The danger is that the reader will accept the tone of balanced rational calm at face value. Looked at more closely the support of Wilson's Government for the employers' case is obvious. The employers are shown as generous and responsible ('urging', 'granted', 'offered', 'pointed out', 'appeal'), whereas the seamen's leaders are represented as a Bolshie lot ('demanding' and 'rejecting', 'militant, bitter', and 'offensive'). Tony Wailey deliberately sets out in his account to re-claim the meaning of what he lived through in 1966 from this distorted representation. He speaks out, forcefully and clearly, through his own sense of what happened, using his own rhythms and words to fit the structure of that feeling for him and his mates. It isn't just personal testimony; it also speaks for a wider group experience of the seamen's strike, shaping their own awareness of what was happening through the process of organizing and then in some cases, articulating that process. The gain is in having ordinary people's experiences validated in a public way, and in the developing awareness that comes with controlling your own experience through your own language. The key aspects of the way language is used in many of these radical projects, especially the local publishing projects, is the emphasis on authentic voice and on the process of learning through publishing. The sheer energy of the vernacular voice, as opposed to borrowed respectability, is to be found everywhere in the taped talk or writing of ordinary, working people in these projects.[4] A trust in the way they say things at home when going public is an important part of developing confidence as a language user for many of these people. Instead of trying to become a skilled ventriloquist through bland and often inadequate imitations most of the best work comes through remaining loyal to their own spontaneous voices. This is clearly a complicated issue; a growing confidence in the way they speak at home is a powerful part of boosting self-esteem, while at the same time they need to operate just as effectively in standard written forms when the occasion demands it.

A Positive Direction

What Can Schools Learn from these New Movements?

I think that they can stimulate the recognition—or at least remind us—that the job of English teachers is to encourage children to look upon themselves as people who also can 'control the word', to see that they can be in charge of the word and not just be on the receiving end of it. In order for that to happen we have to make sure of the shift from the idea of knowledge as 'given' to the idea of knowledge as 'made'; as the Bullock Report puts it: '"What is known" must in fact be brought to life afresh within every "knower" by his own efforts.' We need to create enough space in classrooms for children's resources (their experience, language and knowledge) to be recognized and brought to bear upon the school experience, in order for the unfamiliar to be understood in terms of the familiar, in order that they can reconstruct the significance of the school experience for themselves.

We need to estimate properly what children can do in their handling of language when put into positions of power and respect in school. When encouraged to make meaning through purposeful reading, writing and talking, children can change their view of themselves as language users from docile receivers to initiators with power to determine what they want to use language for.

That involves expanding our teaching styles: moving away from authoritarian 'production management' to more open conversations in which the teacher's voice might be received as one possible way of doing things and not the only way. This move also implies teachers becoming active investigators of what goes on in classrooms as children learn, rather than merely performers of monologues and dispensers of tasks.

What Does this Mean in Practice?

The kind of illustration that is needed here is beyond the scope of an article.[5] All I can do is to focus on a couple of examples that might show the spirit of what I think should be the new emphasis for English teaching.

(1) One possibility is the explicit investigation and questioning of official misrepresentations, in books and in the media, of the particular quality of ordinary people's lives, through, for example, a study of different newspaper accounts of the same incident; or by looking in class at writing produced by working people about their history and their views of the world. Tony Wailey wryly criticizes the silent passivity with which the seamen received Wilson's radio message. That kind of challenging of the official consensus should be on our agenda too.

(2) Being able to have a greater say in what you do and the way in which you do it in the English classroom is very much at the heart of this approach. For example here are some fourteen year olds entering into direct conversations (in writing) with the teacher about what they're doing and what they would like to do:

> I think the way you told us to do our topic work e.g. all on our own was a bit much all at one time. I think it would have been better if you slowly sent us on our own. Get what I mean? All through the school people have been telling us what to do. So you can't expect us to change all at once.
>
> Paula

I am also worried about School dinner. We pay 30p and will soon have to pay 35p and we hardly get anything. All I had yesterday was six ravioli cases, a spatula full of chips and a half full ladle of peas. For the second course I had a 2 by 6 cm piece of pudding and some NICE!! custard. Do you think that I get value for money?

Stephen

Ideas for my own topic.

I am not shore where to start but I could start on the killing of animals in this country like when I first killed a bird and how it felt to be powerful and a crack shot but also how it felt taking a helpless sparrows life.

Some more ideas which I have just thought while I am doing my homework is to write a few stories as I have looked after an owl a bat and I even brought up 2 hares out of six which was not easy and I learn by my mistakes . . . .

Stuart

Uncertainly at first, these pupils are learning how to speak out with confidence. They're using the written word to find out what they're thinking (. . . 'some more ideas which I have just thought while I am doing my homework . . . '), and to comment on and evaluate what they're doing in English ('I think it would have been better if you slowly sent us on our way').

(3) Similarly, through talking and reading children, can construct their own meanings if they genuinely feel that what they have to say is worth something in school. This is a small, self-chosen group of children discussing, without a teacher present, the poems they've written:

A Shall we read another one?
S Yes, let's read David's.
D You read it.
R I'll read it. [Reads.]
    'My grandfather
    He stood deep in thought
    While the milk on the stove
    Boiled over
    His eyes with no sentiment
    Flickered
    Stared on and on and gone
    An old chair creaked as he sank down
    And his mind ticked on.
    In the endless fields of thought
    of great rivers so long
    Of wrought-iron bridges
    To cover the rolling mind
    Of my grandfather.'
    [. . .]

R I read it and thought 'that's good' but then I thought 'well, what have wrought-iron bridges to do with it?'

D Well I suppose, I suppose I did kind of well write it or it kind of came; but I think it is right.

S Why?

D Well the main thing about him is he is like a bridge. I remember, well he's always coped with things, climbed over obstacles, made kind of, well bridges you see across, between things, between us, too. Do you see?

G I suppose so.

D 'Wrought iron' was because he does everything well and because in his day bridges were made of, well were made of wrought iron not cement.

R Yes.

[Confusion of voices.]

G He's thinking of the past, isn't he, things like, that have gone before. He doesn't notice what's happening now.

G Old people are like that, my gran, she remembers everything when she was a girl, but not what happened yesterday.

S Yes.

A That's right.

R Yes.

S I wonder if it's true.

G I think . . .

R If what's true?

S Well, sort of what they remember, like it was always better then, in their day—even the weather.

[Laughter.]

A Or else, 'I didn't have all these things when I was a girl', and 'I wasn't allowed to do that', and 'Think yourself lucky'.

[Laughter.]

R Well, they can't just make it all up, though. It can't be, well, very nice to be old.

S No, and not be able to do things any more.

D Well, we all change things that happen.

A What do you mean?

D Well, if I do something wrong, or get, well, you know, embarrassed, well I think about it, and do it again and again in my mind. I sort of act it out.

G Yes I know.

D I make it, well, better, till it stops worrying me.[6]

Talking is working here as a sifting and sorting process. The group together builds up the connection between the grandfather and the wrought-iron bridge; the idea is then extended in a more general way.

Provisional impressions held privately in single minds are defined more precisely through sharing them; the whole group is then in a position to inspect, modify and re-assess these hunches so that a more considered, collaborative meaning can be established. They do it by homing in on what they know about, by bringing their own stories to bear on the contrast in the poem between unpleasant present happening (the milk boiling over) and the compensatory daydream (the wrought-iron bridge) so that the contrast is brought alive. Brought alive for the writer too, who says later, 'if I do something wrong, or get, well, you know, embarrassed, well I think about it, and do it again and again in my mind . . . .'

Such examples of children taking control can only stand as hints for a way forward. They need to be investigated further and puzzled over; similar experiences of positive practice need to be shared among teachers. They need to be shared particularly because it's very easy for committed teachers working individually to become baffled by the relationship between the large scale of the things happening in the world outside and the small scale of positive things happening in the classroom. There's a clear problem here of demoralization, of thinking 'what possible kind of difference are my small, daily attempts to build up children's confidence making?' That kind of demoralization leads back to an undervaluing of what can happen when ordinary working people master, question and use the word for their own purposes. Sharing your classroom experience with other teachers is a way of thinking positive. It's up to us . . . .

Notes

1 See THOMPSON, E.P. *Writing by Candlelight*, Merlin Press, p. 263.
2 From WILSON, AMRIT (ed.), *Asian Women Speak Out: A Reader*, National Extension College.
3 An article on community publishers by GREGORY, GERRY, 'Working Class Writing', appeared in issue 4 of *The English Magazine*. A round-up of recent community-produced publications appears in the review section of this issue (eds.).
4 See, for example, PRICE, KATHLEEN, 'Dig for Victory (The Pig Muck)' from *Looking Back*, available from Your Own Stuff Press (13 Mona Rd., West Bridgford, Nottingham) 65p inc. postage.
5 See my *Continuity in Secondary English*, Methuen, forthcoming.
6 From *Talking, Writing and Learning 8–13*, Schools Council Working Paper 59, Evans/Methuen.

2
Toward Tomorrow

Introduction

In the General Introduction I argued that the English curriculum of the future will have to concern itself more and more with the context of the world in which school students are growing up and that we cannot allow English teaching simply to exist within a museum of the past. The two articles that follow indicate some of the things that should be on our agenda in English classrooms already but generally are not. As Len Masterman shows there has been plenty of urging from the Bullock Report on for a more positive approach to media studies in schools, and, latterly, especially television studies. But we have been very slow to develop these in our schools and for the videotape-recorder to be used for any other purpose than off-air recording of schools broadcasts for later use is still rare. Now, it seems, we are to be as slow in recognizing the potential of the microprocessor as we have been with television. The government has, belatedly in the view of some, decided to put into operation a scheme to get at least one microprocessor into every secondary school and to train staff to use it. But it is important that this is not something that is restricted to older pupils or to the science and mathematics departments. If these powerful tools of the future society are not to remain in the hands of an elite there is an urgent need to recognize their place within the humanities curriculum and in the education of all pupils before the school-leaving age.

It is not an accident, therefore, that these two articles have been placed together. In a fundamental way they are both concerned with power and with access. It is only by making television for themselves that students will really come to understand how television works and gain power over their understanding and enjoyment of the medium; it is only through 'hands on' experience that real computer awareness can be developed. We ought to have done something about television education long ago; we should start computer education in the context of the humanities now. In their contributions, especially written for this collection, Len Masterman and Daniel Chandler provide some pointers for development by the English teacher.

Television and the English Teacher

Len Masterman
Lecturer in Education, University of Nottingham

English teachers have largely abdicated from their responsibilities over television. In schools and colleges today, those teachers who are taking on the vitally important task of developing a critical media education are perhaps more likely to be social scientists than English specialists. This is curious given the explicit concern of most English teachers to encourage critical awareness, to privilege the experiences of the learner, to develop skills in communication and interpretation and to educate for responsible citizenship within a democratic society. It is even more curious given the training and experience of English specialists in textual analysis. This article will try to explain why and how this situation has arisen. It will also try to indicate the major changes which are necessary in the training and practice of English teachers if they are to take on the responsibility for developing in their students an informed and critical understanding of the most pervasive and potent medium in our culture.

The birth of media education in this country ironically lay in a profound distrust of the media themselves. Traditionally ignored by the educational system, the mass media were drawn to the attention of teachers when they came to be identified as agents of cultural decline, seducers of the innocent, and creeping diseases whose baleful influence clearly needed to be actively fought by the teacher, and counterbalanced by doses of 'inoculative' education. The Spens Report on Secondary Education in 1938, for example, spoke of 'The hoarding, the cinema and . . . the public Press . . . subtly corrupting the taste and habit of a rising generation', and advocated speech training as a way of combating 'the infectious accent of Hollywood' and of abolishing class barriers.[1] Twenty-one years later, the Crowther Report on the education of 15/18 year olds suggested that:

> Because they [the mass media] are so powerful they need to be
> treated with the discrimination that only education can give. There
> is . . . a duty on those who are charged with the responsibility for

education to see that teenagers . . . are not suddenly exposed to the full force of the 'mass-media' without some counterbalancing assistance.[2]

The classic and, for English teachers, almost certainly the most influential argument of the case for discriminatory and inoculative education was put by F.R. Leavis and Denys Thompson in *Culture and Environment*, first published in the 1930s but still widely influential among English teachers in the 1950s and 1960s.[3] *Culture and Environment* begins:

> Many teachers of English who have become interested in the possibilities of training taste and sensibility must have been troubled by accompanying doubts. What effect can such training have against the multitudinous counterinfluences—films, newspapers, advertising—indeed the whole world outside the classroom? Yet the very conditions that make literary education look so desperate are those which make it more important than ever before; for in a world of this kind—and a world that changes so rapidly—it is on literary tradition that the office of maintaining continuity must rest.[4]

What Leavis and Thompson offered to English teachers was a missionary position: a positive and heroic role as a bastion of cultural values in a world of change, change that brought with it mass production, standardization and a levelling down in cultural and material life:

> Those who in school are offered (perhaps) the beginnings of education in taste are exposed, out of school, to the competing exploitation of the cheapest emotional responses; films, newspapers, publicity in all its forms, commercially-catered fiction—all offer satisfaction at the lowest level, and inculcate the choosing of the most immediate pleasures, got with the least effort. The school-training of literary taste does indeed look a forlorn enterprise. Yet if one is to believe in education at all one must believe that something worth doing can be done. And if one is to believe in anything one must believe in education. The moral for the educator is to be more ambitious: the training of literary taste must be supplemented by something more. And there has been enough successful experimenting to show that more might be done, and that it is worth doing. In the attempting the many intelligent men and women who every year go into schools might find assurance of vocation. Certainly there is a function awaiting them that might command enthusiasm. The instinct towards health—the instinct of self-preservation—that we must believe to be in the human spirit will take effect through them or not at all. In a world of depressed and cynical aimlessness there is for them work that, aiming at considerable and considered ends, will yield enough in immediate

effect to make whole-hearted devotion possible ... we are committed to more consciousness; that way, if any, lies salvation.
We cannot, as we might in a healthy state of culture, leave the
citizen to be formed unconsciously by his environment; if anything
like a worthy idea of satisfactory living is to be saved, he must be
trained to discriminate and to resist.[5]

It would be difficult to over-estimate the influence of that call to moral
and cultural resistance, to say nothing of the prevailing religiosity of tone.
Yet for the English teacher of even more fundamental significance were the
practical examples from advertisements, newspapers and journals which
crowded the pages of *Culture and Environment*. True, the correct attitude
to be taken to these examples was not left in any doubt:

'Some advertisers aim at creating the illusion of "personal"
relations between themselves and their prospective customers.
Give examples. When were you last taken in?'
'"Clean cut executive type", "good mixer", "representative man",
"short-haired executive", "regular guy" (Americanism). Why do
we wince at the mentality that uses this idiom?'
'"I would admit that it is better to read a thriller than not to read
at all" (Harold Nicholson). What is there to be said against this
view?'[6]

For all its antipathy to the media, however, *Culture and Environment* was
of crucial significance in bringing media texts out from the cold, and
making respectable their analysis in the classroom. The magnitude of this
step may be gauged by the fact that until as recently as the mid-1970s,
for a teacher in France to have used a newspaper as a teaching text would
have been to risk dismissal. It needs to be emphasized too—particularly
now that anti-Leavisite positions are more fashionable—that it would have
been difficult and perhaps impossible for media work to take root in British
classrooms had it not been for the tone of moral righteousness which
accompanied it.

The movement once begun, however, was to be irreversible, opening the
way in the late 1950s and the 1960s for the classroom use of a wide range of
materials derived from books which cast a much more informed and
sympathetic eye upon popular culture—Richard Hoggart's *The Uses of
Literacy* (1958 in its paperback edition), Vance Packard's *The Hidden
Persuaders* (1960) and Hall and Whannel's influential *The Popular Arts*
(1964).

The increasing availability and use of popular texts was paralleled during
the 1960s by an intellectual and emotional movement away from discrimination *against* the mass media towards discrimination *within* them. The first
signs were just about discernible in 1960 at the National Union of Teachers'
important and impressively well-attended national conference on 'Popular

Culture and Personal Responsibility'. But the old school-masterly rhetoric, fanned both by the inanities of ITV ('Until ITV arrived' as Peter Black wrote, 'the public had never seen anyone earn a pound note for correctly distinguishing his left foot from his right'[7]) and its soaring profits, as well as the catastrophic decline of BBC audiences, did blaze as brightly as ever. Here is Dr Horace King speaking at the conference:

> We inherit from our ancestors a European culture which was the gift of creative artists on the one hand and creative thinkers on the other. The schools, churches and every kind of definite cultural organisation do what they can to pass on this tremendous gift from the past to defend it against onslaughts . . . . On the other hand we have commercial culture which seems to threaten the very existence of the most precious things in the culture we seek to preserve.[8]

It would be tempting, but mistaken, to regard such anxieties, which were expressed again and again at the conference, as the fulminations of stone-aged obstructionists. Rather what the NUT conference provided was a platform for 'responsible' middle-class opinion to express its concern at the tide of commercialism and infantilism which seemed already well on the way to engulfing the nation. It was a concern which was to receive its fullest articulation some two years later in the Pilkington Report,[9] which, though rejected by the government of the day, was to some degree instrumental in ensuring that the worst fears of the NUT conference were not realized.[10]

Yet at the conference the anxious sirens of the day could not quite drown the whisper of the future. A.P. Higgins, a Nottingham teacher, stated: 'I feel this conference has tended to think in terms of defending children against exploitation . . . . Nevertheless . . . if I were asked to sum up in one sentence the purpose of education in film and television I would simply say it is to help children to enjoy to the full all that is best in film and television.'[11]

It was such impulses as these towards a cautious discrimination within the media which were to provide the real growth points from the conference. As Nicholas Tucker in a book developing out of the conference expressed it: 'There is a lot of bathwater, some of it not very clean, but there is a baby as well.'[12] Indeed one of the most important documents to emerge from the conference is not the official record of its proceedings, but the highly influential Penguin book, *Discrimination and Popular Culture*, published in 1964, in which 'serious' attempts were made to arrive at evaluative criteria for different aspects of popular culture. Denys Thompson could still write in his introduction to the book that: 'The aim of schools is to provide children with standards against which the offerings of the mass media will appear cut down to size.'[13] But by now this was coming to be seen as an unproductively elitist stance by many teachers and other voices were beginning to articulate more clearly what was to become the conventional wisdom for the remainder of the decade. In Hall and Whannel's words:

> In terms of actual quality . . . the struggle between what is good and worthwhile and what is shoddy and debased is not a struggle against the modern forms of communication but a conflict within these media.[14]

This was undoubtedly a step forward and *The Popular Arts* contains many fine analyses of popular genres and artists. The book did, however, encourage teachers to assert the existence of a kind of high culture within and even between the mass media. Ironically in *The Popular Arts*, popular films, for example, tend to be described as works to be discriminated *against*. John Ford, for example, is judged not to be a major director since 'he does not bring to the cinema the cultural equipment of a Bergman or a Bunuel.'[15] Hawks' *To Have and Have Not* and *The Big Sleep* are not serious films . . . . But their style rescues them from banality.[16] Cinematic art resides not in the popular cinema at all, but in intellectual foreign-language films. Hawks and Ford are suspect *because* they are popular, and because they work within popular genres. On the other hand, 'no one has to be defended against de Sica, Bergman or Antonioni', and 'we can understand the claims of Renoir, Bunuel, Kurosawa and Antonioni to this area of "high culture".'[17] Hardly surprisingly Hall and Whannel could find little evidence of popular art within television. Treating the medium as a crude and inferior form of cinema, they compare *Coronation Street* unfavourably with the documentaries of Denis Mitchell,[18] whilst of the popular series only *Z-Cars* and *Steptoe and Son* receive even qualified endorsement.[19]

The Popular Arts both reflected and gave sharper definition to a general movement in the 1960s to sift the mass media for newer art forms, which could nevertheless be evaluated by quite traditional aesthetic criteria. In classroom practice this often meant that 'discrimination' could be simply equated with a preference for *Panorama* over *Opportunity Knocks*, for *The Guardian* over *The Daily Mirror* and for films shown at film societies rather than the local *Odeon*. The movement privileged, that is, the rather high-brow 'serious' media tastes of teachers over the popular media offerings most avidly consumed by their pupils.

This movement had received its official imprimatur with the publication of the Newsom Report in 1963. In words directly echoing Crowther, the report spoke of the need for schools to provide a 'counterbalancing assistance' to the mass media, and, in a passage well known to all film teachers, of the necessity of discrimination:

> We need to train children to look critically and discriminate between what is good and bad in what they see. They must learn to realise that many makers of films and of television programmes

present false or distorted views of people, relationships, and experience in general, besides producing much trivial and worthless stuff made according to stock patterns. By presenting examples of films selected for the integrity of their treatment of human values, and the craftsmanship with which they were made, alongside others of mixed or poor quality, we cannot only build up a way of evaluating but also lead the pupils to an understanding of film as a unique and potentially valuable art form in its own right as capable of communicating depth of experience as any other art form.[20]

It has often been remarked that Newsom was of immense importance in encouraging the serious study of film in colleges and schools since 1963. The effect of the report upon the serious study of television, the most potent of all the mass media, has been rarely scrutinized. Note that, in the above quotation, while film and television are condemned for presenting 'false or distorted views', television mysteriously disappears when examples of integrity and craftmanship are mentioned. The report recommends that film studies might develop as the study of an art-form comparable with literature, music and painting. Such an approach clearly has its limitations when applied to television, for though the medium might be said to have produced original works of aesthetic merit, it also serves the functions of, for example, the newspaper, music-hall, sports-area, popular cinema and theatre all rolled into one. Newsom then provided the impetus for the establishment of 'high culture' courses in film at the expense of a medium clearly a more potent influence upon pupils, and a more integral part of their experience. It initiated a trend from which schools and colleges have scarcely yet begun to recover. Paradoxically the effect of Newsom was to arrest the development of the study of television by linking film and television together and encouraging teachers to think of them both in aesthetic terms, by failing to acknowledge the diverse functions of television and by offering no guidelines to teachers on how television might be studied in order to foster discrimination. When teachers began to glimpse some of the pitfalls awaiting them on this particular route it is little wonder that they became reluctant to take the journey.

Two rare teacher guides to the trip were provided by Nicholas Tucker's *Understanding the Mass Media* and Brian Firth's *Mass Media in the Classroom*.[21] Both books contain well-meaning, but essentially defensive, chapters on television teaching; both are hamstrung by the 'aesthetic' criteria they adopt for evaluating the medium; both, perhaps fortunately, lack any direct evidence that the approaches advocated were ever tried out in the classroom. Evaluative criteria tend to be derived from film theory. Tucker, for instance, advocates the study of television techniques and posits the centrality of the television director: 'In every way he is the key figure, and pupils will do well to know some of the directors' names and the sort of work they produce.'[22] The sentiment finds its echo in Firth: ' . . . one could hardly discuss *The Monkees* without pointing out the debt of that series to the Beatles' films made by Richard Lester.'[23] Most television material, not susceptible to this kind of analysis, can be dismissed in one word at the very moment it is being observed: 'Television programmes are not entirely made up of dramatic serials, plays and old films, and some notice might be taken of other standard time-killers—quizzes, "pop" programmes and comedies, for example.'[24] Worse, discussion is advocated, in which conclusions, in Leavis and Thompson style, are already cut and dried:

> Quizzes are often very popular, and the reason must be that there is often a very large money prize at stake. The difference between a quiz and a give-away show can at this point be made clear. Is it skill that enables the contestants to win or merely luck? Is it interesting to watch because it tests the audience's knowledge as well, and tries to bring viewers into the programme or is it because we see people tormented and often humiliated by their desire to get their hands on a big prize? Does the question-master ask his questions directly, or does he coax, hint and generally become the most important part of the show? Some of these programmes are mildy entertaining and occasionally instructive, but for the most part 'they are good for killing time, for those who like their time dead'.[25]

The likely reaction to this conclusion of pupils who actually like watching quiz shows is not elaborated.

Many of these pedagogic difficulties had been foreseen with some perspicacity by Richard Hoggart earlier in the decade. Writing in *The Observer* in 1961 Hoggart argued that active discrimination involved not the application of a pre-formulated class judgement, but rather the separation of 'the Processed' from 'the Living' in each thing of its own kind. It required, that is, close attention to the texts themselves rather than the easy application to them of a fixed 'brow' or educational scale. Hoggart observed the tendency to carry

> . . . into new and confused areas of cultural activity, the old, comfortable grading by height of brow . . . reinforced by an implied social or educational grading . . . . 'Mass culture' is that enjoyed by the 80 percent who have not been to a grammar school . . . . The crucial distinctions today are not those between the *News of the World* and *The Observer*, between the Third Programme and the Light Programme . . . between the Top Ten and a celebrity concert . . . . The distinctions we should be making are those between the *News of the World* and the *Sunday Pictorial*, between 'skiffle' and the Top Ten; and, for 'highbrows', between *The Observer* and *The Sunday Times*. This is to make distinctions . . .

which require an active discrimination, not the application of a fixed 'brow' or educational scale .... Our job is to separate the Processed from the Living at all levels. .... Processed culture has its eye always on the audience, the consumers, the customers. Living culture has its eye on the subject, the material. It expects the same attention to the subject from the members of its audience. Processed culture asks 'What will they take? Will this get most of them?' Living culture asks 'What is the truth of this experience and how can I capture it?'[26]

Of all the shifting notions of media discrimination which we have so far charted, Hoggart's is clearly the most advanced, and the most sympathetic and relevant to the media experiences of working-class pupils. The evaluative rule-of-thumb which it suggests (between the Processed and the Living) is one which at first sight could be readily applied to many media offerings and whilst Hoggart presents here a simplified theoretical blueprint for action, his earlier work, *The Uses of Literacy*, contains many concrete analyses of the popular media (excluding, for historical reasons, television) which exemplify the kind of discriminations he advocates here. In the classroom, however, the problems produced even by this version of discriminatory teaching proved to be as intractable as ever. It is necessary at this point to interrupt the historical account so far presented, and consider some of the reasons why this should be so.

Discriminatory teaching, whatever its form, is based upon the assumption that genuine differences are likely to exist between the teacher's point of view of what is 'shoddy and worthwhile' or 'Processed and Living' and the pupils'. If this were not so, then discriminatory teaching would be unnecessary. These differences carry unequal weight in the classroom, however. There the teacher has the authority provided by his/her social class, education and linguistic competence to elevate preferences to the status of objective judgements. Pupil preferences, lacking this kind of authority, remain merely preferences and vulnerable to attack. What are too rarely raised in classroom discussions of aesthetic value are the social basis of judgment, the assumptions which lie behind assertions of value and the crucial question of 'value for what?' Posited instead is a transcendental notion of value assigned by an ideologically innocent reader to an ideologically pure text. In these circumstances it is unsurprising, perhaps even fortunate, that discriminatory teaching appears to have cut very little ice with large numbers of comprehensive school pupils who obstinately persist in asserting the validity of their own responses. Such obstinacy may be regarded as a form of working-class resistance to the bourgeois hegemony of the classroom.[27]

In addition to this there are particular problems in applying the notion of discrimination to the study of television. It is clearly an inappropriate tool for handling a good deal of television material: there seems little point in trying to discriminate between televised news bulletins, weather forecasts, football matches, race-meetings, quiz programmes or chat shows. And even when it might seem to make sense—with plays, or comedy series, for example—how does one begin to do it? Little consensus exists on what constitutes 'good' and 'bad' television, and attempts to erect and defend generally agreed criteria of judgement have been singularly, even eccentrically, unsuccessful.[28] Hoggart's criteria, apparently common-sensed enough, are, on examination, no exception. For almost all of television consists of what he would call Processed Culture. Certainly most news, current affairs and entertainment programmes could be fairly described in this way. This is not necessarily the pejorative description which Hoggart imagines. For it is inevitable and proper in a medium in which, as it is presently constituted, even minority evening programmes cater for an audience of millions, to have one eye on that audience, and to ask 'What will they take?'—for Hoggart the hallmark of Processed Culture. What Hoggart suggests as antinomies (e.g. eye on audience as opposed to eye on material) characteristic of bad and good programmes, can be observed in most programmes held in legitimate tension.

The kind of theoretical approaches outlined so far in this chapter led, in the 1960s, to a decade of unfulfilled promise for the relationship between English teaching and television. In the 1970s, the failure to initiate new approaches produced a wasteland. A number of documents record these bleak trends. Murdock and Phelps' survey, *Mass Media and the Secondary School*, conducted in the early 1970s noted:

> A considerable number of English teachers said that their main aim in introducing mass media into lessons was to point out the 'dangers' of the media and to provide pupils with a 'defence'. Of the English teachers who answered our question, 36 per cent responded along these lines, and it seems probable that some of those who did not answer would agree with them. This attitude is far more common among English teachers than among teachers of other subjects—only 6 per cent of science teachers answered in this way, and the figure for teachers as a whole is only 19 per cent.[29]

The view of many English teachers that adolescent media audiences were 'captive and defenceless "Zombies"' was felt by Murdock and Phelps not to 'correspond with the real situation' in which young people were constantly making sophisticated choices in their response to the media. 'Nevertheless', Murdock and Phelps were compelled to conclude sadly,

> The 'Zombie' view and its concomitant stress on the need to inoculate pupils against media influences, together with the emphasis on upholding the superiority of literary culture appear to provide the perspective of a number of English teachers.[30]

Murdock and Phelps noted that 35 per cent of English teachers wished 'to encourage appreciation and discrimination', but more interestingly— and more critically—observed that only 6 per cent of English teachers encouraged their pupils to create their own mass media material:

> . . . from the results of this study, it appears that the only contact that the great majority of pupils have with media material is confined to their role as consumers and audience members; very few are encouraged actually to produce media material themselves. Without this perspective any understanding of the way in which the mass media work must necessarily remain partial.[31]

The report of the Bullock Committee, *A Language for Life* (1975), could only express concern 'that a decade after the publication of the Newsom Report there is still little evidence of the kind of study it recommended . . . . We believe that in relation to English there is a case for the view that a school should use it (film and TV study) not as an aid but as a disseminator of experience. In this spirit we recommend an extension of this work.'[32] Bullock, for the first time in an offical report, recognized the independent importance of television, and the significant part it played in the experience of pupils, and urged English teachers to respond to the medium construc- tively.[33] The report however offered no diagnosis as to what had gone wrong since Newsom, and guidelines for future practice was unusefully vague: 'Although there is unquestioned value in developing a critical approach to television . . . . We would place the emphasis on extending and deepening the pupils' appreciation.'[34] Since Bullock, therefore, whilst social scientists and teachers in the visual arts have increasingly colonized media education, there has been a predictable lack of response from English teachers. It is a sad conclusion to over forty years of often frenetic activity during which time English teachers have thought, written, worried, held conferences and passed resolutions about media education. And all to such little effect. Why has so little been achieved? And what would constitute a constructive response from English teachers to the challenges of the future?

Some answers to these questions will already be apparent from the foregoing survey. Two deep themes run throughout these documents:

(1) Most fundamentally, there persists to this day within English studies— it is apparent in even the most liberal formulations—a deeply-rooted distrust of the mass-media, and particularly television, as prime agents of cultural debasement and decline. I have in front of me a paper on *Mass Culture and Mimesis*[35] recently written by Peter Abbs, a teacher passion- ately concerned about the future direction of English teaching and with whose work, in general, I have a great deal of sympathy. His paper attempts to answer the question, 'What should be the function of the school during a period of cultural debasement?'

... the cultural processes engendered by the consumer society ... can be pinpointed quite simply: *there are large and accruing profits to be made from a vast populace rendered intellectually gullible and emotionally indolent.* Cliche, sentiment, glossy patter, stereotyped images, instant jingles round the clock, are easy to manufacture, easy to slot to each other, and providing that within the populace there are no sensitive feelings for aesthetic shape and personal truth, easy to distribute not only across 'the provinces', but around the world. There is nothing, for example, easier than to slot dead cliches together making them sound warm and intimate to lazy half-illiterate readers .... We need to know whether television, by providing so much detail and that so constantly, effaces imagination and, in so doing, develops a deep passivity of mind, an unwillingness to grapple with life, an inability to initiate events. We need to know whether the casual stance adopted by the intelligent young today derives from a profound sense of cultural relativity fostered by the arbitrary flow of the serious and the trivial, the real and the unreal, which marks television entertainment, magazines, newspapers and radio alike. Today's university students form the first TV generation and they manifest a fear of deep seriousness and deep feeling. Is there a connection between the casual stance of the student and television? We need to know whether the electronic media with its instantaneity and completeness precludes the development of inward space. We know that the reading of literature demands privacy and calls upon complex powers of imaginative reconstruction and, thereby, tends to develop a sense of inwardness. Is it true that what comes through electronic culture does not demand or foster the same qualities? Is it possible, also, that in thousands of homes television has now become the dominant socializing force having more influence even than the surrounding family? This would seem to be the case.[36]

That questionable conclusion aside, one can recognize a certain kind of truth in the drift of the argument. It is one strand of the much more complex truth about the role and impact of television in our society. What one objects to are the all-embracing nature of the assertions, the broad sweep of the generalizations, the categorization of real people as 'half-illiterate ... , intellectually gullible and emotionally indolent', the reluctance to engage closely with media texts (one suspects that Abbs wouldn't allow a television in his house), and above all the pervasive pessimism in substance and tone. For that kind of negativity encourages, not the scrutiny and investigation of television, but its dismissal. And that, in an educator, is an abdication of responsibility.

One can state the counter-case quickly and bluntly: that the media can be sources of pleasure and illumination as well as de-sensitizing agents;

that the media shape our perceptions in fundamental ways which we all need to understand if we are to be responsible citizens; that it is possible for students to be taught to look critically at media messages and institutions; that students can themselves communicate with sensitivity and skill in the 'new' media, and, in doing so, begin to challenge dominant codings; that television, in particular, can be the most powerful stimulus English teachers have at their disposal for encouraging reading and—if that is what they wish to do—for encouraging an interest in 'serious' literature.[37]

One final point needs to be made. The gap between the activities, priorities and concerns of most schools, and the very real problems and difficulties which students face in the world outside is now dangerously wide. Yet at the beginning of the 1980s we are standing on the threshold of the most enormous and unprecedented expansion of television and video. Within the next fifteen years, television and broadcasting as we know it will have changed beyond recognition in the face of an enormous de-regulated onslaught from direct satellite broadcasting, fibre-optic cable with the capacity to deliver thirty, fifty or even a hundred channels, and the expansion of video-cassette and video-disc markets. English teachers can ignore or deplore such developments; that is, they can opt for the role of educational dinosaurs. Or they can keep themselves well-informed about these developments, and work alongside their students in discussing, analyzing and explaining the implications of the unprecedented degree of choice they will have in their selection of visual material. There are few more important decisions facing individual English teachers over the next decade.

(2) The second constant theme in the shifting relationship between English teaching and the mass media concerns the reluctance of those teachers who have taken the media seriously to unload very much of the critical baggage acquired during their literary training. It is necessary, here, to state the self-evident: television is not ersatz literature, and is not best understood through the application of aesthetic or moral criteria having their roots in literary or even film criticism. Indeed, as I have suggested, it may not be best understood through the attempt to apply *any* kind of evaluative criteria.

At this point many English teachers will protest. After all, the very *function* of media education in the past is being called into question. Are we to be denied our right and duty to help our students to distinguish the creative from the shoddy, the worthwhile from the third-rate? Some loss, certainly, is involved. It *is* a sacrifice—not least to the ego—not to be able to show precisely why *Family Fortunes* is so appalling or Bob Monkhouse so egregious. Or, perhaps, why *Fawlty Towers* is worth watching. Yet the sacrifice, I believe, has to be made. I have already touched upon some of the problems raised by discriminatory approaches. Here I simply wish to add that the movement from evaluative to descriptive and investigatory procedures can turn media education from a largely negative enterprise— and one for which English teachers have, not surprisingly, shown little appetite—into a more positive one. The change can also open up the prospect of pedagogies which are genuinely more collaborative and less oppositional to pupil tastes. The practical problems of conducting evaluative discussions in the classroom will be far more familiar to English teachers than they are to media theoreticians, as I have suggested elsewhere. Classroom experience suggests

> ... that the objective of arriving at value judgements closes up rather than opens out discussion; that it is too easy to obtain evaluative responses from pupils, and thereafter too difficult to move beyond them; that as soon as a programme is evaluated as bad (or Processed) or good (or Authentic) then the impetus for further investigation disappears and is likely to be seen by pupils as an unnecessary 'pulling to pieces'; that evaluative responses force students to make individual stands and take personal positions, a more threatening procedure and ultimately one less productive of dialogue than say a systematic group exploration; that one of the keys to unlocking responses is to move students towards making statements which seem to them to have some validity, irrespective of their own personal feelings and tastes. If judgement can be suspended and mass-media material simply examined—seen more clearly—so that a wider and more complex range of meanings and values can become apparent, then discussion can flow and the necessity for discrimination, an irrelevance to the process of understanding, withers away.
>
> The movement advocated here from appreciation to investigation is underpinned by a shift away from an elitist definition of culture—'the best that has been thought and written in the world' —to a view of culture which is descriptive of the values manifest in the arts and institutions of a society and the behaviour of its groups and individuals. The gain is intellectual as well as obviously social and political. For under the first definition of culture very little can be said about a wide range of television programmes; they are simply 'trivial', 'processed' and unworthy of serious reflection. Yet such programmes all need elucidation, all need to be read as cultural texts, iconic in character, which can be decoded to reveal large numbers of meanings. The codings themselves will reveal and embody the ideology and professional practices of the broadcasting institutions, demonstrate the constructed and mediated nature of the 'normal' world of the programmes, and invite a comparison with other possible, but suppressed codings. It is with cultural criticism in this sense that the study of television should be concerned.[38]

Suggested here in broad terms is a possible programme for television education. The next section will elaborate upon that outline and attempt to be precise about the role which English teachers might play in such an education.

So far I have described the influence of English teachers on media education in negative terms. What positive and more detailed suggestions can be offered as to the possible constituents of a worthwhile television education? The answer involves, I believe, an almost inescapable logic. For to argue for the study of television is to imply—correctly in my view—that the medium is *non-transparent*. A 'window on the world' view of the medium would make its study impossible. One would not be examining television, but other things—sport, current affairs or drama, for example. The case for television education rests upon the idea that the medium is actively involved in constructing 'reality' rather than neutrally transmitting it. Television, that is, deals in *representations*. The ideological power of the medium resides in the naturalness of these representations, and the plausibility of the professionally polished images, seamless in their continuity, which mask the mediating processes at work. The ideological potency of television arises precisely from the power of those who control and work in it to pass off as 'real' or 'true' an *inevitably* partial and selective (and almost always white, male, middle-class, middle-aged and heterosexual) view of the world.

If television images and programmes are constructs then four areas immediately and logically present themselves for further investigation:

1 *Who* is responsible for these constructions?

2 *How* precisely is the ideological effect noted above achieved (i.e. what are the dominant techniques and codings currently employed within broadcasting)?

3 *What* values are implicit in the world so constructed?

4 *How* are these constructions read?

It will now be apparent why most of the recent initiatives within media education have been taken by social scientists. For the first and fourth areas (the nature of broadcasting institutions, the sociology of the communicating professions, and problems relating to audience response) are of traditional concern to social scientists, whilst the second and third areas involve handling concepts such as 'social construction' and 'ideology', which are as familiar to sociologists as they are alien to most literary specialists. In the analysis of particular programmes it is not always possible or necessarily desirable to treat these four areas discretely for they are often interpenetrating and mutually illuminating. For the sake of clarity, however, the problems and issues relating to each area will be considered separately:

1 *Who Constructs Television's Representations?*

The question has tended to be answered in very different ways by English specialists and sociologists. The former have frequently attempted to search out the presiding creative presence in particular programmes. This hang-over from literary critical practice was applied with some, though not unqualified, success to film studies, breathing life into the *auteur* theory and producing, in the work of a Leavisite critic like Robin Wood, examples of precisely those discriminations within popular culture advocated by Hoggart.[39] Film studies did gain from its association with literary criticism a rigour in textual analysis which it would otherwise have lacked. But particular emphasis upon the director as author placed difficulties in the way of understanding film as a commercial, collaborative and industrial form. The tendency to associate the study of television with film led, as we have seen, to even less convincing attempts at establishing authorship.[40] The appearance as late as 1981 of a volume on *British Television Drama*, a collection of essays on the television work of 'creative' dramatists such as Jim Allen, Alan Plater and David Mercer, merely serves to point the limitations of an 'individualistic' cultural analysis wrenched from the economic and institutional contexts within which television plays are actually produced.[41]

Sociologists, on the other hand, have paid a great deal of attention to media institutions and the routine practices of the communicating professions. Whilst some writers, most notably Murdock and Golding,[42] have argued that media education must *begin* from a concrete analysis of economic relations and the ways in which they structure cultural processes and products, it would be surprising if many English teachers were to be sympathetic to this view, for it carries with it obvious dangers of reductionism—the reading off of the text from its economic 'determinants'—and fails to give due weight to the specificity of the text. The *relative* weight to be attached to cultural and economic analyses is, indeed, a matter of lively debate amongst sociologists, and is part of a more general argument within Marxism about the relative autonomy of superstructure from economic base. For as long as it can be argued, however, that the relationship between aesthetic product and economic base is complex, mediated and indirect, and certainly whilst it is still possible to argue, as Stuart Hall has done, that the symbolic form of the message has a privileged position,[43] then space will certainly exist for the deployment of the kind of skills in close textual analysis which English teachers are well equipped to develop in their students. Such analysis must recognize its own limitations however and be informed at all points by the sociological and economic data available. The work of such writers as Burns, Schlesinger, the Glasgow Media Group, Cohen and Young, Alvarado and Buscombe, and Murdock and Golding will need to be more widely known amongst English teachers than it is at present.[44] These texts are a basic starting point for anyone wishing to analyze television. In short, English teachers who wish to work effectively with the medium must take cognizance of work going on in other disciplines, and be prepared to unlearn some of their own most cherished attitudes and assumptions.

2 How Does Television Construct its Representations?

A critical understanding of television will involve a reversal of the process through which the medium selects and edits diverse images into a polished, continuous and seamless flow. It will involve, that is, the deconstruction of television texts by breaking through the surface of the images to reveal the techniques through which meanings are produced. The project is analogous to that undertaken in the theatre by Brecht, and in the cinema by Godard. Substitute 'television' for 'theatre' in the following quotation, which outlines Brecht's critique of bourgeois theatre, and it becomes possible to see how deconstruction can lead to a more scientific viewing of television programmes, and, indeed, become part of a more totally liberating curriculum for schools:

> Bourgeois theatre, Brecht argues, is based on 'illusionism': it takes for granted the assumption that the dramatic performance should directly reproduce the world. Its aim is to draw an audience, by the power of this illusion of reality, into an empathy with the performance, to take it as real and feel enthralled by it. The audience in bourgeois theatre is the passive consumer of a finished, unchangeable art-object offered to them as 'real'. The play does not stimulate them to think constructively of how it is presenting its characters and events, or how they might have been different. Because the dramatic illusion is a seamless whole which conceals the fact that it is constructed, it prevents an audience from reflecting critically on both the mode of representation and the actions represented.
>
> Brecht recognized that this aesthetic reflected an ideological belief that the world was fixed, given and unchangeable, and that the function of the theatre was to provide escapist entertainment for men trapped in that assumption. Against this, he posits the view that reality is a changing, discontinuous process produced by men and so transformable by them.[45]

However much we may be sucked into the realism of a particular film or play, however, we are always finally aware that we are watching representations—performances which have been scripted, rehearsed and acted—and not reality. This is far from the case with television, where even the most alert critic constantly needs to be on his/her guard against the apparent authenticity of the images on the screen. The necessity for deconstruction in television analysis then is even more imperative than it is in the theatre or the cinema.

A simple start can be made by deconstructing photographs. Harold Evans' compilation, *Pictures on a Page*, and the magazine, *Camerawork*, provide many examples of how photography operates as a system of visual editing.[46] A first step is to draw attention to the unseen presence and intentions of the photographer who has constructed the image, selected *that* moment, that angle, and may even have arranged that composition. A second is to show the ways in which a photographic print, which will represent for most pupils 'the finished product', is merely the raw material for further editing, selecting and cropping. A great deal of well-produced photographic material is now cheaply available which gives pupils practice in constructing their own media products. A number of selection and editing exercises is distributed by the Society for Education in Film and Television (SEFT),[47] Evans provides material which allows scope for creative cropping and layout exercises, in which pupils' work can be compared with the results achieved by the picture editors of different newspapers,[48] whilst a recent simulation, *Choosing the News*, requires pupils to lay out the front page of a newspaper by selecting and cropping photographs, and choosing stories from a wide variety of written and visual material.[49]

Finally, the relationship between photograph and any accompanying text—caption, headline or article—will need to be explored, for an understanding of the relationship will be of critical importance in the eventual deconstruction of television texts. The best available material here is *Teachers' Protest*,[50] a photoplay exercise which includes background information, press reports and packs of thirty photographs and slides which pupils have to manipulate and organize for presentation as documentary material within a number of possible formats. Teachers' notes accompany the pack and suggest many ways of using the material within the classroom. The exercises suggested ('Try telling the story in a deliberately biased way', 'make a police training film', 'make part of a textbook for television camera-men', etc.), are by no means unchallenging and assume some familiarity in handling visual material as well as a basic understanding of the nature and purpose of captions. I have used *Teachers' Protest* with most success when I have prepared the way for its use with one or two simpler caption exercises, which really do sharpen awareness of the relationship between words and pictures, and encourage close scrutiny of the visual evidence presented by pictures:

(i) Prepare a set of cards, each consisting of one newspaper photograph and two captions, the real one, and one which is made up. The fictitious caption should give a completely different interpretation of the picture, but should still be quite appropriate to it. Students must choose the correct caption.

(ii) Prepare a set of cards each consisting of one newspaper photograph and two accompanying *headlines*, one, the headline actually attached to the photograph, the other, a headline which *might* have been attached to it but wasn't. Again, students must guess the correct headline.

Follow-up work to *Teachers' Protest* might include a slide presentation, in which *different* captions which have been attached by the class to the *same* picture are collated by the teacher for class discussion. This exercise draws attention very clearly to the ambiguous nature of much visual evidence, and to the function of captions in anchoring meaning to visual material.

Having cut their teeth on this much simpler photographic material, students should now be able to look critically at the relationship between televised sounds and images. Acquiring the ability to 'shred' the visual image from its accompanying commentary is an important step towards tele-literacy, and the polysemic nature of visual evidence can be demonstrated by showing television news and documentary film without commentary, so that a range of possible interpretations and anchorages may be explored before the commentary is revealed.

This kind of exercise takes the filmed material as 'given', but as with photographic exercises it is necessary to examine the processes through which filmed 'reality' is manufactured. Again, the limitations of simply analyzing the images on the screen need to be stressed. The closest scrutiny cannot reveal what was *not* shot by the film crew nor what ended up on the cutting room floor. Neither does it easily give up the *coded* nature of the information transmitted. Whatever appears on the screen so often seems simply 'natural' rather than the end product of a whole range of choices and options. Hence the importance of simulation as a method of learning, the value of practical video work, and the significance of the production of media materials by the students themselves in which a range of alternative codings can be explored, and the images produced are necessarily seen as 'preferred' ones.

Television does not simply construct events however. It attaches significance to them, gives them meaning. How is this achieved? First of all the act of selection itself marks some events, issues or people as being more important, valuable or significant than others. Television tells us what is important by what it covers, and by what it does not. But the medium also defines the way in which these events should be discussed, and the interpretative frameworks which should be brought to bear upon them. This is sometimes known as television's agenda-setting function. A great deal of research on television news has demonstrated how there is a consistency about the recurrent explanations, evaluations and assumptions which are brought to bear upon the coverage of, say, industrial relations (to take only the most blatant example) and which permeate the very language in which they are reported.[51] In Galtung and Ruge's nice paradox '"news" are actually "olds" because they correspond to what one expects to happen'.[52] Or in the words of a reporter, news is 'simple clichés set to music—you select the right cliché and you write it up to suit the particular circumstances'.[53]

Altheide's research on American television news confirms the point. He shows how most stories are 'already pretty well set before they leave the station . . . . The story is simply the . . . medium through which a definition of an event—the angle—is presented'.[54] The task of the reporter is, for the most part, simply to seek evidence which supports the angle. Halloran *et al.*'s case-study of media coverage of an anti-Vietnam war demonstration provides a classic example of how this works in practice.[55] A preconceived formula of 'expected violence' provided the framework for the media's coverage of the event. When the 'violent' protest turned out to be peaceful, emphasis was placed upon those violent elements present and there was even reference to 'buildings which were *not* attacked'. An extract from the televison news commentary illustrates the nature of the interpretative framework:

> The police were taking care today that the violence of last March would not be repeated. Occasional searches on roads into London produced little result, itself encouraging. The demonstrators continued at least without obvious weapons.[56]

The framework here not only structures and carries the meaning of the event, it excludes, of course, other possible frameworks. It would have been quite possible to have seen the demonstration, as Halloran, Murdock and Elliott point out, as the way in which many thousands of morally right young people were protesting against a barbaric and unjust war in Vietnam.

As to why some interpretative frameworks rather than others should become familiar and well-established, explanations have included the essentially conservative and hierarchical nature of the broadcasting institutions, their susceptibility to overt and indirect political pressure, the middle-class biases of their personnel, a philosophic commitment towards 'balance' and consensual explanatory models, the extent to which journalists are reliant upon established institutions (the police, the army, the law courts, big businesses, football clubs, etc.) as news sources, and the ability of such sources to manage news and set events within their own interpretative contexts, and the over-accessibility of the media to those in powerful and privileged positions.[57]

Some views—those of revolutionaries or the IRA, for example—are scarcely ever offered by television. Other voices are, but they form part of what we might term a 'secondary' discourse which it is the privilege and function of the medium's dominant discourse to place and evaluate for us. Colin MacCabe's discussion of 'the hierarchy of discourses' within the nineteenth-century classic realist text is curiously appropriate to this aspect of television:

A classic realist text may be defined as one in which there is a hierarchy amongst the discourses which compose the text and this hierarchy is defined in terms of an empirical notion of truth. Perhaps the easiest way to understand this is through a reflection on the use of inverted commas within the classic realist novel. While those sections in the text which are contained in inverted commas may cause a certain difficulty for the reader—a certain confusion vis-a-vis what really is the case—this difficulty is abolished by the unspoken (or more accurately the unwritten) prose that surrounds them. In the classical realist novel the narrative prose functions as a metalanguage that can state all the truths in the object language—those words held in inverted commas—and can also explain the relation of this object language to the real. The metalanguage can thereby explain the relation of this object language to the world and the strange methods by which the object languages attempt to express truths which are straightforwardly conveyed in the metalanguage. What I have called an unwritten prose (or a metalanguage) is exactly that language, which while placing other languages between inverted commas and regarding them as certain material expressions which express certain meanings, regards those same meanings as finding transparent expression within the metalanguage itself. Transparent in the sense that the metalanguage is not regarded as material; it is dematerialised to achieve perfect representation—to let the identity of things shine through the window of words.[58]

Brunsdon and Morley in their study of *Nationwide* have shown that the anchorpersons convey through the programme's metalanguage—linking, framing, commenting upon and placing each item—how the programme's other discourses should be read.[59] And it remains true in television programmes of all kinds, even given the inevitable slanting and selectivity inherent in every image, that we are still rarely allowed to judge such images on their own merits. As the audience, we are habitually nudged in the direction of this or that preferred meaning. This is generally established even before the item begins. Here are two conventional and unremarkable examples:

Changing the subject completely, over the last few months quite a few musicals have come and gone on the London stage with themes so varied that it seems song-writers will try anything in their search for success. Well, yet another new formula is being tried out at *Her Majesty's Theatre*. It's called *Fire Angel* and it's based on the unlikely combination of a New York Mafia setting and the story of Shakespeare's *Merchant of Venice*. Well, while the Bard may be revolving in his grave, let's meet the co-writers . . . [60]

There's no end to the questions that MPs put to Ministers. The frequent recipient of hard questions is the Foreign Secretary. The most unexpected question, surely, is one he's received from a Birmingham MP. It's all about the clothes the Queen is wearing on her tour of the Middle East. The questioner wants Her Majesty to stop pandering to what he calls 'the customs of religious bigots' by wearing long covering dresses. Now this, he claims, is insulting to the Queen's own sex. The questioner is Mr John Lee, Handsworth's Labour MP. He talks now to Peter Colbourne.

After the interview with Mr Lee the item was 'wrapped up' by the linkperson with the final comment: 'I think that people will agree that, despite the problems, the Queen is doing a great job'.[61]

The impressions conveyed here—of desperate exploitation by the writers of the musical, or of quirky eccentricity by the MP—were not at all reinforced by the interviewees themselves who seemed bemused by the angle taken. But they *were* reinforced by the interviewers who far from being 'humble seekers after truth' (in Robin Day's well-worn phrase) continually sign-posted to us the viewers—by their tone, reactions, interruptions and gestures—how the words of the subjects were to be interpreted. Here are two further examples taken from the notoriously partial television coverage of the 'winter of discontent' (termed by one writer a 'winter of industrial mis-reporting'[62]) in early 1979: 'Isn't the strike by ambulancemen potentially one of the most disastrous things that could happen to society?' (John Stapleton, *Nationwide*, BBC 1, 16 January 1979). 'How do you justify putting lives at risk?' 'If somebody dies will it be on your conscience?' 'Is more money worth a life?' (BBC News, 19 January 1979).[63]

It takes an extremely confident and accomplished interviewee to challenge such signposting, and construct his own alternative meanings. Arthur Scargill, James Callaghan and Brian Clough are amongst the few who regularly demonstrate the technique:

Interviewer: The coal board does seem to be having some trouble selling all the coal it can at the moment. Presumably that will limit its ability to pay when you do come round to presenting this claim.

Arthur Scargill: Well, if we'd have listened to that sort of argument of course we would never have had the increase in 1972, nor the increase in 1974. The fact that we're not able to sell the coal which we are producing at the moment is due to a number of factors, not least of which is the importation of foreign coal by certain industrialists.

I: So overall you're accepting only a partial defeat today.

A.S.: Overall I'm accepting a total victory today.[64]

> Robert Mackenzie: May I bring your mind to the fact that almost every government in Europe is a coalition . . . . Why is it part of Labour Party dogma to oppose coalition?
>
> James Callaghan: Now, now, now, come on, now don't let you try to get me into a position where you're saying this is only Labour Party dogma. The Conservatives have argued this for years.[65]

> Interviewer (to Trevor Francis on signing for Nottingham Forest for a fee of one million pounds): And when will you play your first game, Trevor?
>
> Brian Clough (interrupting): When I pick him.[66]

Such reversals are exceptional. For the most part presenters remain firmly in control, their status as guarantors of truth reinforced by the medium's dominant visual codings. For example they, like station announcers, newsreaders, and weather forecasters are amongst the small band of people who are allowed to talk direct to camera:

> All these persons have one thing in common. They are there to give us information which we are asked to assume is accurate (as indeed some of it is), unbiased and authoritative, (which it is less likely to be). They have authority vested in them by the television organisations and can be described in a useful phrase as 'bearers of truth'. But there is another and more interesting category. It includes the monarch, the prime minister, cabinet ministers when they make official broadcasts (what are called ministerial broadcasts) and the leader of the parliamentary opposition front bench, who is allowed in certain circumstances to reply to a ministerial broadcast if the broadcasting authorities judge that it was controversial. All these persons—and one or two others including the Archbishop of Canterbury as head of the Church of England—are allowed to address the television audience ('the public' or 'the nation' as the broadcasters call it on such occasions) directly. They do so by reason of their constitutional or political authority. On other occasions (for instance when the Chancellor of the Exchequer is interviewed about the Budget) they are all (with the exception of the Queen) treated like ordinary people; that is to say, they are shown in profile or in such a way that their gaze is not fixed directly on the viewers but on the interviewer who is with them in the studio. In other words their statements have to pass through someone else, as it were—they have to be mediated. If they attempt to take on the role of a person of authority and address an audience directly, the director will cut away from them and go back to a shot of the interviewer . . . . There are, however, certain politically unimportant persons who *are* allowed to address the camera directly

—people like comedians, who are the equivalent of medieval jesters and, like the jesters, are allowed to act as if they had the same privileges as the men and women of power in our society. For that is what the full face picture means: that the man or woman on the screen has power and authority.[67]

The whole area of visual coding deserves specific attention in any consideration of how the medium constructs its meanings. Authority is reinforced or undermined not simply by eye-contact patterns, but by appearance, dress and the way in which the image is framed:

The convention is that in 'factual' programmes they (subjects) should be shot from eye-level and not from above or below, since shots from either of these angles would present an image slanted in more senses than one. The other convention deals with the question of how 'tight' a shot may be. Generally, important figures will be shown in medium close-up which shows them from the waist up. This may be replaced by a close-up which shows only the subject's head and shoulders. It would be very rare for a big close-up—a shot showing only the head—to be used of an important person. Just as in our normal social intercourse we observe certain conventions about how close we come to other people and how close we allow them to come to us, so when choosing their images, television cameras keep a certain distance from their subjects . . . . It is almost inconceivable that one should see on the television screen a big close-up of a figure of authority—of a prime minister or international statesman. The camera stands back from them. But in the case of ordinary people it is not unknown for the camera to come close in, particularly if the subject is in a state of emotional excitement, grief or joy.[68]

Similarly, there are codes of geography within a studio which tell us who is important and who less so, or which indicate the relationship which exists between the subjects on the screen. The positioning of an interviewer between proponents of two conflicting views is a powerful visual reinforcement of the broadcaster's 'neutrality'. On the other hand, in 'chat' shows, interviewees sit together in comfortable chairs in keeping with their role as 'guests'. The Glasgow University Media Group has drawn attention to the dominant codings in the reporting of industrial relations news:

. . . all those things which enhance a speaker's status and authority are denied to the mass of working people. This means that the quiet of studios, the plain backing, the full use of name and status are often absent. The people who transcribed our material here pointed out to us that the only time they had difficulty making out what was said was in interviews with working people. Not because of 'accent', but because they were often shot in group situations, outside, and thus any individual response was difficult to hear. The danger here is that news coverage is often offering up what amounts to stereo-typical images of working people.[69]

Patterns of editing are also worth observing. A significant element in the controversy over the documentary film, *Yesterday's Men*,[70] for example, in which the impact of defeat on senior members of the Labour government which fell in 1970 was treated in a way which infuriated Harold Wilson and many Labour politicians, lay in the programme's break with the traditional codings of political interviews:

> For instance, *Yesterday's Men* indicated a certain stance towards its subjects because of the length of shot devoted to a subject. In 'normal' political interviews the vision mixer cuts between participants which builds up a picture of the standard flow of conversational interaction; if the camera dwells on the subject it 'means' something different.[71]

Tracey, in a detailed case-study of the *Yesterday's Men* affair,[72] argues that problems arose because of 'the presuppositions of politicians about the nature of programmes emerging from the [BBC's Current Affairs] Group.'[73] It was the 'breaking out of traditional formulae that led to the political controversy.'[74] Instead of the 'serious' Panorama-type treatment they expected (and clearly felt they should have been accorded), Labour politicians found themselves the subjects of a 'send-up'.

A conventional visual coding within recorded interviews is worthy of particular attention with school pupils. This is the use of the 'cutaway' from the interviewee either to the interviewer or to a piece of silent film. The purpose of cutaways is to make an edited, constructed event appear 'natural' and unedited by covering over cuts in the original film. The 'jump' cut in which the editing is generally fully exposed to the audience is a more honest device, but it is somewhat infrequently used since it deliberately reveals the illusion behind the 'continuity' of an interview. Silent film will often be used within interviews where it is necessary to cover a large number of edits in a short period of time.

Finally, mention must be made of one of television's dominant techniques for shaping the events it handles: the use of narrative. Television tells stories. News, current affairs programmes, documentaries, sports programmes all create little dramas with their own heroes, villains, conflicts, reversals, rewards and resolutions. Dramatic shaping is endemic to most forms of editing for television. As documentary film-maker Frederick Wiseman has suggested,

> Documentaries . . . are fictional forms . . . . Editing is the assessment and evaluation of individual sequences and the assembling of these disparate, originally unrelated fragments, into a dramatic form. This

process has an internal and external aspect: internal in the need
to compress a sequence down to a usable form, external in the way
individual edited sequences are joined so as to impose a thematic
and dramatic unity on otherwise chaotic material.[75]

The shaping of events and issues into fictional forms has been investigated
by Heath and Skirrow in their analysis of *World in Action*[76] and Bazalgette
and Paterson in their study of television news coverage of the Iranian
Embassy siege which, as they demonstrate, 'is open to analysis in the same
way as any other narrative.'[77] Their suggestion that 'this approach may
offer a way of understanding how the political aspect of events as recounted
in both news and fiction is marginalised, and how they remain interesting
and pleasurable in spite of the lack of explanation, motivation, contextu-
alisation'[78] hints at the dominant fiction which underpins the medium's
penchant for narrative: that there does indeed exist an unproblematic and
disinterested 'position' from which the story may be told. In the deathless
words of the President of CBS News, 'Our reporters do not cover stories
from their point of view. They are presenting them from nobody's point
of view.'[79]

Hence the strength of the assertion that 'narrative is an element that
militates against knowledge ... because it attempts to conceal itself, to
imply that this is how the world is.'[80] But as we have seen 'how the world
is' *contains* the positions fed to the viewer by editing, framing, commentary,
visual codings, etc. This militates against knowledge not because of 'bias'
or the suppression or demotion of alternative viewpoints, but because what
is concealed is the notion of the text as a site for the construction of meanings which need to be considered and analyzed in relation to the position,
interests and intentions of its producers. English teachers might wish to
reflect upon the extent to which printed texts might be similarly susceptible
to the kind of analysis outlined in this chapter. Could reading become more
scientific through the analysis not of a 'finished text' but of the 'position'
of its writer, those offered to its readers, and of the ways through which its
meanings are produced?

3 *What Values are Implicit in the World so Constructed?*

Analysis of the world presented to us by television may proceed through
the elaboration of meanings generated at denotative, connotative and
ideological levels:

(i) *Denotation*. If students are to be encouraged to look at television more
scientifically they will need to be fully aware of the nature of the information communicated by television. As Umberto Eco has expressed it:

> ... if you want to use television for teaching somebody something,
> you have first to teach somebody how to use television. In this
> sense television is not so different from a book. You can use books

> to teach, but first you must teach people about books, at least about alphabet and words . . . [81]

If we wish students 'to use television' then we will need to begin by challenging a view which many of them will hold: that television for the most part communicates simply and unambiguously so that when a programme has been seen 'there's nothing to discuss', for no problems arise from it.[82] Any television teacher then will have two primary tasks. First of all, s/he will need to demonstrate that the act of seeing is fraught with problems and difficulties, and that though visual evidence appears seductively open and innocent, it is invariably partial, ambiguous and open to interpretation. This can be introduced by using some of the many puzzles, tricks and illusions to be found in the literature on the psychology of perception. Secondly, it will be necessary to demonstrate that television images are overloaded with information, through increasing awareness of the variety of non-verbal channels along which meanings may be carried. Both areas of activity will pose new challenges to many English teachers, though Andrew Wilkinson argued some time ago that English teaching ought to be concerned with 'total' rather than mere linguistic communication,[83] and certainly the study of drama (to say nothing of that form of television study which consists of reading published scripts) has been too often impoverished by exclusive attention to the written text.

I have described elsewhere how different aspects of non-verbal communication may be explored and elucidated through the use of role-play, simulation and discussion, and how their relevance to television may be established.[84] Here it is enough to emphasize that the simple cognitive task of describing in detail what appears on the screen is one which must be given its due weight in the classroom. Group perceptions will be enormously rich, and need to be tapped and placed at the disposal of each individual. There will frequently be major discrepancies in perception between individuals which may create major misinterpretations later if they are not quickly identified. And often a simple detail, noted by one person, can open up the ideological implications of a programme for the entire group.

An example: in 1977, *Panorama*, as a contribution to Prime Minister Callaghan's Great Educational Debate, devoted an entire programme to a film by Angela Pope, *The Best Days?*, set in a 'typical' London comprehensive school. 'This isn't a conventional *Panorama* report,' said David Dimbleby in opening the programme. 'There's no reporter and no commentary. It offers, instead, a fly-on-the-wall view of life in one school today.' The film covered a 'typical' school day, and in a key five-minute sequence a particularly disorganized and disorderly history lesson with 'an average third form' was shown in which very little seemed to be taught or learned. The teacher was ill-prepared and the class, clearly bored with the subject (nineteenth-century Prussia), largely ignored what the teacher was saying and talked amongst themselves. The scene represented was the very epitome of comprehensive education as readers of the *Daily Mail, Daily Telegraph* or *Daily Express* would recognize it—less a contribution to the Great Debate than a graphic demonstration of its necessity.

In looking closely at this sequence one of the students thought she noticed something strange which no one else had observed: half-way through the lesson some writing had mysteriously appeared on what had previously been a clean blackboard behind the teacher. We checked the sequence again. The observation was correct. Indeed, *three* entire blackboards had been filled with writing by the teacher. This considerable task had apparently been accomplished in the middle of a difficult lesson with an unruly class.

Then someone else noticed something about the content of the lesson: it made no sense. The class had been given the original task of copying a map. Then, without any explanation offered within the film, we see them all copying down large chunks of writing from the board. The inconsistency was obvious. But again only one person had noticed it. The most likely explanation seemed to be that 'the lesson' was a fiction manufactured from the content of two lessons filmed on separate occasions. There is nothing unusual about this, of course—it is normal and often inevitable practice in film making—but it does undermine the status which the programme claims for the film as document rather than fiction. And the *degree* of compression involved is of some importance. Here we have perhaps eighty minutes of teaching encapsulated in five minutes of film. (How many football fans would ever wish to pass an opinion on a match on the basis of this amount of evidence?) The evidence presented, moreover, is clearly loaded. There is particular emphasis on the beginning and ending of 'the lesson', times when any class will be at its least settled. Since the class was copying material down from the board there would almost certainly have been periods lacking in visual interest (i.e. when the class was working) which we do not see. The criteria by which material was allowed to pass through the director's highly selective sieve are self-evident. Strict limits to the range of material available will of course have been set by the nature of the director's pre-shooting briefing to her cameraperson. The angle will have been established on this particular teacher and his class before the camera began to roll. Again, from the evidence available it is quite clear what this angle was.

A great deal more could be said about this sequence, particularly its reliance on reaction shots (demonstrating how little attention is being paid to the teacher by his class) which are simply the creations of the editing. I only wish to show here, however, how one hawk-eyed student can illuminate for everyone how television, far from being a 'fly-on-the-wall' is continuously engaged in the active construction of meaning.

(ii) *Connotation and Ideology.* I have drawn some attention to the importance of accurate description of television images since the area is not one normally regarded as problematic within the study of literary texts. If I pay correspondingly less attention to connotative analysis it is because this is a level of analysis in which most English specialists will already be well practised and to which, in television, they can bring a much needed rigour. I have tried to show elsewhere how attention to connotative meaning needs to be built in to early exercises on non-verbal communication from the very beginning. In television programmes, as in literary texts, deeper themes manifest themselves as connotative 'clusters', or 'chains' of associations, nuances and suggestions through which structures of meaning (often not evident to their producers) come to be revealed. Whilst in literary study the purpose of attention to connotation has traditionally been to show how the resonances of language produce in the work multi-layered complexities in meaning and structure, in television such meanings have an *ideological* rather than merely aesthetic purchase, as Stuart Hall has suggested:

> The visual sign is . . . also a connotative sign. And it is so pre-eminently within the discourses of modern mass communication. The level of connotation of the visual sign . . . is precisely the point where the denoted sign intersects with the deep semantic structures of a culture, and takes on an ideological dimension . . . . These connotative codes are the 'linguistic' means by which the domains of social life, the segmentations of culture, power and ideology are made to signify. They refer to the 'maps of meaning' into which any culture is organised, and those 'maps of social reality' have the whole range of social meanings, practices and usages, power and interest 'written in' to them. Connotated signifiers, Barthes has reminded us 'have a close communication with culture, knowledge, history and it is through them, so to speak, that the environmental world invades the linguistic and semantic system. They are, if you like, the fragments of ideology'.[85]

Of course, as I have suggested, ideological questions perhaps ought to have a more significant place in the practice of literary criticism and in any examination of the assumptions of that practice than they do. But in television analysis the *centrality* of ideological questions can scarcely be denied given the medium's continual tendency to blur the distinctions between the 'objective' and the selectively constructed, the 'real' and its representation.

How can comprehensive school pupils best grasp the concept of ideology? The question is crucial, but difficult. First of all, the apparent 'innocence' of non-verbal communication, which is one of its most compelling characteristics, needs to be examined. The values implicit in gestures, modes of dress, the function and design of objects, or some of the typical rituals and modes of communication in school can be explored in a way which draws attention both to their apparent naturalness, spontaneity, even 'inevitability', and to the importance of the human choice and control which lie behind them. It is of some importance that students, and even quite young pupils, should not regard non-verbal communication systems simply as worthy of study in their own right, but as inextricably connected with the political, economic and social systems which give them life. The cultural analyses of Roland Barthes in *Mythologies*,[86] in which he considers such phenomena as haircuts in the film *Julius Caesar*, the new Citroen, toys, and the face of Garbo, provide sophisticated examples of the kind of work which can be carried out at their own level by quite young pupils. This chapter has attempted to outline some of the ways in which this work might be taken forward and developed in relation to television in which a constructed world embodying coherent patterns of ideas and structures of belief appears to us as a natural phenomenon. Ideological understanding of television will involve the grasping both of those patterns and structures, and of the significance of their natural embodiment. As I have suggested those patterns and structures begin to *reveal themselves* when we pay attention to connotative levels of meaning. Finally, ideological analysis must begin to grapple with two further questions. What function do these ideas have in our society? (That is, what are their material consequences? What 'work' are they required to do?) And where do these ideas come from? (That is, what material conditions did they spring from? What has been their historic function?) For 'whatever else it signals, the concept *ideology* makes a direct reference to the role of *ideas*. It also entails the proposition that ideas are not self-sufficient, that their roots lie elsewhere, that something central about ideas will be revealed if we can discover the nature of the determinacy which *non*-ideas exert over ideas. The study of "ideology" thus holds outs the promise of a critique of *idealism* as a way of explaining how ideas arise.'[87]

4 *How Are These Constructions Read?*

Problems relating to the differential reading of texts have not generally been of great concern to English teachers. Such problems surface explicitly in the classroom, but an important function of much English teaching has been to short-circuit them by positing the notion of the innocent/objective reader who needs to be self-effacing in his/her relationship to the text. Too often reading in schools has involved not the honing of personal responses to texts, not the making of meanings by pupils, but the subjugation of such responses to the sanctity of the text which can be 'known' through the practice of a criticism as ideologically innocent as the text itself. 'We have a lot to make up for', as Dr Anne Smith, sometime editor of *The Literary Review*, recently remarked. 'So many people have had all the confidence in their own opinions knocked out of them by the academic experts like me.'[88]

By contrast, the effects upon television audiences of the messages they receive have been so much the subject of investigation from the earliest days of the medium, that it is simply not possible to regard the reading of television images as unproblematic.[89] According to Stuart Hall, 'communication between the production elites in broadcasting and their audiences is necessarily a form of systematically distorted communication'.[90] A number of studies have indicated that television broadcasters know little about their audiences:[91] 'We would say that we've been broadcasting to the people along the corridor (i.e. to editorial and managerial superiors) not to the people who are listening', as one BBC newsman expressed it to Tom Burns.[92] Or in the words of another, cited by Schlesinger, 'I'm really writing for myself and the wife . . . the wife's my hardest critic.'[93] Whilst this degree of smugness is hard to take, it remains a matter of bleak fact that we too, as educationalists, know little about how our students decode the media messages they receive. Yet the collection of such basic information is a precondition for any worthwhile media education.

Before examining problems of decoding however it is necessary to look a little more closely at the nature of the television message. For if the message is not an unproblematic, unilateral sign, neither is it completely open to any kind of reading which will gratify the needs of the decoders, as David Morley has pointed out:

> The TV message is . . . a complex sign, in which a preferred reading has been inscribed, but which retains the potential, if decoded in a manner different from the way in which it has been encoded, of communicating a different meaning. The message is thus a structured polysemy. It is central to the argument that all meanings do not exist 'equally' in the message: it has been structured in dominance, although its meaning can never be totally fixed or 'closed'. Further, the 'preferred reading' is itself part of the message, and can be identified within its linguistic and communicative structure . . . . The moment of 'encoding' thus exerts, from the production end, an 'over-determining' effect (though not a fully determined closure) on the succeeding moments in the communicative chain.[94]

To this qualification of the notion of audience response as a mass of differential readings must be added another: the extent to which individual and privileged responses actually fall into sub-cultural patterns:

> We need to break fundamentally with the 'uses and gratifications' approach, its psychologistic problematic and its emphasis on individual differences of interpretation. Of course, there will always be individual, private readings, but we need to investigate the extent to which these individual readings are patterned into cultural structures and clusters. What is needed here is an approach which links differential interpretations back to the socio-economic structure of society, showing how members of different groups and classes, sharing different 'culture codes', will interpret a given message differently, not just at the personal, idiosyncratic level,

but in a way 'systematically related' to their socio-economic position. In short we need to see how the different sub-cultural structures and formations within the audience, and the sharing of different cultural codes and competencies amongst different groups and classes, 'determine' the decoding of the message for different sections of the audience.[95]

Morley himself has provided the only direct evidence we have in the literature of the responses of different groups of students to the same television programmes (*Nationwide*). His report makes salutory reading. Particularly striking is the degree of hostility and alienation expressed by black students towards a programme whose very hallmark is its confident assumption and expression of consensual values.[96] As teachers we will need to engage much more with sub-cultural decodings than we ever have in the past. Some—those which are explicitly racist or sexist, for example—we will wish to challenge. And to some extent sub-cultural variations will scarcely be relevant to the kind of detached, scientific consideration of the ways in which meanings are produced by the medium which I have suggested earlier in this chapter. In other areas, however, the felt and authentic responses of students will be encouraged and worked with by the teacher who will need to understand their location within the patterns of values, ideas, emotions, beliefs and practices which constitute the students' sub-cultures. A teacher who is able to say in advance and with some degree of certainty how, say, *Mastermind* or *The Two Ronnies* is likely to be read by students of Indian, West Indian or white working-class origins will possess a skill of inestimable value and one worth working hard to acquire.

Teaching about television need not be an elaborately complex business. It is something which many hundreds of English teachers could do simply and effectively. Their failure to do so has meant that since Newsom there has passed through our schools *an entire generation*, of whom few have been given even rudimentary guidance on how television communicates its meanings. This is an omission of great magnitude. There are few signs of its being rectified, a situation which is likely to continue until English teachers again place the question of how they can best contribute to our children's understanding of television firmly upon their agendas. If the question is to be answered satisfactorily, however, more open attitudes will be necessary. Attempts to recuperate the study of the medium to this or that specialism will give only partial and distorted answers. Satisfactory solutions are more likely to be found by those able and confident enough to step outside of their own discipline, taking from it whatever is appropriate, discarding what is not, and by those intellectually curious enough to explore the contributions which other disciplines might make. It is those English teachers who regard their discipline not as a 'pure' retreat within which to withdraw from pressing practical problems, but as an intellectual tool which can contribute to their solution who will ultimately do most to ensure credibility for their subject. That is the challenge of the future. It is one important and worthy enough to be taken up by every English teacher.

Notes

1 *Report on Secondary Education* (Spens Report) (1938) HMSO, pp. 222–3.
2 *15 to 18* (The Crowther Report) (1959) HMSO, Vol. 1, para. 66.
3 LEAVIS, F.R., and THOMPSON, D. (1933) *Culture and Environment*, Chatto and Windus.
4 *ibid.*, p. 1.
5 *ibid.*, pp. 3–5.
6 *ibid.*, pp. 111, 121, 143.
7 BLACK, P. (1972) *The Mirror in the Corner*, Hutchinson, p. 111.
8 NUT (1960) Verbatim Report of Conference on *Popular Culture and Personal Responsibility*, NUT, p. 50.
9 *Report of the Committee on Broadcasting* (The Pilkington Report) (1962) HMSO.
10 Through its proposal that facilities be given to the BBC to provide BBC2 and its impact upon the Television Act, 1964, which strengthened the ITA at the expense of the companies and which led to the re-jigging and revoking of some of the franchises by the Authority in 1967.
11 NUT, *op. cit.*, p. 104.
12 TUCKER, N. (1966) *Understanding the Mass Media*, CUP, p. 2.
13 THOMPSON, D. (1964) Introduction to THOMPSON, D. (ed.) *Discrimination and Popular Culture*, Penguin, p. 20.
14 HALL, S., and WHANNEL, P. (1964) *The Popular Arts*, Hutchinson, p. 15.
15 *ibid.*, p. 109.
16 *ibid.*, p. 207.
17 *ibid.*, pp. 39 and 50.
18 *ibid.*, pp. 257 ff.
19 *ibid.*, pp. 127–30 and 265–8.
20 *Half Our Future* (The Newsom Report) (1963) HMSO, paras. 475–6.
21 TUCKER, *op. cit.*, and FIRTH, B. (1968) *Mass Media in the Classroom*, Macmillan.
22 TUCKER, *op. cit.*, p. 121.
23 FIRTH, *op. cit.*, p. 68.
24 *ibid.*
25 TUCKER, *op. cit.*, pp. 136–7.
26 HOGGART, R. in *The Observer*, 14 May 1961, reprinted as *Culture—Dead and Alive*, in *Speaking to Each Other, Vol. 1: About Society* (1970) Chatto and Windus, pp. 131–3.
27 See TAYLOR, R.L. (1978) *Art, an Enemy of the People*, Harvester, p. 47.
28 See ABRAMS, P., 'Radio and Television', in THOMPSON, D. (ed.) *op. cit.*, pp. 50–73.
29 MURDOCK, G., and PHELPS, G. (1973) *Mass Media and the Secondary School*, Macmillan, p. 48.
30 *ibid.*, p. 49.
31 *ibid.*, p. 51.
32 *A Language for Life* (The Bullock Report) (1975) HMSO, para. 22.14.
33 *ibid.*, para. 22.4.
34 *ibid.*, para. 22.14.

35 ABBS, P. (undated) 'Mass Culture and Mimesis', *Tract*, No. 22.

36 *ibid.*, pp. 10 and 18.

37 See MASTERMAN, L. (1980) *Teaching about Television*, Macmillan, pp. 173 ff.

38 *ibid.*, pp. 19–20.

39 See, for example, WOOD R. (1965) *Hitchcock's Films*, Zwemmer; (1967) *Arthur Penn*, Studio Vista; (1968) *Howard Hawks*, Secker and Warburg.

40 For a rare and creditable attempt to compare directional styles in light entertainment programmes see DYER, R. (1973) *Light Entertainment*, BFI Monograph, No. 2, esp. p. 14.

41 BRANDT, G.W. (ed.) (1981) *British Television Drama*, CUP. More satisfactory approaches to the study of televised drama are suggested in *Screen Education*, 35, summer 1980.

42 MURDOCK, G., and GOLDING, P. (1977) 'Capitalism, Communication and Class Relations', in CURRAN, J., GUREVITCH, M., and WOOLLACOTT, J. (eds.) *Mass Communication and Society*, Arnold.

43 HALL, S. (1973) *Encoding and Decoding in the Television Discourse*, Paper published by Centre for Contemporary Cultural Studies, University of Birmingham.

44 BURNS, T. (1977) *The BBC: Public Institution and Private World*, Macmillan; SCHLESINGER, P. (1978) *Putting 'Reality' Together*, Constable; GLASGOW UNIVERSITY MEDIA GROUP, (1976) *Bad News*, RKP, and (1980) *More Bad News*, RKP; COHEN, S., and YOUNG, J. (1973) *The Manufacture of News*, Constable; ALVARADO, M., and BUSCOMBE, E. (1978) *Hazell: The Making of a T.V. Series*, BFI/Latimer; MURDOCK, G., and GOLDING, P., *op. cit.*

45 EAGLETON, T. (1976) *Marxism and Literary Criticism*, Methuen, pp. 64–5.

46 EVANS, H. (1978) *Pictures on a Page*, Heinemann; *Camerawork*, published six times each year by the Half Moon Photography Workshop, 27 Alie Street, London E1. The notion of photography as a system of visual editing is from Szarkowski, quoted in SONTAG, S. (1979) *On Photography*, Penguin, p. 192.

47 *Teachers' Protest, The Visit, Swallow Your Leader, The Market, The Station*, available from SEFT, 29 Old Compton Street, London W1V 5PL, and for ILEA teachers only from the ILEA English Centre, Sutherland Street, London SW1V 4LM.

48 EVANS, H., *op. cit.*

49 SIMONS, M., and BETHELL, A. (1979) *Choosing the News*, ILEA English Centre.

50 *Teachers' Protest* devised by Michael Simons and Cary Bazalgette with additional material by Andrew Bethell and Simon Clements, obtainable from SEFT and the ILEA English Centre.

51 GLASGOW UNIVERSITY MEDIA GROUP, *Bad News* and *More Bad News*, *op. cit.*

52 GALTUNG, J., and RUGE, M. (1965) 'The Structure of Foreign News', *Journal of International Peace Research*, No. 1, reprinted in COHEN and YOUNG, *op. cit.*, p. 64.

53 CHIBNALL, S. (1977) *Law and Order News*, Tavistock, p. 35.

54 ALTHEIDE, D.L. (1976) *Creating Reality: How TV News Distorts Events*, Sage, pp. 76 ff.

55 HALLORAN, J.D., MURDOCK, G., and ELLIOTT, P. (1970) *Demonstrations and Communications: A Case Study*, Penguin.

56 *ibid.*, p. 223.

57 See BURNS, T., *op. cit.*, CHIBNALL, S., *op. cit.*, and HALL, S., *et al.* (1978) *Policing*

the Crisis, Macmillan (especially the chapter on 'The Social Production of News').

58 MacCabe, C. 'Realism and the Cinema', Screen, Vol. 16, No. 2, p. 8.

59 Brunsdon, C. and Morley, D. (1978) Everyday Television: Nationwide, Television Monograph No. 10, BFI, p. 61.

60 Pebble Mill at One, BBC, April 1979.

61 Midlands Today, BBC 1, 20 February 1979.

62 MacShane, D. (1979) 'There's a new bitterness ... ', The Media Reporter, Vol. 3, No. 3.

63 TUC (1979) A Cause for Concern, TUC, p. 30.

64 News at One, (ITN) 12 October 1978.

65 Panorama, 7 October 1974. Cited in Hall, S., Connell, I., and Curti, L. (1976) 'The Unity of Current Affairs Television', Cultural Studies, No. 9, p. 81.

66 ATV Today (ATV) 1 February 1979.

67 Hood, S. (1981) On Television, Pluto Press, pp. 3–4.

68 ibid., p. 5.

69 Glasgow University Media Group, op. cit., p. 26.

70 See Tracey, M. (1977) The Production of Political Television, Routledge, Ch. 10, and 'Yesterday's Men—A Case Study in Political Communication', in Curran, Gurevitch and Woollacott, op. cit.

71 Dyer, G. (1978) 'Teaching about Television Interviews', Screen Education, No. 27, p. 45.

72 Tracey, M., op. cit.

73 Tracey, M., in Curran et al., op. cit., p. 262.

74 ibid., p. 268.

75 Wiseman, F. (1981) 'Pride, Patience and Prejudice', The Guardian, 17 March 1981.

76 Heath, S., and Skirrow, G. (1977) 'Television: A World in Action', Screen, Vol. 18, No. 2.

77 Bazalgette, C., and Paterson, R. (1980/81) 'Real Entertainment: The Iranian Embassy Siege', Screen Education, No. 37, p. 55.

78 ibid., p. 56.

79 Altheide, op. cit., p. 17.

80 Williams, C. (ed.) (1980) Realism and the Cinema: A Reader, Routledge and Kegan Paul in assoc. with British Film Institute, p. 152.

81 Eco, U. (1979) 'Can Television Teach?', Screen Education, No. 31, p. 15.

82 See Masterman, op. cit., pp. 40 ff.

83 Wilkinson, A. (1972) 'Total Communication', English in Education, Vol. 6, No. 3.

84 Masterman, op. cit., Chs. 3 and 4.

85 Hall, S., 'Encoding and Decoding ...', op. cit., pp. 12 and 13.

86 Barthes, R. (1972) Mythologies, Cape.

87 Hall, S. (1978) 'The Hinterland of Science: Ideology and the "Sociology of Knowledge"', in Centre for Contemporary Cultural Studies, On Ideology, Hutchinson, pp. 10 and 11.

88 'The Prime of a Scottish Reviewer', The Guardian, 23 September 1981.

89 For a resumé of the principal modes of investigation see Morley, D. (1980) The 'Nationwide' Audience, Television Monograph No. 11, BFI.

90 Hall, S., 'Encoding and Decoding ...', op. cit., p. 1.

91 Burns, T., op. cit.; Gans, H.J. (1970) 'Broadcaster and Audience Values in the

Mass Media', *Transcription of the Sixth World Congress of Sociology*, September 1966, International Sociological Association; SCHLESINGER, P., *op. cit.*

92 BURNS, *op. cit.*, p. 200.

93 SCHLESINGER, *op. cit.*, p. 119.

94 MORLEY, D., *op. cit.*, pp. 10 and 12.

95 *ibid.*, pp. 14 and 15.

96 *ibid.*, pp. 71–4, 78–9, 87–8.

The Potential of the Microcomputer in the English Classroom

Daniel Chandler
Coordinator, 'Microcomputers in English' Group,
Schools Council Computers in the Curriculum Project

> They turned the pages, which were yellow and crinkly, and it was awfully funny to read words that stood still instead of moving the way they were supposed to—on a screen, you know. And then, when they turned back to the page before, it had the same words on it that it had when they read it the first time.
>
> ('The Fun They Had' by Isaac Asimov, from *Earth is Room Enough*)

Asimov's short story concerns two children of the future who discover a book about schooling as it is today. Neither of them has ever seen a book before, and 'school' for Margie and Tommy consists of sitting alone at home in front of a 'mechanical teacher' which simply asks questions, gives tests, calculates marks and (ironically) sets homework. To some teachers, Asimov's presentation of this doomsday vision would represent their own fears. One might trust any English teacher to agree that if s/he could be replaced by a computer then s/he ought to be: we are, after all, concerned with the exploration of the imagination and not with mechanistic instruction. However, it is to be hoped that sensitive teachers will not allow the image of the teaching machine to deter them from using the new microcomputers as a creative and liberating resource. Indeed, only if they were to neglect this responsibility would the model of learning implicit in the Asimov nightmare be likely to become unconsciously adopted in schools. It would be deeply tragic if the new technology were to serve only to reinforce retrogressive educational strategies.

If students are to remain in control of microelectronic technology they must become familiar with the uses and the limitations of computers, as well as learning how to use a keyboard, read a screen and select information. Certainly, as teachers concerned with overall competence in language, we cannot afford to neglect the fact that from now on 'illiterates' will not simply be those who cannot read 'words that stand still', but those who do not have the skills required to use a microcomputer with the same confidence that they might use a pen.

There are, I think, four main ways in which a microcomputer might be regarded by English teachers as being a useful classroom resource: for simulation gaming; for language games; as a word-processor of the sort that a journalist might use; and, with a 'viewdata' system, for what is beginning to be called the 'fourth R'—Information Retrieval.

Before I discuss these uses it may be in order to explain just how feasible it is for a microcomputer to be available in the English classroom. Basically, a simple microcomputer consists of a keyboard (containing the Central Processing Unit, or CPU), a video monitor (or even an ordinary television), and a data-storage system which can be simply an ordinary audio cassette-recorder (see Figure 1). The only new item you would be likely to need would be the keyboard unit—and it is already possible to buy an adequate one for around £300. At that price any English Department ought to be able to argue the case for one. Two desirable optional extras might best be made available as a central resource in the school (if they are not already): a printer (for 'hard copy' of what you type on the screen) and 'disk drives' (a faster and more versatile alternative to the cassette-recorder).

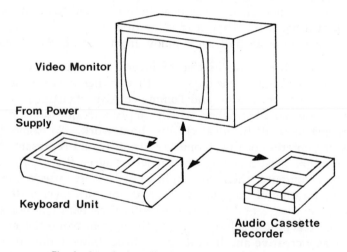

Video Monitor

From Power Supply

Keyboard Unit

Audio Cassette Recorder

Fig. 1. A typical small microcomputer system

If the reader is beginning to be haunted by visions of silent children staring into video screens I would like to emphasize that in my own view the best educational 'software' should assume that students will be using microcomputers in small groups, and should exploit this situation. An obvious way in which this can be done is by the use of simulation programs requiring group decision-making.

Computer-based simulation is rather different from the kind which focuses on dramatic role-play. No programs of this kind have as yet been developed specifically for English as far as I am aware, but I hope that some of the potential of this approach for the English classroom will become apparent after I have outlined two examples. One is an 'orthodox' computer-based simulation exercise and the other can be regarded as a type of simulation game.

Route is a program developed by Hertfordshire Advisory Unit for Computer-based Education to form part of an examination course in Environmental Studies*. It is concerned with the building of the A1M link through Hatfield in Hertfordshire and aims to encourage students to think of the associated environmental problems. Students are required to consider three types of road and the environmental cost of each of them, and then to plan a route through or around the town within a reasonable budget. The computer is able to perform complex calculations which might otherwise have been an obstacle to their understanding of the main issues and indeed to their enjoyment of the whole decision-making process. In such simulations it is possible for the computer to produce rapidly and graphically the results of suggested alternatives. Group discussions of controversial issues which might normally result in the ritualized exchange of clichés can, with such a focus, result in some real refinement of thinking and the language used to express it. Programs of this kind might not be out of place in English lessons in the context of the exploration of a suitable theme.

A program which appeals rather more to my own imagination and which I have found highly successful with students is a commercial game called 'Mission Impossible'. Although it was produced as a home entertainment program rather than as educational software it seems to me to have considerable potential as far as English is concerned. It is one of a series of 'Adventure' programs in which players must explore unknown territory by telling the computer exactly what to do. There are no 'graphics': the different locations in which the players find themselves are described on the screen as and when they are discovered. The object, as in the well-known role-play game of 'Dungeons and Dragons', is usually to find and accumulate 'treasures' in a fantasy world of sword and sorcery.

In 'Mission Impossible' the setting is modern, and the object is to prevent a nuclear reactor from exploding by finding and defusing a saboteur's time-bomb. It is intended to be a game for one player, but I have used it with many small groups as the centrepiece of a variety of language activities including code-breaking, map-making, role-play and crosswords. It would be no exaggeration to say that students find the game highly addictive, and the animated interaction that groups become involved in is always imaginative and co-operative.

A brief description of the game and of the way in which I have used it may be useful. Students are divided into groups of between four and six and the groups take it in turns to use the computer. Whilst one group sits

---

Route was developed with funding from the Schools Council Computers in the Curriculum Project and will be published by Longmans.

at the keyboard, the others are given assignments such as decoding passages which contain clues to help them when they take their turn. Those at the keyboard are told that they must allow the computer to be their 'puppet' and that they can issue commands in the form of two word sentences by using the keyboard as a typewriter. These commands ('go north', 'sit down', 'look around' and so on) enable them to explore the building and to manipulate anything they find there.

In Figures 2a and 2b 2a illustrates roughly what the screen looks like to those at the keyboard when the game begins. They are told which room they are in, what can be seen in it, and the direction they must go in order to leave the room. After giving the additional information shown, the computer waits to be told what to do. The only way in which the typing of their 'input' differs from using a typewriter is that at the end of a sentence they must press the white button labelled ENTER (other machines use the word RETURN or NEWLINE). With simpler programs I have found that even five-year-olds are quick to understand the principle of 'telling the computer you've finished'.

I AM IN A BRIEFING ROOM. VISIBLE ITEMS:

LARGE TAPE RECORDER.

    SOME OBVIOUS EXITS ARE: WEST

←--→

A MINUTE AGO SOMEONE RAN OUT OF THIS ROOM! BY THE WAY I SEEM TO BE CARRYING SOMETHING!

------------------------→   TELL ME WHAT TO DO?—

Fig. 2a. 'Mission Impossible': screen at beginning of game

I AM IN A BRIEFING ROOM. VISIBLE ITEMS:

LARGE TAPE RECORDER.

    SOME OBVIOUS EXITS ARE: WEST

←--→

GOOD MORNING MR PHELPS. YOUR MISSION (SHOULD YOU DECIDE TO ACCEPT IT) IS TO PREVENT THIS AUTOMATED NUCLEAR REACTOR FROM BEING DESTROYED BY A SABOTEUR'S TIME BOMB!

THE SABOTEUR (WHO ALSO REWIRED THE SECURITY SYSTEM) IS A HEART-PATIENT. HE PLANS TO COMMIT SUICIDE WITH THE REACTOR! HE IS STILL LOOSE IN THE BUILDING.
YOU'LL FIND SECURITY KEYS & A MAP IN THE MANILA ENVELOPE LYING NEXT TO THE TAPE PLAYER.
------------------------→   TELL ME WHAT TO DO?—

Fig. 2b. 'Mission Impossible': example of computer response during game

(Reproduced by kind permission of Molimerx Ltd, authorized
UK distributors for Adventure International software)

The usual response to the initial situation is for one of the group to type in 'follow him' (referring to the person who ran out of the room). The computer's response is, 'I see no-one here': students quickly learn to avoid imprecise commands!

Some teachers might regard it as a limitation that students are able to use sentences of only two words in length, with its consequent contortions of conventional grammar. On the contrary, I have found that the computer's responses to words it does not understand ('I don't know how to . . . something' and 'I don't know what . . . is') have been very useful indeed as a dynamic demonstration of the concept of verb and subject. Students tend to treat their group as an instant thesaurus when the computer insists, 'I must be stupid but I don't understand what you mean'.

Before the group can discover the object of the game they must instruct the computer to play the tape-recorder referred to in Figure 2a. Sometimes the computer has to suggest that they should 'try starting it' before they see the output illustrated in Figure 2b.

And so the game proceeds, through rooms and corridors, with students having to decide how to open locked doors, evade security cameras and ultimately defuse the bomb. As one student commented, 'the advantage of playing the game in a group is that you can all put your ideas forward of what to do next', with the result that all of the groups which have used the game have made more progress in an hour than I made in a week! Another student added the profound comment that working in a group makes the game more than just 'a private struggle against the machine'.

One of the things that students learn from the game is that using a video display does have its difficulties: they have to learn to notice that the screen is constantly changing in response to their inputs, and whilst those with whom I have discussed this have replied that they have had no difficulty in actually reading the words, one observed, 'I found it hard to go straight to the appropriate information on the screen.' The concentration required, as students often commented, was far greater than that required in their everyday reading of print, and yet with highly motivating material such as this they were able to sustain that kind of concentration in groups of five and six for more than an hour on occasions.

I have also used this game with a group of student teachers of English at Cambridge University, and it seems to me that an interesting lesson can be learnt from the fact that whilst the computer's occasional frank admission that 'I must be stupid' resulted in no comment from the school students other than that 'computers only understand what they've been told', a more common attitude amongst the university students was to regard this as a manifestation of the total inadequacy of the computer. As two journalists recently put it: 'Sit a child in front of a computer and s/he immediately uses it, relates to it, plays with it, laughs and cries over it, learns from it. When, and if, an adult layman approaches a computer, it's with an air of suspicion, hostility and often fear.'[1]

Appropriate word games on a microcomputer can be highly motivating with students who have particular difficulties with spelling: I have used my own version of Hangman to reinforce a dyslexic student's recognition of the patterns he had found most difficult to remember. I heard recently of an imaginative program called Spell Invaders, a modification of the infamous arcade game, in which children had to shoot down the correct letters to form a word.

Programs are already commercially available which can generate words and play the partner in simple word games based on anagrams, Hangman and 'Word Search' puzzles. I have also seen a program which generates crosswords from words chosen by the user and for which students could devise clues. However, the usefulness of such games is limited. With most ready-made programs of this type the teacher would have to know enough about programming to be able to adapt them to individual needs. This can be a very time-consuming process, although trying to do so is perhaps the easiest way into learning how to write your own programs. The best games, of course, would be those which teachers had produced for their own students and which formed an integral part of their schemes of learning activities.

Good commercial word games for a microcomputer are hard to find. Most tend to be trivial games for two players with the role of one of them usurped by the machine: hardly an imaginative use of a sophisticated tool. One game which does have considerable potential for small groups is based on the popular parlour game of Twenty Questions. A simple version can be found in David Ahl's book, *Basic Computer Games*. I will outline my own version and suggest how it might be used by an English teacher with a mixed-ability group.

In my version, called 'Creatures', the computer asks for the players to think of a living creature and then tries to guess what it might be. It asks, 'Is it an insect?', 'Is it a fish?' and so on, imitating the human technique of narrowing the options. The computer has very little chance, in fact, of guessing the correct answer at the beginning of the game since, in my version at least, it knows only thirteen creatures. What is interesting about the game is that when the computer admits defeat the students have to tell it what the creature is, and frame a question that would distinguish their choice from the computer's last guess. In this game the students are 'teaching' the computer because it stores and uses the new questions. In the process students have to devise questions involving increasingly subtle distinctions.

To illustrate how the game proceeds and to show just how challenging it can be, here is how some student teachers of English quickly found themselves in rather a tight spot!

CREATURES

THINK OF A LIVING CREATURE
AND THE COMPUTER WILL TRY TO
GUESS WHAT IT IS.

IF IT DOES NOT GUESS IT, YOU
WILL HAVE TO TEACH THE
COMPUTER!
ARE YOU THINKING OF A CREATURE?
YES
IS IT AN INSECT? NO
IS IT A FISH? NO
IS IT A BIRD? YES
IS IT A BIRD OF PREY? YES
IS IT A KESTREL? NO
THE CREATURE YOU WERE THINKING
OF WAS A? HAWK
PLEASE TYPE A QUESTION THAT
WOULD DISTINGUISH A HAWK FROM
A KESTREL . . .

This game has obvious potential in English lessons. Here is an excellent program to generate constructive discussion, requiring students to make effective use of reference sources and to take great care in the framing of questions. It also acts as a dynamic demonstration of the way in which language fashions information into 'trees' of interrelated classifications, a model which can prove useful when discussing the use of viewdata, as will shortly become apparent. Far from making the teacher redundant, this game would provide an ideal opportunity for the English teacher to concentrate on helping students to develop what is surely the most important learning skill of all: the ability to ask the most significant questions. There could be useful discussions about whether a group had taught the computer to ask the most helpful questions or whether the students could increase its speed of guessing by repositioning the questions in its branching system.

If you have access to a printer, one powerful use for a microcomputer is as a word-processor. With a word-processor one can draft material on the screen using the computer's keyboard like a typewriter, edit out errors and neaten up a page at the touch of a button, and then print out on paper what you have on the screen. Sophisticated word-processors have revolutionized offices, since they can perform all the standard functions of a typist in a quarter of the time.

A simple word-processor has considerable potential in the English classroom. Professional word-processors are very expensive machines indeed, but it is quite possible to obtain relatively cheap programs which will enable one to use an ordinary microcomputer as an elementary word-processor.

Using a 'typewriter-style' keyboard can help children who normally have difficulty with writing in several ways: it is often easier to develop a rhythm, it enables the user to concentrate on content, and it helps with spelling because 'word shapes' are always identical and thus easier to remember. For a student who finds handwriting and inaccuracies a major obstacle to written expression, the chance of drafting writing in a way that will allow instant and invisible alterations and which produces printed versions at the touch of a button is a considerable incentive. As Seymour Papert, an enlightened Professor of Education at MIT has recently written, 'for most children rewriting a text is so laborious that the first draft is the final copy, and the skill of rereading with a critical eye is never acquired': an observation familiar to English teachers. Professor Papert declares that 'this changes dramatically when children have access to computers capable of manipulating text . . . . I have seen a child move from total rejection of writing to an intense involvement (accompanied by rapid improvement of quality) within a few weeks of beginning to write with a computer.' This is, as Papert argues, a far more creative method of developing a child's mastery of language than the far more widespread use of the computer in American schools for drill in grammar and spelling or multiple-choice comprehension tests. And yet, the use of the word-processor by students in school could easily be overlooked, since one can easily imagine 'adults, including teachers, expressing the view that editing and re-editing a text is a waste of time ("Why don't you get on to something new?" or "You aren't making it any better, why don't you fix your spelling?").'[2]

With a word-processor groups of students could easily produce their own books. A declaration by Ken Worpole several years ago in *Teaching London Kids* is even more true today: 'we have the technological potential now to completely abolish the traditional distinction between writers and readers (producers and consumers) . . . and . . . English teachers can make themselves central to this process.' Even without a printer students could store their screen-writing (as I do) on ordinary audio-tape: a sixty-minute cassette-tape could easily contain a substantial 'book'. Indeed, there are obvious ecological reasons for preferring this method.

I have avoided recommending the use of microcomputers for 'programmed instruction' because I consider that we have a responsibility to show students how to remain in control of the new technology rather than to allow themselves to be manipulated by it. Whilst a small number of children with specific reading and spelling difficulties might well benefit from structured reinforcement using a microcomputer, this is by no means a question of transferring 'slot-and-filler' exercises to the video screen. Interesting work is being done in this field by the specialist team at the Walsall Education Development Centre, which is concerned primarily with word recognition, word attack skills and strategies for improving reading speed. However, it would be difficult even for class teachers already fluent in programming to find sufficient time to devise worthwhile programs for children with specific learning difficulties.

Programs are already available for teachers which purport to take care of the computing whilst the teacher concentrates on what s/he wants to teach. One of the dangers of teachers using computers without themselves learning how to program them is that they could unconsciously adopt a model of programmed instruction, particularly when they feel that they are dealing with 'the Basics'. There would perhaps be less danger of this if teachers were to regard the production of suitable programs as a team responsibility; it would certainly be unfair for individual teachers in English departments to find themselves given the extraordinarily time-consuming task of producing all of the programs which might be required.

Earlier in this article I mentioned 'viewdata'. Both viewdata and 'teletext' are information retrieval systems which use modified television sets to display 'frames' of information: in the case of viewdata these are transmitted via the telephone lines and with teletext they are broadcast along with television pictures. In Britain, a viewdata service called Prestel is provided by the Post Office, whilst teletext systems consist of the BBC's Ceefax ('see facts'!) and the IBA's Oracle (Optional Reception of Announcements by Coded Line Electronics).

Whereas the teletext systems are run as a public service, Prestel is a commercial system which charges its 'Information Providers'. The obvious advantage of the Post Office system is that it has at present around 250,000 pages whilst the teletext services for technical reasons transmit only three or four hundred frames. Teletext tends to be rather like an electronic magazine: the topics covered by Ceefax and Oracle include news, weather, sports results, travel information, stocks and shares, food prices, entertainment guides and subtitles for the deaf (superimposed on the television pictures). Prestel, on the other hand, is a vast mine of information for which substantial directories are published. Apart from the small additional cost of the modified television set Ceefax and Oracle are free, whereas Prestel televisions are still very expensive, and the user has three charges to pay: the cost of the telephone call, the cost of 'on-line' computer time, and in most cases a charge for each frame consulted. The surprise of the Asimov children when they discover that their book 'had the same word on it that it had when they read it the first time' is a reminder of the advantage that these systems have over print in displaying up-to-date information.

With the teletext services all that is needed is a specially modified television set and a keypad rather like a calculator. When a number is entered by the user, the set waits for the relevant page in its fixed sequence and then displays it for as long as is required.

Teletext has far less educational potential than Prestel, but it is not without its uses as a resource. It is a convenient, if limited, source of up-to-date information which would be useful to students involved in project work. It could be an interesting focus for the study of selectivity in news-editing and would provide an easy introduction to the selection of information from screen textual displays.[3] Prestel, however, is a much more versatile resource.

The full public launch of Prestel was in September 1979, but it is still in its infancy in schools. After the installation of Prestel facilities in thirty-two 'centres of learning', a detailed study of its educational potential was initiated by the Council for Educational Technology in September 1980. The trial aims to assess Prestel as a learning resource and as a means of giving students experience in using on-line computerized information; a report will be published. There is already a trial curriculum index with references provided by subject headings including 'English Language and Literature'.

I have used Prestel with fourth-year students at one of the experimental centres—Stantonbury Campus, an innovative community comprehensive for the 12 to 18 age range in Milton Keynes. I did not use the curriculum index: it is as yet fairly limited in its usefulness (at least as far as English is concerned). I was rather more interested in showing students how the whole indexing system operated. I will use one of our tours of the system as an introduction to its use and structure.

The Campus model is a Deccafax Viewdata system which consists of a video display unit and a remote control keypad (see Figure 3). If you have a microcomputer it is now quite possible to avoid buying an expensive terminal by investing in a 'Prestel adaptor' for your computer instead. To operate the Prestel unit all that one needs to do is to plug it into a telephone socket, switch it on and press the 'viewdata' key on the keypad. A list of alternative telephone numbers appears; when one of these is selected the system dials it automatically. When the call is connected the words 'Welcome to Prestel' appear on the screen and the user types in his pass code. Pressing the # sign reveals page 0, the general index.

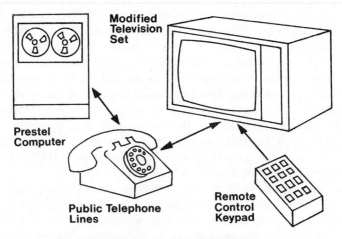

Fig. 3. The Prestel viewdata system

At this point it will be necessary to look at Figure 4. Although the flow chart moves naturally down the page it is more useful to imagine the structure as a tree which one climbs branch by branch, with the option, in Peter Large's words, of leaping 'like a supercharged squirrel' from one

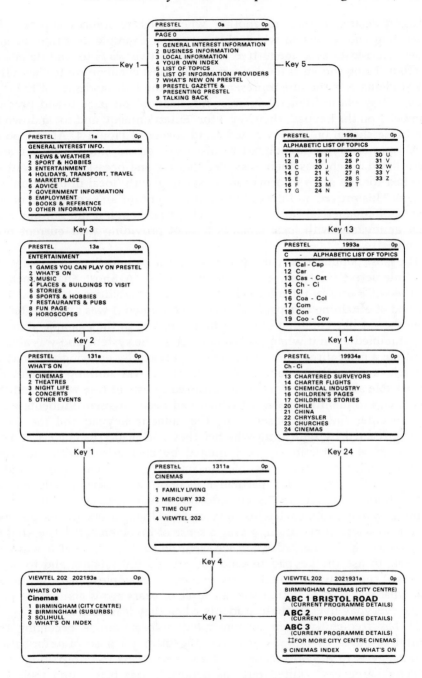

Fig. 4. Use of Prestel viewdata system

(Reproduced by kind permission of British Telecom)

distantly-related branch to another when cross-references appear. The branching choice system which this particular example illustrates (sometimes referred to as a 'menu-tree') represents two ways to find details of the films being shown at local cinemas. The most common route chosen by my students was the one represented down the left-hand side of the diagram. They chose 'General Interest Information' on page 0 and pressed number 1 on the keypad, then key 3 for 'Entertainment' and so on down to the frame shown on the lower left-hand corner of Figure 4. At this point they were always disappointed to discover that no cinemas in our area were listed. Such was their disbelief that on one occasion they double-checked for the same information by starting with 'local information' on page 0. This proved an interesting starting-point for an explanation of the system of commercial Information Providers (although it did not diminish their annoyance with local cinemas for not providing their current programmes!).

The most popular destinations for our journeys into the unknown were the 'interactive' sections. One of them—called 'A Short Sharp Spelling Test'—will serve to introduce the interactive capabilities of Prestel. Our method of obtaining this page whenever we wanted it was rather different from the cat-like climbing of the information tree in the example above. I had stumbled upon it when browsing through the system, and was able to illustrate a more direct 'homing-pigeon' approach by entering an asterisk, the relevant number and the # sign. There was nothing particularly remarkable about the test itself: it consisted of lists of five words, and the object was to identify the word which had been misspelt. Students were able to enter their responses using the numeric keypad and the video display reacted by indicating whether they had made the correct choice. This kind of interaction is very limited by comparison with the more 'educational' interaction possible on ordinary microcomputers, and I would hardly justify this particular example as a serious educational application. However, it has considerable advantages, as Martin Banks points out, over available teletext services in obliging users 'to take positive actions to select information, giving a sense of involvement'.[4] The kind of discussion which emerged when we went on to discover that it was also possible to use the keypad to send for printed information and to book tickets at the Aldwych (to take only two minor examples) made me realize that what was science fiction only a couple of years ago is going to be part of the everyday lives of these students when they leave school.

As has frequently been demonstrated, information is becoming the central resource in our society, and the main purpose of information technology is to provide widespread and fast access to information. But, as Peter Large has pointed out, 'as databanks get bigger and their use spreads beyond the computer professionals, the problem of pin-pointing what you want becomes greater . . . . Even . . . a structure of pre-defined chunks of information, presented on the screen as separate pages, with each page offering pointers to the following pages ... can become confusing.'[5]

It is vital for us to foster information literacy if students are not to be lost in information (or indeed led by those who may manipulate it). Guided tours of the technology are not enough. Knowing how to find and use information in all its forms is an essential reading skill. Bearing in mind the astounding spread of information technology I hope it will be clear that we have a responsibility to ensure that our students become familiar with the kind of information retrieval I have described. Apart from the obvious personal advantages of knowing how to find the information one wants, using a viewdata system can be very expensive indeed if the user adopts a 'butterfly' approach and this could be a school-leaver's quickest route out of a job. Even if schools cannot afford a Prestel terminal or a Prestel adaptor for their microcomputer, they can teach some of the skills needed by viewdata users. Students can be shown, for instance, how to select likely sources for the information they require, how to make sensible use of the directories and how to 'climb the information tree' in a logical manner. As one managing director recently put it in a *cri de coeur*, 'Computers open up a world of information .... But how do we select the information? How do we isolate the particular piece of information needed? That is what the teachers ought to be teaching!'[6]

In teaching students how to use computerized information systems we need to be aware of other characteristics of the medium. The video screen as a reading medium is quite different from the printed page. The 'pages' are much smaller: on viewdata or teletext screens only about 130 words— two or three short paragraphs—can be displayed at any one time. Reading a screen requires far more conscious effort than reading a printed page: it is not easy to read a large number of 'pages' with one's full concentration (one writer has described it as being like 'reading a newspaper through binoculars'!). One cannot browse through such a system as easily as through a reference book. And yet people will need to learn how to read an electronic text display if they are to benefit from what may soon be the natural medium for routine information.

In 1968 Marshall McLuhan foresaw the development of computerized information systems as a revolutionary mass medium. Certainly, in a society where information is power, it is desirable that every individual should have access to such a medium. The technology is already available for an information system which is both global in scope and individualized by personal selection. Whether the computer does indeed become a medium for the masses rather than a tool for the technocrats must depend in part on education. If we do not equip all of our students for a world in which microelectronic technology is already widespread we will be sowing the seeds for a blindly Luddite reaction. If on the other hand we embrace, with the microcomputer, the 'programmed' model of learning which is commonly adopted in the United States we will be leaving our students open to exploitation.

In much the same way that we have questioned assumptions such as the authority of print and the reality of the reel we must also question any tendency to accept that the terminal tells the whole truth. Whilst using the computer as a creative tool we must be aware of the 'massage' of this powerful new medium, since, as McLuhan warned, 'electric information environments . . . alter our feelings and sensibilities, especially when they are not attended to'.[7]

English teachers already have a significant role in the creative and critical use of the media in schools, and I believe they are well placed to develop 'convivial' and 'appropriate' approaches to the use of the microcomputer. Certainly, 'computer literacy' involves dramatic extensions to the traditional skills of reading, writing and fact-finding, and it seems to me at least that the microelectronic revolution, far from being remote from the concerns of English specialists, ought to be central to them.

Notes

1 RODWELL, PETER, and TEBBUTT, DAVID (1980) *Personal Computer World*, November.
2 PAPERT, SEYMOUR (1980) *Mindstorms: Children, Computers and Powerful Ideas*, Harvester Press, p. 30. A provocative answer to the doubting adults mentioned by Professor Papert is that word-processing programmes already exist with inbuilt vocabularies of 50,000 words, which are capable of correcting the user's spelling slips if required, and that many professional writers use them.
3 For a discussion of the educational potential of teletext see ANDERSON, JOHN (1980) 'Exploring Teletext as a Resource', *PLET*, 17, 1 (February).
4 BANKS, MARTIN (1980) *Living with the Micro*, Sigma Technical Press, p. 111.
5 LARGE, PETER (1980) *The Micro Revolution*, Fontana, pp. 56–7.
6 FIRNBERG, DAVID (1980) *Personal Computer World*, April.
7 McLUHAN, MARSHALL, and FIORE, QUENTIN (1968) *War and Peace in the Global Village*, Bantam, p. 36.

Suggested reading

Although a booklist on a topic such as this is likely to be hopelessly out of date almost as soon as it is published, I would like to suggest some helpful starting points for teachers who may be thinking of using a microcomputer.

Perhaps the most readable general guides to the microelectronics revolution are *The Mighty Micro* by the late Dr Christopher Evans (revised Coronet edition, 1980) and *The Micro Revolution* by Peter Large, technology correspondent of *The Guardian* (Fontana, 1980). A slightly more technical introduction is *Living with the Micro* by Martin Banks (Sigma Technical Press, 1980).

For serious treatments of the social issues I would suggest *The Microchip: Appropriate or Inappropriate Technology?* by Dr Alan Burns (Ellis Horwood, 1981). *The Microelectronics Revolution*—a collection of essays edited by Tom Forester and particularly useful for its essays on the Information Revolution (Basil Blackwell, 1980), and *Computers and Social Change* by Murray Lever (Cambridge University Press, 1980). For a controversial discussion of the future of conventional literacy in the context of the technological possibilities the reader is referred to Chapter 6 in John Oxenham's *Literacy: Writing, Reading and Social Organisation* (Routledge and Kegan Paul, 1980).

Useful books on viewdata are: *The Viewdata Revolution* by the inventor of Prestel, Sam Fedida, and Rex Malik (Associated Business Press, 1979); *The Electronic Bookstall* by Rex Winsbury (International Institute of Communications, 1979), who argues against the concept of the tree metaphor as applied to viewdata; and *Viewdata: A Public Information Utility* by Dr Adrian Stokes (Langton Information Systems, 1978). For a copy of the current Prestel directory and up-to-date news of viewdata developments the teacher may wish to obtain a copy of one of the quarterly guides: *The Prestel User* (from Printel Ltd, Elliott House, 130 Ber Street, Norwich NR1 3AQ) or *The Viewdata and TV User* (from the publishers of Educational Computing, listed below).

A book I would strongly recommend to English teachers is *Mindstorms: Children, Computers and Powerful Ideas* by Professor Seymour Papert (Harvester Press, 1980). Although it is partly concerned with describing the development of a new computer language to help children to learn mathematical concepts, Papert provides stimulating alternatives to the 'programmed instruction' model of computer-assisted learning and visionary insight into education which I can only compare with the writings of A.S. Neill. I do not feel able to recommend any of the other books on educational computing which I have seen, since they are either science-based or propound a model of learning which involves 'programming the child'. The best way to keep informed of current developments in educational computing is to read the commercial monthly, *Educational Computing* (from IPC Business Press Ltd, Oakfield House, Perrymount Road, Haywards Heath, Sussex RH16 3DH) and the termly *CAL News* (free from CEDAR—see list of addresses), and to join MUSE, who publish the quintannual *Computers in Schools* (see address list).

If you wish to learn programming (and I would recommend it both as a creative activity in its own right and as the only way of ensuring that programs you use are an integral part of your scheme of activities with students) I would strongly advise you to purchase your own microcomputer. Consult a computer science teacher for advice on which machine will best meet your needs. Before committing yourself you may find it useful to browse through some of the general computer magazines obtainable on magazine stalls: the most helpful are *Personal Computer World* and *Computing Today*.

Two useful background books for beginners are *The Personal Computer Book* by Robin Bradbeer (MCB Publications, 1980) and *The Good Computing Book for Beginners* by Dennis Jarrett (ECC Publications, 1981). I taught myself by trying to understand and adapt some simple games programs, and if this method is likely to suit you I would recommend David Ahl's *Basic Computer Games* and *More Basic Computer Games* (Creative Computing, 1979). If you prefer a structured guide, try Donald Alcock's *Illustrating Basic* (Cambridge University Press, 1977), although it is usually best to buy a text written specifically for the 'dialect' of 'Basic' that your own machine uses. An excellent reference book is latest edition of *The Basic Handbook* by David Lien (Compusoft Publishing). Such books are most easily obtained at the computer shops which are opening up all over the country.

Addresses of bodies providing information and advice

Advisory Unit for Computer-Based Education
　　Endymion Road, Hatfield, Herts AL10 8AU
Association for Computer-Assisted Learning
　　c/o Educational Computing Section, Chelsea College, Pulton Place, London SW6 5PR
British Broadcasting Corporation (Ceefax)
　　Engineering Information Department, Broadcasting House, London W1A 1AA
British Computer Society
　　13 Mansfield Street, London W1M 0BP
CEDAR (Computers in Education as a Resource)
　　Imperial College Computer Centre, Exhibition Road, London SW7 2BX
Computer Education Group
　　North Staffordshire Polytechnic Computer Centre, Blackheath Lane, Stafford ST18 0AD
Council for Educational Technology
　　3 Devonshire Street, London W1N 2BA
Independent Broadcasting Authority (Oracle)
　　Engineering Information Service, PO Box 29, Winchester, Hampshire SO21 2QA
Microelectronics Development Team
　　Education Development Centre, 36 Wolverhampton Road, Walsall, West Midlands WS2 8PN
MEP (Microelectronics Education Programme)
　　Cheviot House, Coach Lane Campus, Newcastle upon Tyne NE7 7XA
MUSE (Micro-Computer Users in Secondary Education)
　　Oundle School, Oundle, Peterborough PE8 4AQ
Prestel International
　　4th Floor, Telephone House, Temple Avenue, London EC4Y 0HL
Schools Council Computers in the Curriculum Project
　　See Association for Computer-Assisted Learning
TEACH (Technology: Education and Change)
　　London House, Mecklenburgh Square, London WC1N 2AB

3
Assessment and Language Development

Introduction

In the addendum to his article Bill Mittins draws attention to 'the excessive allocation of the most able teachers of English to examination groups.' One invariable component of the examination system in English has been the writing of the formal essay, though our growing awareness of the need to be aware of the importance of *context* in writing, the development of a sense of audience, purpose and awareness of form in the writer, makes the usefulness of the formal essay as a means of assessment of increasingly doubtful value. As we are in the process of reconstructing the examination system it seems clear that we shall have to come to recognize the necessity of course work assessment as the only available means of examining pupils' writing across a wide range of purposes. So far (1981) all the working groups that have been preparing English criteria for the new examination have argued for at least a combination of coursework with more traditional examining methods. The case for coursework as the major means of examining has also been set out in detail.[1] But, for our teaching as well as our assessment procedure, we need much more knowledge about how children develop as writers and there are the beginnings of research in this area at long last. I had hoped to be able to include in this volume an important article by Donald Graves, 'A New Look at Writing Research',[2] but have failed to obtain permission to reprint it. It is nonetheless recommended to anyone who wants to obtain a picture of research into writing and the development of writers at the present time.

The two articles that follow explore two aspects of student writing and our assessment of it. 'A Historical View of Marking Essays' summarizes what work has been done upon the validity and reliability of the essay as a means of assessment; 'The Development of Writing' summarizes the work of Andrew Wilkinson and his team in 'the Creditor Project'.[3] Both articles should help us to have a more adequate appreciation of what we are doing when we judge students' work.

Notes

1 SCOTT, PATRICK (1980) *Coursework in English: Principles and Assessment*, NATE Examinations Booklet No. 3.

2 GRAVES, DONALD (1981) 'A New Look at Writing Research', in HALEY-JAMES, SHIRLEY (ed.) *Perspectives on Writing in Grades 1–8*, National Council for Teachers of English, Illinois.
3 The work described here is extended and discussed in further detail in WILKINSON, ANDREW (1980) *Assessing Children's Language*, Oxford.

A Historical Review of Essay Marking*

Mike Hayhoe
Lecturer, School of Education, University of East Anglia

> We need to set out some of the problems of assessment and correction
> and supply some of the answers.
>> (*English: A Programme for Research and Development in
>> English Teaching*, Schools Council Working Paper No. 3,
>> HMSO, 1965)

This brief paper deliberately limits itself to the issue of marking essays.
There is much discussion about the design of the means by which we will
assess the language performance of young citizens in the years to come—
norm and criterion referencing; profiling; continuous or terminal assessment; internal or external marking; common or 'banded' papers. Whatever
decisions are made, it is likely that the 'essay' will remain a frequent
component of such assessment.

There are those who have reservations about our reliance on the 'essay'.
Knight (1977) talks of the 'tenacity of this national institution' and Rowntree
(1977) compares us with ancient China as an 'essay-ridden' nation. His
attitude is clear:

> Essays and other written offerings do lend themselves to being
> pored over and quantified by examiners with an ease that on-going
> *processes* (e.g. conversation, acting, debating, team-work, etc.) do
> not.

Perhaps a more generally accepted justification for assessment essays is
that of Deale (1975):

> It would be difficult to imagine any English course which did not
> place emphasis on writing ability and equally difficult to conceive
> of any test of this ability except the essay or composition paper.

---

*This paper was originally written for a one-day conference organized in 1980
by the National Association for the Teaching of English as part of discussions
leading to new proposals for English in the General Certificate of Secondary
Education. It has been revised especially for this collection.

Whatever views may prevail in the coming decades about how to assess young citizens and their language, it is likely that looking at their performance in continuous writing will remain one of the main devices we will use, be it the timed essay based on a limited choice of topics as part of terminal assessment, or a student-initiated extended project, or course work items.

Here lies the rub, for the problem of being fair and consistent has long troubled those who have to assess such work. Rowntree has found concern about marker reliability in the 1880s! Raleigh (1980) suggests that an error of 25 per cent in grading an essay may be a conservative estimate, and it has been suggested that the problem of unreliability in marking essays exists in 'internal assessment' as well as 'external'.

This paper brings together comment on some of the problems that continue to face examiners in the marking of essays. Whatever may be done to improve the reliability, comparability and validity of overall and particular examination design in English, markers will face 'essays'—and problems.

Reliability, Validity and Values

Research into assessment has looked at reliability and validity. Research on markers of essays has tended to concentrate on reliability but, as Willmott (1975) has commented, reliability is inextricably linked with validity. Much work has looked at how consistent a marker is and how he compares in his performance with others. Implicit in some of this has been his 'validity' as a marker. If an examination's validity can be described in terms of the degree to which it 'measures well' what it is intended to measure (Raleigh) then it may be legitimate to talk of a marker's validity: the degree to which he 'measures well' what the assessment system set out to measure. Much research suggests that reliability and validity can be difficult to achieve, whether it be in 'content' essays or in Deale's 'free-response' essays.

Rowntree's quoting the unreliability of essay assessment in the 1880s is only one example of work on this aspect. Finlayson (1951) in Britain and Dittmer (1974) in the United States have been among many who have found problems. A marker may well assess an essay very differently on two occasions. It is very likely that markers will disagree in their grading of a composition. Thorndike (1968) sees the problem as being exacerbated as a topic becomes more discursive and doubts whether reliability can ever be compatible with 'uniqueness', the feature of much work in English.

'Uniqueness' raises the issue of divergence and convergence in much English work. How far, and in what ways, is a particular marker affected by divergence—the individuality of the work he is assessing, its 'uniqueness'? How far, and in what ways, is he affected by convergence—notions of correctness and orderliness as priorities?

Some research has been carried out on assessors' value bases. British and American researchers have suggested that markers tend to group together. Wiseman and Wrigley (1958) identified two schools of thought: those who valued the 'imponderables' of vitality, freshness and fluency and those who tended to see the writer as 'a craftsman able to show his skill whatever type of material he works in.'

Britton (1963) found some evidence to suggest that teachers may well group towards valuing one end or the other of two poles:

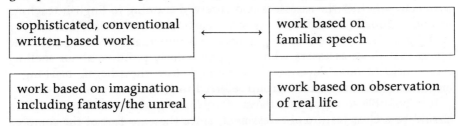

American work suggests that teachers tend to cluster in favouring certain criteria—ideas, form, 'flavour', mechanics, wording—and that the cluster of criteria adopted by a teacher can affect grading.

Deale feels that 'adequacy of writing' rather than of ideas affects the marks awarded when assessing essays but others are less sanguine. Soloff (1973) argues that it is possible that lack of consonance between the writer's values and those of the assessor on a topic may affect the grade awarded. In its pamphlet *Assessing Compositions* (1965), the London Association for the Teaching of English expressed concern about how an assessor may react to experiences and attitudes in an essay which are unfamiliar to him and the potential for under-or over-assessing the work.

In spite of the anxieties expressed by Soloff and LATE, the notion of a marker being affected by a writer's values and ideas suggests that he is reading interactively, responding to more than the surface features of the language in front of him. This 'engagement' with the piece of writing is probably inevitable; I believe that most readers of this paper would hold it to be essential. Marshall (1960) suggests that assessment in terms of the features of a piece of work which 'float' to the examiner—his intuitions about the text—is the proper activity of an alert and sensitive marker. This is akin to Raleigh's comment that such marking is based on 'opinion'.

Some of the research mentioned above has suggested possible problems where experience or values in a piece of work do not square with those of the examiner: where there is some form of divergence. Better known, perhaps, is the research into 'flawed convergence', where a writer fails to conform with certain writing rules.

In the process of assessment, perhaps particularly when it is under some pressure, as can happen with some terminal GCE and CSE essay marking, markers can be affected by visual features at the expense of such aspects as organization, fluency, appropriateness in terms of task and audience, and so on. This may be because the visual features are more immediately obvious, especially when they are flawed, and because there is a greater degree of consensus about them than there is about what 'coherence' or 'clarity' or other more global criteria may be.

Much of the research on this aspect of assessment comes from America and suggests that 'non-content errors' can affect grading quite powerfully— in that country, at least! Marshall (1967) looked at 'content' essays in history and found assessors particularly affected by errors of spelling and grammar, whether the assessors had received training in English teaching or not. Scannell (1966) found assessors particularly adversely affected by spelling errors, with errors of grammar and punctuation coming next. He found that those assessors who were particularly punitive about spelling errors held strong views about spelling before they began marking— members of the 'mechanics' group referred to above.

It is possible to argue that flaws of spelling, grammar and punctuation should be a clear feature of assessment, since they are part of the complex means of realizing language on the page, although this leaves unexplored such matters as types and frequency of flaws and what has caused them— carelessness, ignorance, commendable ambitiousness in a search for the appropriate word or structure, and so on.

What also gives concern is the impact of handwriting. Chase (1968), Briggs (1970) and Soloff (1973) have been among the many researchers who have demonstrated the power of this surface feature in affecting marking. In his more recent work, Briggs (1980) goes further, suggesting that there may be borderline areas in grading in which this visual aspect of a piece of writing may be the major factor in deciding what it is worth. Disturbingly, he is not sanguine that bias over handwriting, be it in the form of over-marking or under-marking, will be removed by double marking or by moderation, since there is no guarantee that the bias is not shared across the assessors concerned. Briggs sees this as a problem which it may be 'professionally embarrassing to acknowledge'. It may also be more amenable to further work, both in terms of research and affecting assessors towards greater reliability, than some of the other features of potential bias discussed here.

There may also be links between some forms of examination design and problems which markers encounter. Thorndike (1971) and Dixon (1979) have questioned the reliability of timed examinations, with their premium on speed of writing and speed of word selection and idea formation. Given that not all pupils are 'fast' and that not all 'slow' pupils are 'poor', work produced under these conditions may present problems for the examiner who is trying to identify a candidate's true performance. Another feature of some examinations is the provision of one chance to write on one of a choice of essay topics. Vernon and Millican (1954) and Britton (1963) have shown how performance is affected by choice of task. Braddock (1963) found that bright pupils may well penalize themselves by tackling more demanding tasks, e.g. essays involving description or discussion. The solution to this problem may well lie in terms of provision of a range of tasks over a period of time, but should the practice of the terminal essay paper continue it raises considerable problems for the marker as he tackles the small amount of evidence before him.

There are many other variables which affect overall judgement. Yates and Pidgeon (1957) found that the siting of an essay affected the marker's response. If an 'average' piece of work followed several fine pieces, it was likely to be marked hard; if it followed several poor ones, it was likely to be upgraded. Soloff found, unsurprisingly, that fatigue affected marking adversely. It may be that such factors as these are the proper business of those who organize and regulate assessment schemes. It seems quite evident that the 'uniqueness' of much written work in English demands alert assessors if the writers are to be given justice. This may have implications for the numbers of pieces of work examiners should be allowed to tackle, for the conditions in which they should be required to work and for the amount of time which should be taken in the work's assessment.

Comments on In-Text Features

It has been suggested that long-term knowledge of the writer and his work may well help in making a 'deep' assessment of his performance, but much marking depends on knowledge of in-text features alone, as in the case of some GCE and CSE essay papers and in the case of much moderation. Boards, Panels and Mode III schemes have their various documents outlining what is to be valued in assessing 'essays' in English, often suggesting in which mark band particular levels of ability in particular features should appear. Some of these schemes are public; some are not. It would be of more than idle interest to have access to such papers and to see where lie their points of match and of mismatch, as a preliminary to further discussion about *what* we are looking for and how we grade it.

Perhaps an outline of some of the work of the last two decades in trying to identify features of writing may help to promote fuller discussion about the features and factors an assessor should have in mind when marking the work of a fifteen- or sixteen-year-old. Much of this work has been concerned with younger students and with looking at writing for studying developmental processes, but its perceptions may be of interest. The findings of four workers are summarized in Figure 1.

Young (1962) suggested a very simple four-feature model, which raises several points. His first and second items seem to be concerned with the 'uniqueness' of an essay and to fit Wiseman's exhortation (1949) that behind assessing a piece of writing the marker is assessing the writer. His other two items fit the 'mechanics' school of thought. Comment about relative weighting of these items is absent. The problems of assessing 1 and 2 and

YOUNG (1962) (Age 11)	PERCIVAL (1965) (Age 11)	BERSE (1974) (Age 11)	BRITTON (1966) (Age 16)
1. LANGUAGE CONTROL (a) Vocabulary	7. EFFECTIVE LANGUAGE* — accuracy of choice — sensory vocabulary — effective literary devices — effective use of associated words and phrases	2. VOCABULARY RANGE	APPROPRIATE AND VIVID WORDS/PHRASES
(b) Variety of sentences	2. SENTENCE LENGTH 3. CO-ORDINATING CONJUNCTIONS 4. SUBORDINATING CONJUNCTIONS	3. PRE-VERB LENGTH 4. WEIGHTING OF TYPES OF MODIFYING CLAUSES	
(c) Organization of ideas 2. IDEAS/ORIGINALITY/ IMAGINATION	6. UNITY OF STRUCTURE	5. SEQUENCE	COHERENCE/ORGANIZATION* INTELLIGENT INVOLVEMENT*
3. SPELLING/ PUNCTUATION/GRAMMAR	5. PUNCTUATION (Later) SPELLING* (Later) AVOIDANCE OF COMPOSITIONAL ERRORS* (e.g. grammar; some punctuation)	1. ACCURACY (SYNTAX/ ACCIDENCE)	MECHANICAL ACCURACY*
4. HANDWRITING AND PRESENTATION	1. NUMBER OF WORDS*		
	* = Four nearest to teachers' marking.	NB sub-feature on developing complexity of characterization: characters unrelated; related through ritualized action; related through action; related through feeling; related through feeling and action.	* = Three most used by assessors. NB a minority added RELEVANCE.

Fig. 1. Summary of selected research on features of writing

the ease of identifying 3 and 4 are tackled too briefly. Organization of ideas is seen as a sub-feature of Language Control.

Percival (1965) worked on a narrow area, basing his research on work stimulated by pictures. He hoped that these would promote writing involving narrative, description, characterization and dialogue. His first five features could be called 'objective' but 6 and 7 are clearly subjective and large and raise again the issue of whether such features receive some sort of weighting according to the task being assessed—in other words, how such 'big' features affect an individual marker and are effective across markers.

Percival did not see his list of features necessarily applying to other sorts of writing, and the more recent work of such people as Britton (1975), in disputing the old rhetorical categorizations of writing, makes his caveat all the more interesting to pursue.

In his slightly later work, Percival (1966) found a significant correlation between impression marking by experienced teachers and the four features marked with an asterisk in Figure 1. This may prove the reliability of the marking. It may show that, no matter how we mark, these are among the features that affect us most powerfully. If that is so, it raises again the issue of the relative power of particular features—and the apparent, disconcerting absence of feature 6.

Whatever questions Percival's work may raise, his celebration of an 'essay' is likely to have many supporters:

> A piece of composition is not the sum of the number of words, sentences, punctuation marks, and so on, but is rather the spontaneous integration of all these elements to produce a single, composite work.

Berse (1974) set up postulates which pay more attention to the points clustered in Young's first item. He suggested five features which have some bearing on the 'goodness' of a young writer's work:

1 Accuracy	such features as number and subject-verb agreement;
2 Vocabulary range	number of different verbs, nouns, etc.;
3 Pre-verb length	based on the premiss that length of subject may indicate complexity of thought;
4 Modifying clause weightings	modifying clauses weighted according to their degree of sophistication in the structure of a sentence;
5 Sequence	internal cohesion and development.

Berse's work suggested that items 2–5 had most to do with quality, although 3 can be misleading. While Young had seen accuracy as an important item,

Berse found that his version of it in item 1 bore little relation to his other indices of 'goodness'. Again, the subjective item, in this case 5, is 'large' and raises questions.

In the course of his work, Berse produced a set of descriptive features of levels of characterization skills which suggest a sympathy with Wiseman's exhortation to seek out the quality of the writer in the writing:

> Characters unrelated;
> related through ritualized action;
> related through action;
> related through feeling;
> related through feeling and action.

Auden once suggested that one of the proper purposes in reading a poem is to try to work out 'what kind of a guy' inhabits it, and it may be that Berse here is moving towards a similar responsive, inquiring approach to 'essays'. Implicit in this approach is not only an assessment of linguistic adeptness but an attempt to see something of the writer's development as a person—of his world view. This seems to be an early relation of the more developed work of Wilkinson *et al.* (1979), which postulates four 'measures' —stylistic, affective, cognitive and moral. This work is significant, not only for spelling out in greater detail what it understands by such terms but for its arguing that the affective, cognitive and moral cannot be omitted. While not specifically looking at assessment in terms of grading, Wilkinson's Crediton Project may help to identify features in 'essays' which will help markers to move beyond simple notions of writing performance, or what Fox (1979), in his attack on the more recent and more well-known work of the Assessment of Performance Unit (1978) berates as a concern for the 'politer skills' and 'minor abilities' rather than communicative competence. Fox notes the five areas of assessment criteria set up by the Language APU in its initial stages:

> 1 orthographic conventions;
> 2 grammatical conventions;
> 3 style;
> 4 structure;
> 5 content.

He raises yet again the issue of the power of 1 and 2 to affect assessment, even when not observing these conventions does not bring about 'communicative interference'. He also raises yet again the subjectivity and 'largeness' of areas 3–5.

Perhaps the best-known work on assessment remains that of Britton (1966) in which he explored the use of impression markers to assess 16 + essays. The tone of his advice to his markers echoes Percival's comment in the same year that a composition is a unique event which cannot be dismantled as if it were a piece of machinery. Its first sentence suggests his awareness of the problem of being affected by flaws, and its entire tone seeks to promote a responsive approach to the writer and his maturity:

> Look for excellences rather than penalise deficiencies. Look for a general language sense, expressed by appropriate and vivid words and idioms, by coherence (unity and shapeliness of the whole piece within the writer's terms). Reward the writer who is involved enough to write in a direct and expressive way, and detached enough to show, by direct comment or implication, his own consistent point of view.
>
> In short: how interesting do you find the piece of writing?

Britton went further, urging his markers not to be over-affected by mechanical flaws, telling them that this would be the business of a fourth, 'accuracy' marker, although it is doubtful whether they did manage to obey his instruction that errors and slips 'should not be taken into account'. His assessors found three factors affecting their decisions: involvement, organization and mechanical accuracy—and some suggested a fourth, relevance. It could be argued that these factors value the writing conventions but also contain a notion of the marker 'meeting' the writer in some of the areas more fully outlined by the Crediton Project. Britton himself values here informed and collaborative intuition—the professional use of opinion.

Raleigh points out that almost all of our marking is based upon 'opinion', and that we need to ensure that that opinion is informed, so that assessment increases in reliability, comparability and validity. This paper has tried to outline some of the problems that face assessors about *how* to mark and *what* to mark. If we accept Raleigh's notion of 'informed opinion' as being important for the improvement of our assessment procedures, two brief questions arise. Firstly, what should be that more fully informed opinion? Secondly, by what means can all those responsible for marking bring about such 'informed opinion'—and ensure its application?

References

ASSESSMENT OF PERFORMANCE UNIT (1978) *Language Performance*, Department of Education and Science.

ASSESSMENT OF PERFORMANCE UNIT (1978) *Criteria for Assessing Writing*, Department of Education and Science.

ASSOCIATED EXAMINING BOARD (1974) *Criteria and Assessment in English*, Occasional Paper 1974.

BERSE, P. (1974) 'Criteria for the assessment of pupils' compositions', *Educational Research*, No. 17.

BRADDOCK, LLOYD-JONES, AND SCHOER (1963) *Research in the Teaching of Composition*, National Council of Teachers of English, USA.

BRIGGS, D. (1970) 'The influence of handwriting on assessment', *Educational Research*, 13.

BRIGGS, D. (1980) 'A study of the influence of handwriting upon grades using examination scripts', *Educational Review*, Vol. 32, No. 2.

BRITTON, J. (1963) 'Experimental marking of English compositions by fifteen-year-olds', *Educational Review*, Vol. 16, No. 1, November.

BRITTON, J., MARTIN, N., and ROSEN, H. (1966) *Multiple Marking of English Compositions*, Schools Council Examinations Bulletin 12, HMSO.

BRITTON, J., BURGESS, T., *et al.* (1975) *The Development of Writing Abilities (11–18)*, Macmillan.

CHASE, C. (1968) 'The impact of some obvious variables on essay test scores', *Journal of Educational Measurement*, Vol. 5, No. 4.

DEALE, R. (1975) *Assessment and Testing in Secondary Schools*, Evans/Methuen.

DITTMER, G. (1974) 'Grading compositions', *High School Journal*, Vol. 57, No. 4.

DIXON, J. (1979) *Education 16–19: The Role of English and Communication*, Macmillan.

FINLAYSON, D. (1951) 'The reliability of the marking of essays', *British Journal of Educational Psychology*, Vol. 21.

FOX, B. (1979) 'Communicative competence and the APU', *Language for Learning*, Vol. 1, No. 3, November.

KNIGHT, R. (1977) 'Examiners' English', *English in Education*, Vol. 11, No. 2.

LONDON ASSOCIATION FOR THE TEACHING OF ENGLISH (1965) *Assessing Compositions*, Blackie.

MARSHALL, J. (1967) 'Composition errors and essay examination grades reconsidered', in *American Educational Research Journal*, Vol. 4, No. 4.

MARSHALL, M. (1960) 'The flotation technique', *Improving College and University Teaching*, Vol. 8.

PERCIVAL, E. (1965) 'The nature of ability in English composition', *Educational Review*, Vol. 18, No. 1, November.

PERCIVAL, E. (1966) 'The dimensions of ability in English composition', *Educational Review*, Vol. 18, No. 3, June.

RALEIGH, M. (1980) *English Exams at 16*, London Association for the Teaching of English.

ROWNTREE, D. (1977) *Assessing Students: How Shall We Know Them?* Harper and Row.

SCANNELL, D. (1966) 'The effect of selected composition errors on grades assigned to essay examinations', *American Educational Research Journal*, Vol. 3, No. 2.

SHERIDAN, W. (1974) 'Open-ended questions', in MACINTOSH, H. (ed.) *Techniques and Problems of Assessment*, Edward Arnold.

SOLOFF, S. (1973) 'The effect of non-content factors on the grading of essays', *Graduate Research in Education and Related Disciplines*, Vol. 6, No. 2.

VERNON, P. (1957) *Secondary School Selection*, Methuen.

VERNON, P., and MILLICAN, G. (1954) 'A further study of the reliability of English essays', *British Journal of Statistical Psychology*, 7.

WILKINSON, A., BARNSLEY, G., *et al.* (1979) 'Assessing language development: The Crediton Project', in *Language for Learning*, Vol. 1, No. 2, June.

WILKINSON, A., and HANNA, P. (1980) 'The development of style in children's writing', *Educational Review*, Vol. 32, No. 2.

WILLMOTT, A., and NUTTALL, D. (1975) *The Reliability of Examinations at 16+*, Macmillan.

WISEMAN, S. (1949) 'The marking of English compositions in grammar school selection', *British Journal of Educational Psychology*, Vol. 19, No. 3.

WISEMAN, S., and WRIGLEY, J. (1958) 'Essay reliability: the effect of choice of essay title', *Educational and Psychological Measurement*, Vol. 18, No. 1.

YATES and PIDGEON (1957) *Admission to Grammar Schools*, Newnes.

YOUNG, D. (1962) 'Examining essays for eleven plus classification', *British Journal of Educational Psychology*, 32.

The Development of Writing*

Andrew Wilkinson, Gillian Barnsley, Peter Hanna and Margaret Swan

Introduction

All teachers have a responsibility for the personal development of their pupils, and the responsibility is felt especially by those concerned with language, language being a major means by which it takes place. Thus the literature abounds with terms like 'growth', 'development', 'maturity', but these terms are notoriously ill-defined.

By far the most significant attempt to come to terms with the problems involved has been that of the London Writing Research Unit. The earliest project resulted in J.N. Britton's paper, *What's the Use?* in 1969, and though effectively nothing was added to the theory during the seventies the Unit developed its practical applications. No findings have had more influence on the theory of English teaching. Concepts such as the expressive, function categories, sense of audience, have resulted in the enlargement of our awareness of the nature of language, and of the process of writing. In the thunderous applause which has greeted work of the Unit no voices have been raised more loudly than our own. We wish to make clear our own debt to Professor Britton and his collaborators since in what follows we must dissent from them, and we would not have it thought that we are wild and sour detractors of an eminence we cannot hope to emulate.

Our main criticism would be that the research does not effectively describe 'the development of writing abilities' which is the title of the report (1975). Britton admits 'an error in choosing the title' (1979, p. 34) but in fact more than the title is in question. The purpose of the research is to substantiate 'a major hypothesis regarding the development of writing ability in school' (p. 82) and indeed elsewhere it is conceded that this hypothesis is not substantiated (p. 197). We wish to go further, and to

*This article was first published in *English in Education*, Vol. 14, No. 3, Autumn 1980, edited by Mike Torbe for the National Association for the Teaching of English.

suggest that the model on which the hypothesis is based is anyway in-adequate. It is our intention to come back to this point later and discuss it in the light of the Crediton Project, to which we shall now turn.

The Crediton Project

With a view to obtaining a clearer picture of the language features of pupils at particular ages, post-graduate studies have been carried out at the Language in Education Centre of the University of Exeter. The initiating paper was that of A. and E. Wilkinson, published in *English in Education* in 1978. The authors have been amazed and delighted at the way the ideas of this paper have seeped through into the work of writers elsewhere so quickly that they have not had time to acknowledge them. At Exeter the work has been extended by Carlin (1978), Marshall (1978), Taylor (1979) and Witcombe (1979), and the most recent project, the Credition Project, has specifically investigated the written language. A team from the University worked in collaboration with teachers in Crediton, Devon, using a simple research design.

Four different compositions—two personal, two discursive—were re-quested from groups of children at seven, ten, and thirteen respectively, in the context of their normal lessons. These were a piece of autobiography on their happiest or saddest day, a narrative suggested by one of three pictures provided, an explanation (of a game), and an argument ('would it work if children came to school when they liked, and do what they liked there?'). It seemed that these four topics required differing and important uses of written language. The same four subjects were given to each group so that the compositions could be more easily compared.

How were these compositions to be assessed? Commonly used 'linguistic' criteria, as in many marking schemes, are often limiting, and do not take into account the writer as a developing being. But the Project was concerned to look at just this; at the nature of the thought, the feeling, the moral stance, as well as at the style, manifested in the writing.

Hence four models were devised to serve as systems of analysis—in the fields of cognition, affect, morals and style. Earlier versions of the first two appeared in the original article in *English in Education*. The complete models are printed in Wilkinson *et al.* (1980). In summary, they are as follows:

> Cognitive. The basis of this model is a movement from an un-differentiated world, to a world organised by mind, from a world of instances to a world related by generalities and abstractions.
> Affective. Development is seen as being in three movements—one towards a greater awareness of self, a second towards a greater awareness of neighbour as self, a third towards an interengagement of reality and imagination.

Moral. 'Anomy' or lawlessness gives way to 'heteronomy' or rule by fear of punishment, which in turn gives way to 'socionomy' or rule by a sense of reciprocity with others, which finally leads to the emergence of 'autonomy' or self-rule.

Stylistic. Development is seen as choices in relation to a norm of the simple literal affirmative sentence, which characterises children's early writing. Features, such as structure, cohesion, verbal competence, syntax, reader awareness, appropriateness, undergo modification.

These models are not intended to be used as day-to-day marking schemes, but to heighten levels of awareness. Their detail enables them to pay due regard to the varieties of activity going on in the process of writing. In one sense they are assessment instruments, but only in the sense that assessment is an essential part of education—we need to make assessments of development to help further development.

In what follows, instead of applying the models in detail we shall attempt to lay out some of the general findings arising from the Project. The types of performance will differ with writer and situation, and we do not wish to argue that at a particular age a child's writing 'ought' to exhibit this or that characteristic. With this reservation we shall attempt a general description of some of the features we have found.

The Writing of Seven-Year-Olds

Young writers will often write slowly. Processes which will be automated in adult writing—letter and word formation, spelling, punctuation, conventional groupings—have not yet become so. Some children will produce few words, others over a page. Spelling may vary from the completely original (which covers a clear story with a thick crust of opacity) to the completely conformist. Punctuation even with the best writing will tend to be forgetful; with the worst it will be non-existent or splendidly random.

A basic problem is construction. Writing tasks are nearly all extended, whereas for instance conversation is often a mutually supported exchange of short items. In writing one form of obvious organization offers itself—the narrative. Because life is chronological—events happen in time—to relate what happens comes naturally. But the writers are often unselective. Teachers will be familiar with the ritual obsession with getting up, breakfasting, going to school, and so on, till watching television and going to bed. Actually this represents a stage beyond that in which insufficient information is supplied, as in the following two complete compositions.

The saddest was when my dog got knocked down

One day we were walking by the country side

> And I wanted to look in a field and my dad
> Walked on and chased him and I fell over on my face

The omission of a word in each case is not significant in terms of our understanding, but does indicate the writers have not monitored the pieces and it is likely are unable to do so. We also probably feel anyway that the stories are incomplete. The first corresponds to what Labov calls an abstract, the summary we commonly give of an anecdote or joke, for example, before telling it. This *partial information* we find a characteristic of young children's writing, indicating a limited organizing ability, writing span and sense of reader needs. Themes which help children to write coherently, on the other hand, are those for which they have some underlying pattern—a fairy story, or other model from literature or TV. One that recurred was that of virtue rewarded, vice punished, where the pay-off line is clear.

In learning to write children come up against a major difference between spoken and written language. In the spoken emotion is conveyed primarily through paralinguistics—the pace, tone, rhythms, timing, all serve this end. In the written it has to be carried by stylistic devices of all kinds—the connotations of nouns and verbs, the enrichment of adjective and adverbs, a whole range of metaphorical language, and so on. These have to be learned, and young children have usually not learned them. Thus their writing will often consist of matter of fact statements, conveying information rather than emotion, as in the above examples. We are not for one moment saying that the emotion may not be felt, but that they have not the resources to communicate it.

Even so this is a generalization which needs qualification; witness the following piece:

> The saddest day was when my Grandad died and his wife was very upset becáuse she had lived for 60 years with him and me and my sister were very very very upset to. We all had to go up to my Grandads house to comfort my Grandmother and stop her crying—
> and we stoped for two days i went with Granmar with my sister
> The End of my Story

In this case the intensity of the experience (needless to say it is a real experience of bereavement) comes across. It is likely that the moving phrase 'because she had lived for 60 years with him' has been uttered by an adult and the writer has been sensitive to it; she has thus been given a language for her grief. Again the word 'upset' is restricted but she uses what resources she has to intensify it by 'very very very'.

Because they are secure in narrative children may use it also in writing for which it is inappropriate. Thus seven-year-olds cannot think analytically in the way required by the argument. We ask them to write on—whether school should be voluntary and subjects a matter of choice. Instead some of them made a decision and developed it into a hypothetical story of the *first I would do this, then that* variety. Clearly narrative has little use in this connection, and without it writers found themselves in considerable difficulties of organization:

> I think school is nice because thursday is my best day because we have drama and in the afetre noon we have p e. I wuode like to come in Monday Wednesday thursday firday are my very very best days in school. I would like wok onely in the morning

This, argumentative, task also requires the ability to objectify—to see the effect of the decision on others—parents, teachers, the school as a whole. Few young children can do this—they tend to express their personal preferences. This egocentricism is in fact characteristic of much of their writing, taken together. Of course when they are asked for a piece of autobiography it is to be expected that the writers themselves will be the centre of attention, but in this case it is particularly significant to see how far other people are involved, and the kind of interest shown in them. In the narratives we would expect the egocentricisms to be manifest in such devices as the first person narrator, and indirectly in the degree to which the characters are revealed as individual identities. Realization takes place through giving them significant dialogue, the mentioning of significant actions, the insertions of interpretative comment, and so on. Most seven-year-olds, whilst showing an awareness of others are unable to manifest them to any great extent as separate beings. Again, the writer's own emotions are expressed but not self-critically.

It is a truism that the early style of children is a spoken style. There are marks of the spoken language—simple active sentences linked by obvious conjunctions, particularly *and, then, so*. The spoken style is less likely to substitute pronouns, use ellipsis, more likely to move from topic to topic without connection. Verbal competence is obviously restricted. There is much use of general verbs—*be, have, go, say, take, put*—and though these are amongst the most common verbs their use seems proportionately more common in the writings we have examined. Nouns also are general—*man, boy, lady, policeman*—often without qualification, and in fact the use of qualifiers to focus the meaning of a noun or verb is not common. Words tend to have a simple connotation, and to be concrete rather than abstract. This having been said about the spoken idiom, it must be pointed out also that by no means all children's sentences are of this kind. They very soon acquire the sense of a written sentence, doubtless from their reading, and of literary forms—*one day, once upon a time*, etc.—and indeed of the sort of spoken language a written story uses. One writer has her policeman saying, 'Hello, Hello, what's up here then?'

The Writing of Ten-Year-Olds

In the writing of ten-year-olds the narrative mode is used at greater length. Stories and autobiographies are predominantly chronological, but an ability to modify this emerges. Writers no longer need to get up, eat a series of meals, and go to bed. They can begin with a significant incident which plunges us *in medias res*, and end with a further significant incident. Retrospection is possible: on the one hand, with a short reference, perhaps by way of explanation, to some prior event; on the other hand, the major part of the writing may be a flashback from an event described at the beginning, which is led up to once again at the end. This last however is not very common among this group. It is more usual to find extended writing in chronological mode, sometimes with two or more incidents described in fair detail, without the writer being sure about the relative priority to be given to each.

A piece by a ten-year-old, Catherine, will illustrate some of these points:

It Fails

'Come on brother aren't you hungry'
George ran down the stairs first dropping his hanky and
then his slipper fell off.
'Youre breakfast is in the oven George'
shouted Mum going out of the back door to work.
'What shall we do today David'. Ask's Gorge dropping
is fork on the floor. 'Well I was thinking
What about robbing a bank'. Answers David.
'Youre' jokeing' says Gorge. 'No I am not'
'Well I don't know if we should realy David'
'Don't be an ass' shouts David going and picking
up his shoes. 'Mum wont know or are you a coward.'
'No I'm not I know we haven't much money but.'
Says Gorge 'But what. O do hurry up and eat that
breakfast' O I'm so sorry.'
David ran up stairs and washed. 1 hour later they
were getting their coats on. 'Well David which
bank are we going to rob if any.' 'Were going to rob
Lloyds bank' but that Welsh' 'So what I'm shore
they have English money.' They caught the bus and
went into town as they lived in London it was very
busy. They paid the driver and got of. 'Now where
do we go now?' asks Gorge 'To the back of the bank.'
'I dont really know if I should trust you.' 'O come on
squirt.' Answears David walking of. 'Wait for me im in
this Loot with you.' Shouts Gorge running after him.
It took them 1 hour to get to the back of
the bank. When they got there it was 11 o'clock
in the morning. 'I'm hungry'. Complains Gorge.
'Well you should have fineshed you breakfast.'
Oh be quiet'. Mouth David says Gorge in a boasting

manor. 'Look hear's an apple and be quiet.'
'Do you want the London police after us!' 'Look
stop talking to me as if I was a baby.'
'Well you are.' 'Oh come on David' 'Or write
Gorge I'm coming.' They quickly stopped when the
saw a sighn.

Do you   NO ENTRY   think we ought to go
in David?'   ascked Gorge

'Of course we can baby. You really are a baby
Gorge. I'm not shore if you won't tell anybody
about what were going to do.' 'Of course I won't
I wouldent let you down now would I.'
'Well I suppose you wouldent. Come on any way.'
They went into the building and looked around.
They saw a large door on the right. They heard a
few voices behind the doors 'I'm scared David'.
'I thought you would be Gorge.'
'Hay whats that noise David.'

'Your under arrest kids.' 'Its the police David.'
'I know Gorge I know.'

Catherine is not bound by a strict sequence of events in the way many younger children are, though there are still signs of the impulse to include everything—incidents like paying the bus fare, for example, which are unnecessary. What is notable however is the way she can begin *in medias res*, with a piece of dialogue. There are really two themes—the interaction between the boys, and the robbing of a bank—both of which are neatly tied up in the last exchange. The second theme is very much subservient to the first, revelation of character being far more important than the narration of unlikely events which are presented with no suspense or anticipation, and fall a little flat. Catherine is in control of suitable cohesive devices. In this type of narrative which moves through dialogue conjunctions are scarce, lexical cohesion and previous reference quite extensive. It is common with this story convention that the first sentence should alert us, the second provide a context: 'brother' in the first becomes 'Gorge' in the second. Mum is introduced by reference to Gorge, and George introduces David; mention of 'breakfast' allows a reference to 'fork' by lexical collocation; later George is 'hungry' not having finished breakfast. Continuatives—'well', 'anyway'—which throw attention back to the previous statement; ellipsis, giving the impression of natural dialogue—'No I'm not', 'I suppose you wouldn't'; and synonyms—'squirt', 'coward', 'baby'— all add up to a very skilled use of cohesion. Syntactically the story does not require complicated structures, particularly as it is mainly in spoken idiom: it several times uses the present participle to add action to words—e.g. 'answers David, walking off'. The diction and phrasing tend to be stock, largely from the Blyton model—'ass', 'squirt'. On one occasion where an exact word is required instead of 'boasting'—'Oh be quiet, mouth David' 'Says Gorge in a boasting manner'—this repertoire does not provide it. The language is appropriate to the period Blyton model, taken with a pinch of salt. The reader is kept in touch, but is sometimes confused—about what happens in the bank and why the boys should at one stage change roles—George becoming dominant and giving David an apple. Effective in many ways, partly from its lightness of touch, the story does not relate the two themes and stops at the climax of the robbery.

Catherine does not express emotion directly in 'It Fails', but shows an ability to understand it in the characters of the two boys. They are consistent (except for one place), David being the dominant entrepreneur, George the one with scruples and anxieties. There is some well chosen detail: David's action in picking up his shoes reinforces his disagreement with George:

'Don't be an ass,' shouts David going and picking up his shoes.

The writing is of course on the fantasy level written with tongue nicely in cheek: the reader, as we have seen, is carefully considered. The boys are deliberately presented as behaving at two different moral levels, David from self-indulgence and George from scruples which David ascribes to fear. Amusingly David only offers two reasons to George for not robbing the bank: 'Mum wont know or are you a coward'. Cognitively the story operates—as so much narrative essentially must do—at the level of reporting.

Time is an element which is present in the work of writers of all ages; space is not. It is only at ten or so that location is established, as in the work of Catherine. It is part of an increasing reference to the reader. The events young children write about often take place in a nowhere. Most members of the ten-year-old group can indicate a context, even set a scene. Details of environment—landscape, for example—can be used to create atmosphere. In fact there is sometimes overmuch detail. The expression of emotion by other means—e.g. adjectival, adverbial, metaphorical—is not common, though if prompted by a title many writers will say 'I felt happy/sad'. The outlining of sad or happy events, however, is of course perfectly possible.

The viewpoint in many cases is still egocentric, and scarcely anyone evaluates his own emotion. More attention is paid to other people, and in the stories characters are portrayed, though often not beyond the single dimensional level. The point having been made, it should be said that there is the occasional writer who explores character and emotion with considerable skill and depth.

As far as the argumentative and explanatory writings are concerned many writers still attempt to apply narrative to a task for which it is unsuitable. Here, for example, is part of the piece from Sandra, aged ten:

I think some times that we are better at school and that
home.
Mam says Sharon in a way you are much better being at
school.
But Mum can I just to day can I stay home no Sharon please
please Just to day no no Sharon.
When you come home you can go to bed do I have to go to bed
yes Sharon
When I got home I did have to go to bed but I that that I
was best to go to school because I learn more at school and
what I will at home like are mum's or dad's can not give us
exmahams.

In an explanation of how to play a game narrative needs to be superceded by, or at least supplemented by, a classificatory system. Thus aims, methods of winning, apparatus, layout, rules, progress of the game, must all be present; and some form of superordinate thinking is important. No writer of this age gives a fully classificatory account of the game; but where a chronological account is offered it may include ordered rather than random lists of information. However the advance that the ten-year-olds significantly make over the seven-year-olds is that their accounts are more complete. They are very aware that there is a reader who has needs, whether or not they succeed in meeting them completely.

In narrative some writers have a sense of register. In explanations there is some sense of presentation derived from rule books. In the 'voluntary schools' task there is no ready model available anyway, and the analytical procedures which produce a rational and objective organization from scratch are not accessible to writers of this age. There is a bigger repertoire of syntax than the seven-year-olds have. The question of using it is now more pressing than the question of possessing it, and few children use it appropriately over an extended stretch of writing, though there are areas of success. On the whole the use of vocabulary and idiom is more competent: a written register is more common. There is some ability to employ technical terms. Some writers begin to experiment with 'fine writing'—phrases not their own for experiences they will later find their own words for. These are obviously not to be condemned as cliches but encouraged as signs of an exercise of growing powers.

The Writing of Thirteen-Year-Olds

In the work of the thirteen-year-olds one of the immediately noticeable features is their ability to differentiate usage. Their sense of the 'appropriate' register and form for a particular type of discourse has developed considerably. This is partly due to growing cognitive powers—the ability to classify which is valuable in the explanatory task also suggests a way of presenting this task. Again on the argumentative task their growing ability to hypothesize has in some cases suggested the outlines of the form. Thus Arthur generalizes and then goes into detail: 'This system would be dubious unless several regulations were introduced'. Of course the ability to use particular registers must also come from acquaintance with them, and there are obvious literary models behind much of the writing, particularly the narrative. The importance of acquaintance with literature in helping children develop their individual forms of writing is borne out by our study. The eighteenth century would have thought this obvious. Writers as diverse as Pope and Blake (how diverse can you get?) went through a self-imposed apprenticeship of 'imitation', and whilst we would not advocate this, it is clear to us that acquaintance with good models is necessary. Thus Enid Blyton's style proves helpful to children as far as the narrative line is concerned but also leads to stereotyping in character.

On the whole writers at thirteen are much more in control of the core narrative. Necessarily it will be chronological, but the time sequence can be adjusted with confidence with prospects and retrospects, and much gratuitous information has been excised. There are also the elaborations which put flesh on the basic structure. These are the devices which make the writing context-free by constantly giving the reader information and explanation. Sometimes the writers are unsure here (one piece is characterized by a staggering number of 'asides') but they are not in doubt of the need to cater for a reader. In a few cases the core narrative as such is missing, and the story is carried in dialogue or in a stream of consciousness. Another feature which distinguishes the work of the thirteen-year-olds from that of the younger groups is their concern with emotion. Younger children can certainly describe events which concern the emotions—death, for instance—but the emotions are not usually expressed or interpreted. In the writings of some of the thirteen-year-olds however there are the beginnings of self-awareness and of awareness of others as psychological beings. In the sense that an awareness of self shows some ability to objectify self, this, as well as the growing understanding of others, carries on the general movement away from egocentricity which we have noticed in the developing child.

Often the writers' very eagerness to write well can produce an impression of 'insincerity' where the language seems second-hand and the emotions expressed exaggerated. Sometimes the reaching out for metaphorical language, even the 'objective correlative' of the story, seems to result in exaggerated or melodramatic emotion. Where there is a specific literary model this feeling of overwriting, and of second-hand emotion may be particularly strong. It behoves us to be careful however. Certainly emotion may be insincere in the sense that it is merely copied; but frequently we find it seems that writers have a unique experience but not, at this stage a unique language. Stratta, Dixon and Wilkinson (1974, pp. 15–20) write of the process whereby a writer attains to a three-fold uniqueness—of self, expression, form. The writer works through the stock language and stereotype perceptions associated with it to an individual perception expressed in individual terms. This is a hard won end—we can scarcely expect children to have gone through the process by the age of thirteen.

As far as language is concerned there is a much more confident choice of syntax in relation to meaning in all but the less successful writers. Normal cohesive devices such as reference and substitution are commonly used as a matter of course. The development comes in the way some writers use them as a deliberate device of style—repetition, parallelism, etc. Some writers can employ irony and disjunction. As already mentioned there is sometimes overwriting, and a search for metaphor which varies in its success. As against this the command of technical vocabulary in the description of certain games is impressive.

Many of these points may be demonstrated in the following piece:

> . . . The first thing we did was to have assembly,
> when I was the only (one) able to answer the
> Headmaster's question. I was nicknamed
> 'Magnus'—a bad start. I knew everything
> in the lessons, I could answer every question
> by means of a lecture, though I had not
> mastered the art of friendliness. As one or two
> fists told me.
>
> My popularity in the class was abismal. I was
> rated as an outcaste by everyone. I was bullied
> perpetually and brutally by gangs. Whenever the
> teacher turned her back they attacked. Often
> when she was looking. She took little action.
>
> I hated the school. I learned absolutely nothing.
> I was in a backward class with an intelligence better
> than most of the top class. Just because of my age.
> The 'supervision' was about as effective as a
> catapult used in war between Russia and America.
> Or worse.
>
> The worst part of the day was changing back from
> swimming. The entire class of boys threw their
> wet trunks at me. At short range. Hard. Being
> a female teacher no supervision could be given.
> This happened nearly every day . . . .

Here we have a piece which conveniently illustrates the development of the writer in many dimensions of our model. As far as affect is concerned the piece is characterized by an intense but well controlled anger against the teacher, the system and the bullies, but at the same time the writer recognizes the complexity of the situation—he is to blame, for being arrogant and unfriendly, as well as the others. The writer not only describes but interprets, and distances by means of irony. He is not dependent on narrative; after the first incident, he makes general statements about what used to happen; and about his general position in school; returning to what was customary in the last paragraph. The implied moral judgement is that it was unjust, but that he had brought some of it on himself.

In style the piece demonstrates a feature which is emerging with the writing of some thirteen-year-olds—the consciousness of the writing as an artifact, the conscious shaping of the work in relation to the reader. Structurally the piece rates highly, each paragraph well organized, with a laconic comment at the end. The syntax is completely under the writer's control, even to the ability to use incomplete sentences. The deliberately exaggerated vocabulary ('abismal', 'absolutely nothing') and the ironic 'supervision', for example, indicate great verbal ability. We have here a very competent writer indeed.

The London Model

We will now return as promised to the work of the London Writing Research Unit. The model offered is based on the Expressive—utterance that 'stays close to the speaker' and hence is fully comprehensible only to one who knows the speaker and shares his context. It is a verbalization of the speaker's immediate preoccupation and mood of the moment' (p. 82). Another category is the Transactional—'the language to get things done', to record facts, exchange opinions, construct theories, conduct campaigns. And the third category is the Poetic. Here language is used as an art medium. 'A piece of poetical writing is a verbal construct, an "object" made out of language'. It exists 'for its own sake, and not as a means of achieving something else' (p. 91). The Expressive is the 'seed bed' out of which the other two can grow: 'in developmental terms, the Expressive is a kind of matrix from which differentiated forms of mature writing are developed' (p. 82).

The Expressive is first defined in spoken terms ('speaker', 'audience', etc.): it leads to 'differentiated forms of mature writing'. Work at Credition leads us to doubt whether this in fact is true. If we take the major form which predominantly constitutes the Poetic—narrative—then we find it highly developed in pre-school children. Lucetta tells us

> A little girl drawed her mummy Then the mummy
> got mad at her and she cried. She lost her
> mummy's cookies. She got mad at her again. And
> she drawed her mummy again. And her mummy got

mad at her again. And her Daddy got home. That
was Julie.

(Applebee, p. 60)

Our work suggests a strong line of development of the narrative proceeding directly from spoken to written mode, which does not need to be
explained by a concept such as the Expressive. Indeed there are reasons
for believing that narrative is a basic way of processing experience, and
thus a basic mode of language, precisely because man thinks and acts in
time. This is reflected in the nuclear sentences of language which are Actor-
Action (SV, SVO) where they are not descriptive. We have found that
young writers use the narrative form for many extended tasks for which
adults would not consider it appropriate. We have given examples of this
in the previous section. And certainly autobiography is written as narrative.
We thus have doubts about whether the Poetic develops in the way Britton
says it does.

However our main criticism of the Project is directed not upon the
Expressive as a concept, but on the descriptive power of the model as a
whole. It is our view that this descriptive power is very limited. It will be
remembered that the Expressive is said to become differentiated, on the
one hand, to the Poetic, and, on the other hand, to the Transactional. No
degrees of development are indicated in the Expressive, nor in the Poetic.
The Transactional, on the other hand, divides into the Conative (subdivided
into *regulative* and *persuasive*), and the Informative (subdivided into
record; *report*; *generalized narrative* or *descriptive information*; *analogic*,
low level of generalization; *analogic*; *analogic-tautologic* (*speculative*);
tautologic).

Under the headings Expressive and Poetic then there is only blank paper.
Nothing is described about the development of emotion, the growth of
moral judgement, the development of style and linguistic uses at particular
levels. What we have is a list in cognitive terms in the Piaget/Bloom tradition, being effectively a development of categories suggested by Moffett
(1968) as is generously acknowledged. It is a pity Moffett's confusing
terminology has to be taken over, and that something of his sense of context
in human experience is missing. Nevertheless the Transactional (informative) category must be considered a valuable addition to our tools of
analysis. Even though the Unit was frustrated in its attempts to validate
the model by the concentration of the schools on lower level transactional
tasks, it is probable on theoretical grounds that under less constrained
conditions some sort of hierarchy as posited would be discovered. So much
can readily be agreed. The gravamen of our comment is that by failing to
define Expressive and Poetic in developmental detail the model is unable to
describe large areas of human experience as manifested in language, and
is thus the less effective.

123

Andrew Wilkinson, Gillian Barnsley, Peter Hanna and Margaret Swan

Comment

In this paper it has been possible only to outline the Crediton models. They have the advantage that they do not require a single categorization to be made of a whole piece. Levels of activity clearly vary, say from sentence to sentence, and the models are delicate enough to cope with this, but it means that they are fairly detailed. Enough will have been said, however, to indicate the nature of the insights they are intended to prompt.

Inevitably they are very tentative since there is no precedent for the affective and stylistic models, and little for the application of any models of this type to writing. However rather than hoping forlornly to bring them to a gleaming perfection we are instead offering them for comment and improvement. Again, the Crediton sample is small; but it is not a sample, it is children. It may be that children elsewhere are not very different.

References

APPLEBEE, A.N. (1978) *The Child's Concept of Story*, University of Chicago Press.

BRITTON, J.N., BURGESS, T., McLEOD, A., and ROSEN, H. (1975) *The Development of Writing Abilities*, Macmillan Educational.

BRITTON, J.N., with BARRS, M., and BURGESS, T. (1979) ' "No, no, Jeannette": A reply to Jeanette Williams' critique of the Schools Council Writing Research Project', *Language for Learning*, 1.1, pp. 23–41.

BRUNER, J.S. (1975) 'Language as an instrument of thought', in DAVIES, A. (ed.) *Problems of Language and Learning*, Heinemann.

CARLIN, E.S. (1978) *Theories and Measures of Writing Development*, Unpublished M.Ed. Dissertation, University of Exeter.

MARSHALL, E. (1978) *Criteria Internalised by Impression Markers*, Unpublished M.Ed. Dissertation, University of Exeter.

MOFFETT, JAMES (1968) *Teaching the Universe of Discourse*, Houghton Mifflin Co., Boston.

TAYLOR, G. (1979) *The Development of Language*, Unpublished M.Ed. Dissertation, University of Exeter.

WEIR, R. (1962) *Language in the Crib*, Mouton, The Hague.

WILKINSON, A., BARNSLEY, G., HANNA, P., and SWAN, M. (1980) *Assessing Language Development*, OUP.

WILKINSON, A. M., and WILKINSON, M.E. (1978) 'The Development of Language in in Middle Years', *English in Education*, 12.1, pp. 45–52.

WITCOMBE, C.M. (1979) *Developmental Aspects of Children's Language in Junior School*, Unpublished M.Ed. Dissertation, University of Exeter.

4
Learning and Personal Development

Introduction

The next three articles are concerned with the way in which the process of learning is related to a process of change in the learner, that it is not just a matter of the acquisition of knowledge seen as 'commodity'. All three see affinities between the ways in which adults learn and the learning of children and all reserve a central place for personal development in and through the arts. It is clear that all three have been greatly influenced by such seminal works for the English teacher as Hourd's *The Education of the Poetic Spirit*[1] and Witkin's *The Intelligence of Feeling*.[2] All the authors of these articles are involved in teacher education, especially the preparation of English graduates to teach English in schools. There is a strong commitment amongst them to the view that teaching is learned best through the personal development of the student teacher, that the acquisition of a number of 'tricks of the trade' is not enough. The articles have all grown out of the work done with students, intending teachers, but they all have powerful implications for the classroom also. Michael Benton's article is a revised and expanded version of an essay that originally appeared in *The First Two Rs*.[3] Eric Hadley's contribution grows directly out of his initial and in-service work in the training of teachers and demonstrates powerfully the continuing relevance of sensitive teaching of literature to English students in the 1980s and beyond. Finally, the joint article by Anthony Adams and Eric Hadley takes English as a case study to raise some important questions about teacher education in general.

Notes

1 HOURD, MARJORIE (1949) *The Education of the Poetic Spirit*, Heinemann.
2 WITKIN, ROBERT (1974) *The Intelligence of Feeling*, Heinemann.
3 BENTON, MICHAEL (1978) *The First Two Rs*, Department of Education, University of Southampton.

How Authors Write . . . How Children Write: Toward a Rationale for Creative Writing*

Michael Benton
Lecturer in Education, University of Southampton

Responses Are Not Enough

In 1854 Dickens published a searing attack on the utilitarian attitude to education in his novel *Hard Times*. Had he been writing in the 1980s, the celebrated opening to that book might have come out rather differently— something like this, perhaps:

> 'Now, what I want is, a Response. Teach these boys and girls nothing but How to Respond. Responses alone are wanted in life. Plant nothing else and root out everything else. You can only form the minds of reasoning animals upon Personal Responses: nothing else will ever be of any service to them. This is the principle on which I bring up my children, and this is the principle on which I bring up these children. Free the child's Creative Responses, Sir!'[1]

This is a caricature of our times just as Dickens' had been over a century earlier but it serves to convey the message of our modern 'gradgrindery': facts are out; responses are in. During the vogue for 'creative writing' there has been an enormous amount of stimulus-response work in English lessons, work that has gone on without any underpinning rationale and often with a distorting concern for ends rather than means. With the child's response at such a high premium, it is easy to see how some teachers have been tempted to accept *any* response as admissible. A response becomes enough in itself, particularly if it can be 'prettied-up' and put on the wall. In extreme cases this can lead to the withholding of criticism, to the feeling that anything goes and to the abrogation of our responsibility to teach children to write.

If this diagnosis has any sort of truth in it, there is little wonder that some children have developed a knowing cynicism about the nature of

*This is a revised and expanded version of an essay published in BENTON, MICHAEL (1978) *The First Two Rs*, Department of Education, University of Southampton.

'creative writing'. They become used to writing to order, used to reacting to the stimuli we offer them and, as I have already hinted, accustomed to the teacher's concern with the finished product, the poem, story or essay, rather than with the creative process that brought it into being. This is why I want us to shift our attention to the process of writing and, in doing so, to attempt a synthesis of ideas offered from three different perspectives: the pedagogical, the psychological and the literary. I shall be looking for the connections between what Robert Witkin says in *The Intelligence of Feeling*[2] about the nature of the creative process in the teaching context, what psychologists tell us about the writer's thinking, and what authors say about what they do. If our familiarity with the first two perspectives has increased in recent years, largely through the work of two Schools Council projects,[3] the third one seems to have been largely ignored. This is surprising since the evidence is plentiful and lies in an area close to the heart of the English teacher's concern. What poets and novelists say in essays, diaries, marginalia and letters about their work is, of course, enormously varied but there does seem to be a discernible pattern; and, moreover, it is a pattern which, as I hope to show, relates remarkably closely to the ones which emerge from the other two perspectives. Indeed, I would go so far as to claim that the combined evidence from the three sources I have mentioned goes a long way towards meeting the criticism voiced in *The Bullock Report*. Speaking of 'creative writing', Bullock said: 'This lack of agreed definition reflects the absence of a clear rationale for the work to which it refers . . . (11.5).[4] I think we are at a stage now where we can begin to see some sort of developing rationale and I hope that I can sketch in the outline and muster some of the evidence, in particular, the literary evidence since, while it is obvious that English teachers are not in the business of trying to make their pupils into professional poets or novelists, it is equally clear that we all have a lot to learn about the art of writing by attending to the accounts of the best practitioners.

Where Stories Start: The Idea of Inspiration

The idea of 'inspiration' is fundamental to any discussion of composition. There are those who claim it can be 'anatomized'[5] and others who believe it will forever elude man's understanding.[6] We do well to begin, then, with a text that is generally acknowledged to be the most detailed and penetrating study by a major novelist of his craft, Henry James' *The Art of the Novel*,[7] a series of Prefaces that, according to C.E. Montague, divulges 'the closest workshop secrets that any novelist has yet confided to non-novelists'.[8]

James talks of 'germs'. He opens his 'Preface' to *The Spoils of Poynton* with the celebrated account of some table-talk at a Christmas Eve dinner which produced

> ... one of those allusions that I have always found myself recog-
> nising as 'germs'. The germ, wherever gathered, has ever been for
> me the germ of a 'story', and most of the stories straining to shape
> under my hand have sprung from a single small seed ...[9]

James goes on to identify three linked qualities of a 'germ': firstly, its
minuteness, it is 'a mere floating particle in the stream of talk' and, as such,
too much detail will clutter and stultify. Secondly, its 'needle-like quality'
by which he means a sort of diagnostic element that pin-points the significant, 'a power', as he puts it, 'to penetrate as finely as possible'. Thirdly,
he mentions the 'fruitful essence' of a germ, its potential as a growth point
for fiction.

The ability to recognize such 'germs' is one that authors commonly
remark upon: recognition may emerge over a period of time as an increasing
awareness of the significance of a particular image or, more commonly,
strike the writer with the sudden revelatory power that convention and
tradition conspire to call 'a flash of inspiration'.[10] The writer's acuteness at
recognition implies a disposition to look. In this respect, his observational
'eye' and his alertness to connections between the disparate experiences of
life that comprise his source material are qualities that the writer shares with
all artists, whatever the medium. So, too, perhaps is the unpredictable
nature of such recognitions: art cannot be pre-planned, it has to be waited
for. But, if there is an arbitrariness about how the mind chooses its focus
of inspiration, what John Fowles calls the 'accidentality of inspiration',[11]
there is a clear methodological principle for the writer once he has recognized the subject with which he must wrestle. Henry James expresses it
thus:

> ... the first thing to be done for the communicated and seized
> idea is to reduce almost to nought, the form, the air as of a mere
> disjoined and lacerated lump of life, in which we may have
> happened to meet it. Life being all inclusion and confusion, and
> art being all discrimination and selection, the latter, in search of
> the hard latent *value* with which alone it is concerned, sniffs round
> the mass as instinctively and unerringly as a dog suspicious of some
> buried bone.[12]

James' final metaphor gives new meaning to one's notion of a portrait
of the artist as a young dog! The writer's initial activity is seen as an
abstracting process, the drive to reduce the significant idea to a bare schema
that will at once encapsulate essential meaning and reflect its necessary
form.

Other writers arrive at a similar conclusion by different means. Often
the 'germ' that constitutes the inspiration for a poem or story is conveyed
through the notion of an image or mental picture. Sassoon speaks for
many writers when he says:

> I have never been fond of ideas for their own sake. In fact they
> have played a comparatively unimportant part in my literary life.
> My thoughts—if one can call them that—have been (when allowed
> to have their own way) a series of mental pictures. Thinking in
> pictures is my natural method of self-expression.[13]

The incidence and nature of such mental 'picturing' is explored later in
the discussion of the writer's thinking during composition. Mention of
'picturing' is made here not only because it is the commonest means
writers use to describe the recognition of the initial impetus to create,
but also because what Sassoon goes on to say in his lecture adds a further
dimension to James' concept of 'germs'. Sassoon continues: 'I have always
been a submissively visual writer ... mind-sight eliminates what is
inessential, and achieves breadth and intensity by transmuted perception.'
The abstracting mechanism is noted but its corollary is the development of
a more intense mental image through a process of psychic transmutation.
The moment of inspiration (as distinct from the idea of a 'flash' or 'spark'—
metaphors merely suggesting an instantaneous event) can thus be located
at the intersection of two complementary recognitions: the one is characterized by the drive to eliminate the inessential, a mental précis through
which the writer narrows down his attention on to a single significant
focus; the other consists in the recognition that within this focal idea or
image lies the latent growth of story; inspiration implies that germination
not only can but *must* take place. The movement of the abstracting process
is centripetal; the movement of the germination process is centrifugal.
'Inspiration' incorporates both elements. This dualism appears to be
consistent with conventional usage in that the lay use of this term describes
the thought 'that creation is the result of *inspiration*—a breathing in by
some exterior spirit'.[14] The inward movement of the writer's muse finds
its corollary in the outward direction of his expressive work. In our
'unpacking' of the meaning of inspiration above, we have the same notion
in less magical language.

The clearest contemporary account of these twin elements of inspiration
is given by John Fowles in his essay 'Notes on an Unfinished Novel'.
Reflecting upon his writing of *The French Lieutenant's Woman*, Fowles says

> It started four or five months ago as a visual image. A woman stands
> at the end of a deserted quay and stares out to sea. That was all . . . .
> These mythopoeic 'stills' (they seem almost always static) float
> into my mind very often. I ignore them, since that is the best way
> of finding whether they really are the door into a new world.[15]

The image has been abstracted from the 'dense hinterland' of the unconscious. Ignored, it persists; indeed, it insists upon recognition. Steadily,
according to Fowles, he became aware 'that it held some sort of imminent
power' that commanded his attention and this recognition he describes in

terms of his mind making the image more specific. Details of a latent 'new world' begin to cluster round this focus until the image will not be denied. Abstraction and germination coalesce. The more intently the mind focuses upon the specific image in order to grasp its essence, the more insistently the mind spawns the details of the 'new world', the mental arena, in which the image resides.

The initiation of storying, the moment of inspiration, is a complex event which, from the evidence and argument given so far, assumes the shape of a psychic hour-glass! The mind is seen as eliminating the inessential, abstracting, focusing, narrowing down to the nexus of inspiration: the writer's recognition of the significance of this nexus is spoken of through metaphors of growth and power which imply the inevitability of creation, once the mind has turned the hour-glass over. Whether or not the writer identifies the initiation of storying in terms of an idea caught in the form of words as James does, or an idea encapsulated in an image as Fowles describes, seems to be as unpredictable and varied as the nature of the creative act itself. Stephen Spender suggests this variety of starting-points when he says:

> My own experience of inspiration is certainly that of a line or a phrase or a word or sometimes something still vague, a dim cloud of an idea which I feel must be condensed into a shower of words.[16]

Spender's vivid metaphor describing the linguistic dimension of the creative process anticipates our discussion of the phases of composition. Prior to the writer's activity of distilling ideas into language comes the mood that is suggested by Spender's imperative 'must'. If we ask what it is that writers mean by this sense of compulsion, their answers appear to take two forms. On the one hand, there is their feeling that the story or poem exists already, that inspiration places an onus upon the artist to use his skill to release the story from the inchoate mass of images and give it form; on the other hand, there is the sense that inspiration is not simply an instantaneous 'flash' but more of a continuous mood that helps to sustain the writing. These two notions concerning the affective elements in being moved to write are discussed briefly below: the first involves the writer's sense of responsibility to his craft, the second his awareness of the appropriate atmosphere that surrounds his creative work. Such an awareness is present both in the writer's initial recognition that he has the 'germ' of a story and in his ongoing feeling of the conditions of creativity during writing. Some consideration of creative mood, therefore, not only arises naturally in a discussion of inspiration but it also leads inevitably towards the notion of the 'phases' of the creative process.

Alan Garner expresses the feeling that the story is already 'there', as follows:

> It is a pure hallucination, but there is always the feeling that the

book exists already, and the task is not so much invention as clarification: I must give colour to the invisible object so that other people can see it.[17]

Elsewhere in the same article, Garner speaks of his job as one of showing, not telling and, in so doing, allies himself with one of the central ideas of literary creation, for he expresses both the writer's sense of responsibility to his craft and a fundamental principle of criticism that is held by critics as different as Percy Lubbock and Wayne Booth. The former makes the point thus:

> ... the art of fiction does not begin until the novelist thinks of his story as a matter to be *shown*, to be so exhibited that it will tell itself.[18]

The idea of the writer *showing* his story appears to derive directly from his feeling that it already exists. In this sense, all literature consists of 'found' poetry or 'found' stories, which is not to deny the special qualities of the creative artist in bringing about the clarification which Garner mentions. Rather it describes the relationship between an author and his material through the sculptural analogy of *taking away* superfluous matter instead of the painterly one that sees the artist attaining results by *laying on*. Indeed, it is in one of Michelangelo's sonnets that we find this notion of hidden form awaiting expressive release:

> The marble not yet carved can hold the form
> Of every thought the greatest artist has,
> And no conception ever comes to pass
> Unless the hand obeys the intellect.
>
> Sonnet XV[19]

The feeling that the artistic shape already exists, whether a sculpture locked in stone or a sonnet or story imprisoned in formless words and images, is an important element in what is generally understood by the word 'inspiration'. In her anatomy of the term, Rosamond Harding concludes by relating this sense of a pre-existing form awaiting discovery to the idea of creation as the 'inbreathing' of a poetic spirit in a phrase that was quoted earlier. Here is the whole extract.

> The artist is, so to speak, given his themes and, once given, he must follow their unfolding. While he transcribes it is dictated to him: it is not the deliberate outcome of his will; and it is this that has given rise to the thought that creation is the result of *inspiration* —a breathing in by some exterior spirit.[20]

The writer as secretary to his muse, transcribing the involuntary images that emerge in his consciousness, suggests an autistic element in his thinking; but the writer is also a maker who fashions these transcriptions into consciously-shaped forms. The interplay of autistic and directed thought is to be seen repeatedly when we come to consider the nature of the writer's thinking during composition. Suffice it to note here that Rosamond Harding implies that both types of thinking are involved when we speak of the creative process as being initiated by 'inspiration'. 'Clarification', in Alan Garner's term, means both *seeing clearly* what has been given and *making clear* what it is that is being expressed.

This dual nature of artistic thinking, with its receptive and creative elements, also invests any discussion of creative mood. The second part of Rosamond Harding's book is given up to 'An Essay on the Creative Mood' and she is quick to point out '. . . the twofold influence of the mood in attracting the right material and in fusing this to fit the conception'.[21] Her essay discusses many examples of writers who testify to the nature and importance of mood both at the start of composition and throughout the process. Drawing heavily on Coleridge, her argument is that the controlling power of composition lies in the 'creative mood'[22] and that to see inspiration as an instantaneous 'flash' is an unnecessarily limited view which does not do justice to what authors tell us. For they say that, to quote Wordsworth's celebrated account, the origins of literary composition are in the interaction of memory and emotion. A 'species of reaction' (what one assumes Sassoon means by his 'transmuted perception') takes place within the writer's psyche such that remembered feeling 'does actually exist in the mind'. Composition means giving form to this feeling. So, Wordsworth continues, 'In this mood successful composition generally begins, and in a mood similar to this it is carried on.'[23] The affective nature of the inspired writer is thus closely allied with the concept of 'mood' and the term 'inspiration' is stretched to mean an enveloping atmosphere that occurs whenever writing is proceeding rather than a once and for all catalyst to start a process. Armed, then, with a concept of inspiration that comprises both the writer's primary focus, his initial insight, and the state of feeling in which composition takes place, let us now look at what authors say about the writing process as a number of phases.

The Phases of the Writing Process

One of the most exhaustive accounts by a writer of his process of making a single novel is Irving Wallace's book *The Writing of One Novel*,[24] in which he gives a detailed description of the experiences and work that went into his composition of *The Prize*.

He conceived the idea of a novel about the Nobel Prizes in Stockholm during 1946 and finished work on the book and saw it published in 1962. As his account makes clear, the novel was something that he lived with as a real part of his life for the whole of this period of sixteen years. How he organizes his account demonstrates the phases of writing activity as he experienced them. Significantly, he divides his book into three sections and uses the commonest metaphor that writers employ about their art in order to link them: Part One is labelled 'Conception', Part Two, 'Gestation' and Part Three, 'Birth'. In the period that lies between the conception and publication there can be identified several phases which occur both in Wallace's and other writers' accounts of the creative process. As a means of identifying, illustrating and developing this area of the argument, the accounts of two novelists, two poets and two children's authors are discussed and related, firstly, to the general survey of Harding (*op. cit.*) in which the main evidence is drawn from earlier centuries, notably from nineteenth-century writers and, secondly, to Wallas's influential account of the creative process in *The Art of Thought*.[25]

It is tempting to think of the phases of the writing activity as a sequence. Indeed, writers' accounts often encourage this notion. However, it may well be more exact to view the phases as a number of recurring states of mental activity that vary in duration, order and importance and, in so doing, contribute to the uniqueness of every creative venture. This uniqueness makes comparison and generalization difficult. Nonetheless, there do appear to be certain phases that can be recognized in the accounts of many writers. We have already considered one, the *inspirational phase*. The others might be called the *preparatory phase*, the *incubatory phase* and the *making phase*.

Irving Wallace records his moment of inspiration as occurring on a particular Sunday at noon when be looked down from the window of his Stockholm hotel and 'idly watched and listened as the King's band played before his enormous Royal Palace across the way'. Two ideas came together, the 'postcard grandeur, the outer reality of it . . . ' and the 'plainer, cruder human events' that his interviews with the Swedish Nobel judges had revealed.

> And that was the moment of conception. At once, I knew what must be done . . . . From that moment, I was possessed of a brain-child, faceless, almost shapeless, that I would not be delivered of for a decade and a half.[26]

The ensuing sixteen years up to publication were characterized by the four types of activity indicated above.

The preparatory phase for this or any other novel could be described in terms of the author's whole life, his accumulated experiences and the uses to which his memory puts such experiences. More particularly, the preparation for *The Prize* consisted of notes, articles and several sketchy outlines, rather like scenarios, all related to the Nobel theme which occupied Wallace during the 1950s. The mental activity was one of conscious searching and researching; of seeking a voice in which to tell the tale and of establishing the details that would authenticate the fiction.

The incubatory and making phases could also be defined widely to include all the activities to do with the author's gestation of the story after 1946 and all his bits of writing that contributed to the final draft. As with the other phases, however, it is more useful to distinguish them in terms of the mental activity involved. The labels themselves suggest a differentiation between two types of thinking, dominated by unconscious and conscious thinking respectively. Irving Wallace describes these psychic processes thus:

> The inner creative process, in that period, was of two kinds, assuming that it can be accurately described at all. Sometimes I would consider my characters and a scene I had planned for them, and the end that should grow naturally out of the scene, and I would sit and think rationally, logically, of how these characters would behave in this situation. Or I would rise, and pace my study floor, as I consciously, objectively, considered what should be done, could be done, or what these people of mine might have done.
>
> But more frequently a different kind of creative action took place inside my head. It was a process over which I had little control. In this process, I would study my sketchy outline of what might follow after what I had already written, and gradually the characters and background and situation would drift from outline into my mind, and there the characters would behave on their own, moving as they wished, speaking to one another as they liked, behaving in the manner that best suited each one of them. These mental playlets, staged in my head, seemed not to result from the conscious me, and I would sit in my chair and watch them with my mind's eye as if I were merely a spectator. Then, suddenly realizing that I was more than a mere spectator, realizing that I was the recorder of the emotions and dialogues and activities of these people, I would grab up a pencil and try to capture what I had just witnessed inside my head. And then, from these hastily scrawled transcriptions, I would write, with care, applying as much art as I could to these episodes.
>
> Few authors have been able to explain the miracle of these near-spontaneous, unprompted inner playlets, but most novelists I've asked have confessed that this was the way it happened to them when they wrote their books, too.[27]

The distinction between the rational, ordered, consciously focused mode of thinking and the uncontrolled, autistic images that comprise the mode of unconscious thinking is already a familiar one. It is sufficient to note for the moment that they constitute two complementary phases of writing activity, ones to which Wallace repeatedly has recourse in order to describe the actual composition of *The Prize* during the twelve months beginning in October 1960.

Of all contemporary novelists, John Fowles is the one who makes his readers most conscious of the writer's craft. We have seen already how the initial image of *The French Lieutenant's Woman* insisted on recognition and became the inspiration for that novel. Fowles describes how this 'mythopoeic still' of the lady on the quay detached itself from his memory store. This store, 'all sorts of flotsam and jetsam from the last two or three centuries, relics of past lives . . . ', seems unwittingly to have made up the preparatory phase for the novel. The incubatory and making phases are also indicated in his reflections while writing. He speaks of the importance of both unconscious and conscious activity. On the one hand, there is the need for 'accidentality . . . unplanned development of character, unintended incidents, and so on . . . '; on the other, he is aware of the role of 'cold experience' both in the parts that reason, knowledge and culture play in the actual making and in the very different job of revising drafts.[28] Fowles's awareness of the creative process expressed in this article also spills over into the novel itself. The covert dialogue with self is transmuted into an overt dialogue with his reader in Chapter 13 of *The French Lieutenant's Woman*. With Shandeyean daring, he dislocates the fiction and exposes the workings of the novelist's imagination. The effect is to spotlight the 'virtuality' of the text and the parts that autistic and directed thinking play in story-making. Fowles expresses this in terms of planning a fiction:

> You may think novelists always have fixed plans to which they work, so that the future predicted by Chapter One is always inexorably the actuality of Chapter Thirteen. But novelists write for countless different reasons . . . . Only one same reason is shared by all of us: *we wish to create worlds as real as, but other than the world that is*. Or was. This is why we cannot plan. We know a world is an organism, not a machine. We also know that a genuinely created world must be independent of its creator; a planned world (a world that fully reveals its planning) is a dead world. It is only when our characters and events begin to disobey us that they begin to live . . . .[29]

There is a disarming sophistory here. Such an interpolation could not exist within a fiction without careful planning! In a later novel, Fowles is clear about the drive towards form and the planning that contributes to the achievement of a finished product that 'is in intention as rigid and pre-conceived as a piece of machinery or an architect-designed building'.[30] The conscious mind creates the model and controls the free play of the unconscious within limits consistent with the maintenance of that model. By such interplay, consciously-designed plans come alive and the shifting imagery of the preconscious is given form and meaning and prevented from vapouring off unused.

The best known account of the phases of the creative process described by a poet is that of A.E. Housman. It has an appealing neatness, the sense of an inevitable sequence of stages and an earthy style, characteristics which have led to its popularity with anthologists of the creative process. Housman's account of the making of a poem is as follows:

> Having drunk a pint of beer at luncheon—beer is a sedative to the brain, and my afternoons are the least intellectual portion of my life—I would go out for a walk of two or three hours. As I went along, thinking of nothing in particular, only looking at things around me and following the progress of the seasons, there would flow into my mind, with sudden and unaccountable emotion, sometimes a line or two of verse, sometimes a whole stanza at once, accompanied, not preceded, by a vague notion of the poem which they were destined to form part of. Then there would usually be a lull of an hour or so, then perhaps the spring would bubble up again. I say bubble up, because, so far as I could make out, the source of the suggestions thus proffered to the brain was an abyss which I have already had occasion to mention, the pit of the stomach. When I got home I wrote them down, leaving gaps, and hoping that further inspiration might be forthcoming another day. Sometimes it was, if I took my walks in a receptive and expectant frame of mind; but sometimes the poem had to be taken in hand and completed by the brain, which was apt to be a matter of trouble and anxiety, involving trial and disappointment, and sometimes ending in failure.[31]

Notice the four phases of the process that Housman describes. Firstly, he is in a relaxed condition of body and mind sustained by a two or three hour walk and a special stimulus (beer, in his case!). Secondly, there is a 'flowing into the mind of verses ... with sudden and unaccountable emotion ... accompanied ... by a vague notion of the poem'. This is followed by a lull and a 'bubbling up' of lines, even whole stanzas, from the abyss of the unconscious. Finally, he records the stage of writing down the verses on arrival home, 'leaving gaps' and hoping for further inspiration. Notice, too, that Housman is describing not an isolated incident but a familiar, recurring pattern.

Amy Lowell is even more explicit. She says:

> Long poems are apt to take months preparing in the subconscious mind; in the case of short poems, the period of subconscious gestation may be a day or an instant, or any time between. Suddenly words are there, and there with an imperious insistence which brooks no delay. They must be written down immediately or an acute suffering comes on, a distress almost physical, which is not relieved until the poem is given right of way.[32]

Because their composing process is generally of shorter duration and of more intense nature, poets are often more precise than novelists about the phases they experience. Certainly these accounts encourage one to view the activities that produce a poem as four *sequential* phases: a period of preparation which may involve conscious work, perhaps setting up the conditions for writing; an incubatory phase, where ideas are gestating in the unconscious; a moment of inspiration, when the writer suddenly has a focus, the words become available and he knows what he must write about; and a period where the business of actually making the poem, of realizing its form, are the writer's concerns.

Of course, this sense of a creative pattern is not confined to work with words: it has been noted in studies of creativity in various fields (see below). At present, however, it is more to the purpose to ask whether or not such phases, sequential or otherwise, appear in the accounts of what children's authors say about what they do. Our two witnesses here are Alan Garner and Philippa Pearce.

By 1968, Alan Garner had published four books for children and established himself as a major children's author. Reflecting upon his work in an article that appeared in that year, he describes the 'internal activities' of writing as following a flexible pattern:

> It is this. An isolated idea presents itself. It can come from any-where. Something that happens: something seen: something said. It can be an attitude, a colour, a sound in a particular context. I react to it, perhaps forget it; but it is filed away by the subconscious.
>
> Later, and there is no saying how long that is, another idea happens involuntarily, and a spark flies. The two ideas stand out clearly, and I know that they will be a book. This moment is always involuntary and instantaneous, a moment of very clear vision.
>
> But the spark must be fed, and I start to define the areas of research needed to arrive at the shape of what the story is going to say . . . . The period of research varies in length. It has never been less than a year, and the most was three years.[33]

Alan Garner's account, like his stories, is close to the poet's precision; Philippa Pearce's is more ruminative, more in the manner of the novelists we examined. Nevertheless, the four phases that comprise the creative pattern are clearly present in her description of the process of writing her story, *A Dog so Small*.

> The idea of a story springs from experience—from what had been seen and heard and done and felt and thought, going back for weeks, months, perhaps years—perhaps even to birth, or earlier.[34]

Her concern here is with identifying the fruitful idea and cultivating it to a point of clarity of presence. After a period of conscious work and preparation, she meets all sorts of difficulties. What happens?

> For me, the important thing at this stage was to wait—to think about the story only when I wanted to; and even then not to think

too hard, not to reason, but to let the mind rove freely, almost lazily. In any bit of time when one hasn't positively to be thinking of something else, the mind can be wandering about in a half-grown story, exploring its possibilities.

Gradually falling asleep or waking up, dozing—these are often useful times. Sleepiness and sleep free the mind to try out possibilities that might otherwise seem too bizarre; but one of them may fit, or lead to another that fits. You can half-dream the answers to questions.

This period of incubation, in which ideas were 'drifting around in my mind', continued until

... I seemed to hear a click in my mind, like the sound of a key turning in a lock, opening something. At last I saw the way through, that my story could go, naturally, without any forcing.

This moment of illumination is followed swiftly by the writing of the story.

Finding myself there, at the beginning of the story, I wanted to start writing at once. I knew there were gaps in the story ahead, particularly towards the end. There was some mistiness elsewhere, as well; but both the gaps and the mistiness were a good way ahead. So I didn't let them deter me. I don't believe in putting off writing if one really wants to, even if everything isn't fully planned.

The character of this final phase, the 'making', is a distinctive one; stamina and perseverance are at a premium.

So far we have derived the notion of a four-phase process of creative activity from the testimonies of recent authors. How does it match up to the more general survey given by Harding? The answer is given in the opening three chapters of her book, entitled, respectively, 'Preparation', 'The Appearance of Inspiration' and 'General Procedure', for, as these headings suggest, the phases we have discussed are only lightly masked by her different terminology. Harding lays considerable emphasis upon the writer as dreamer in her discussion of the preparatory phase and is able to call upon a wealth of nineteenth-century evidence to illustrate the importance of what Freud was later to characterize as the 'dream work'. In so far as her examples demonstrate that the writer's receptivity to the mind's imagery is an important, common quality they are helpful and relate especially closely to the experiences described by Fowles, Garner and Pearce above.

The phases we have labelled 'incubatory' and 'inspirational' are subsumed in Harding's second heading. She comments first on 'the suddenness with which an idea of value makes its appearance'[35] and says this is a characteristic of all creative thought. George Eliot, Hardy, Keats, Shelley and many others are summoned as witnesses both to the existence of this moment of inspiration and to the trance-like state which seems to be a condition of its appearance, a state in which the conscious and unconscious mind operate together and upon each other.

The account of the writer's 'general procedure' after inspiration has occurred corresponds to what we called the 'making' phase. Harding notes the variety of procedures that writers adopt, ranging from brief, disciplined note-making, frenzied, immediate absorption with the work, deliberate setting-aside of the subject, painstaking labour on a first draft, and so on. The most significant factor, one which Harding fails to bring out clearly enough, is that there is no 'general procedure' as such. Instead, there are a number of procedures, all of which a writer is likely to use in the course of his 'making'. Indeed, the main problem of characterizing the creative process in terms of phases is the pressure it exerts towards a description of a predetermined sequence of easily identified categories of mental activity. If the evidence presented so far suggests such an unnaturally neat pattern, then a note of caution is appropriate, for it takes but a moment's reflection to realize the immense variety that exists within the phases of the process. For example, the periods of time involved will vary enormously. From just the authors quoted we know that the incubatory period for Alan Garner's *The Owl Service* was three years, for Wallace's *The Prize* fourteen years, for Housman's poems generally less than three or four hours. Similarly, we know that the defining of an idea for a story, the preparation, and the 'making' of it into a finished novel may take years if you are Alan Garner or Philippa Pearce, or days if you are Enid Blyton. Or again, the inspirational phase, the spark (in Garner's term), may be a slow-burner, smouldering within the period of incubation, so that it is difficult to distinguish the two as separate phases. The variations in the pattern are innumerable. Each writer makes his own unique design but, equally it would appear, each writer experiences these four phases in one form or another.

Finally, how does this literary evidence, both ancient and modern, relate to the orthodox psychological view of the creative process?

The classic statement of creativity as a series of stages was first formulated by Wallas (1926). He put together the testimonies of Helmholtz, the nineteenth-century German physicist, speaking in 1891 and Poincaré, the French mathematician, to propose a four-stage process of creative activity: *Preparation*, the stage during which a problem is investigated from all angles; *Incubation*, in which conscious thought on the problem is abandoned to allow unconscious mental events to occur; *Illumination*, the appearance of what he calls the 'happy idea', quoting Helmholtz, which may be preceded by intimations of creative expression but occur with great suddenness; and, finally *Verification*, the conscious activity of testing and expressing an idea.[36] Two points are worth stressing in Wallas's elaboration of his theory in Chapter 4 of *The Art of Thought*. Firstly, he acknowledges that not all forms of creative thinking (and he cites the 'poet exploring his own memories' amongst his examples) fit easily into a 'problem and solution' scheme, yet, even in aesthetic enterprises, the four stages can generally be distinguished from each other. He allows, therefore, for a transfer of his scheme from the realms of science and mathematics to that of literary creation. Secondly, although he speaks of the four stages as comprising a sequence in time, he also says that in the daily stream of thought these different stages constantly overlap each other as we explore different problems. If so, 'stages' seems an inappropriate term. As we discovered in discussing the literary evidence, the continuing ebb and flow of different types of mental activity is better rendered by the word 'phases'.

Wallas' formulation has been taken up by a number of writers and researchers, notably Patrick (1935), Ghiselin (1952) and Rugg (1963) each of whom, although working in very different ways, comes to broadly similar conclusions.[37] Patrick's enquiries into the creative thought of artists and poets were carried out in strictly supervised and controlled conditions and attempted to find evidence to substantiate Wallas' four stages. Ghiselin adopts Wallas' terminology in his effort to synthesize the evidence of his symposium of nearly forty creative thinkers. Rugg develops his theory of imagination from the same basis. All agree that, although four distinct phases can be discerned, a rigid chronology for their occurrence is distorting: overlap and fusion of these phases appear to take place according to the temperamental idiosyncrasies of the creative individual. Hence, the paradox that any creative activity has both a discernible common pattern and particular, unrepeatable characteristics. The act of creation is both generalizable and unique.

The Writer's Thinking during Composition

Even so, all that the above gives us is a 'timetable'. We need a fresh perspective on creativity, one that is less concerned with phases in a process and more with such matters as the mental space the writer inhabits, the landscape of his imagination, the sources of his raw material and the nature of his thinking. In short, if phases in a process describe a temporal dimension, we now need the complement of a spatial dimension.

There appear to be three linked issues upon which writers comment in relation to the nature of their creative thinking:

(a) the role of memory in providing the source material for their art;

(b) the mental imaging in which these memories are often cast and its relationship with language; and

(c) the interaction of conscious and unconscious thought processes during composition.

These matters are dealt with in turn below.

Memory

The features of memory to which writers often refer, either directly or obliquely, are interrelated in such complex and little understood ways that it would be foolhardy to be more than tentative in describing them. It is possible, however, to tease out four characteristics of memory: its role as a store, its action as a means of particularizing the significant, its temporally ambiguous nature and its creative function in the service of art. A brief comment upon each might be helpful.

Among recent critics, Barbara Hardy[38] has been especially forthright in arguing that narrative is a primary act of mind, and the novelist's art is to select and refine this function through language. Hence, the novelist is both ordinary and extraordinary: he works with the everyday stuff of stored memories, but in his 'making' lies his special skill. It follows that novels will necessarily be composed of a multitude of anecdotes and stories, believed or disbelieved; true, half-true or false; dreamt, experienced or invented, just as daily life is made up of such narratives and just as memory organizes them and presents them to our consciousness. Memory then is used by the creative artist as his store of raw material but, clearly, it performs other functions than simply to provide content.

It is more than the author's mental warehouse. It has an active function, for memory is also a means of focusing on the significant, an instrument to single out the important experience from the irrelevant mass. Robert Louis Stevenson speaks of allowing his 'memory to choose out what is truly memorable by a process of natural selection . . . ', implying that this diagnostic feature is the way that memory contributes to the inspirational phase of writing discussed earlier. With Wordsworthian overtones, Stevenson describes his recollections in tranquillity as follows:

> Very much as a painter half closes his eyes so that some salient unity may disengage itself from among the crowd of details, and what he sees may thus form itself into a whole; very much on the same principle . . . I allow a considerable lapse of time to intervene between any of my little journeyings and the attempts to chronicle them.[39]

The role of memory then is to particularize and once the selection has occurred, other, more complex features of memory appear in the process of the writer's making.

Spender illustrates the temporal ambiguity of memory. He says that, although his memory for daily trivia like phone numbers and addresses is bad, he does possess

> . . . a perfect memory for the sensation of certain experiences which are crystallised for me around certain associations. I could demonstrate this from my own life by the overwhelming nature of associations which, suddenly aroused, have carried me back so

completely into the past, particularly into my childhood, that I have lost all sense of the present time and place.[40]

The memory of past experiences can be so strong as to blot out our awareness of the primary world; in reverie, the memory can create its own secondary world. Spender goes on to explain the temporal ambiguity of memory by quoting a fragment from his notebooks, describing a sunlit countryside, dating from fifteen years previously. He continues:

> And this memory connects with the sun that shines through my window in London *now* in spring and early summer. So that the memory is not exactly a memory. It is more like one prong upon which a whole calendar of similar experiences happening through-out years, collect. A memory once clearly stated ceases to be a memory, it becomes perpetually present, because every time we experience something which recalls it, the clear and lucid original experience imposes its formal beauty on the new experiences. It is thus no longer a memory but an experience lived through again and again.[41]

Memory operates ambiguously in time. The 'prong' upon which associa-tions cluster acts like a magnet on the images of past and present such that the secondary world thus created has elements of both. So it is with fiction. As John Fowles has said: 'A novel is written in the two past tenses: the present perfect of the writer's mind, the concluded past of fictional con-vention'[42]—a remark which leads us to consider a final and more general issue, memory as the fictional mode.

Langer (1953) and Hardy (1975) have written penetratingly about the role of memory in literary composition. Two general features are suggested by their work and warrant comment here both because they are ones about which the psychological evidence on memory has little, if anything, to say and because they are intimately related to children's creative writing. The first is to do with the moral quality of memory and, as such, concerns the affective history of the individual consciousness of the writer; the second is to do with aesthetic quality, with the literary formulation of that history. Both are readily illustrated from a celebrated passage in Book Twelve of *The Prelude*.

> There are in our existence spots of time,
> That with distinct pre-eminence retain
> A renovating virtue . . .
>   . . . Such moments
> Are scattered everywhere, taking their date
> From our first childhood. I remember well . . .[43]

Wordsworth then describes the recollection of a boyhood experience of getting lost in the hills and the memory of encountering 'a girl, who bore a pitcher on her head' against the backdrop of the 'moorland waste'. These images spawn others from a different period of his past, such that the associations of the scene from his childhood, together with those of his youth when he roamed the landscape with his 'loved one at my side', merge inextricably with those of the mature poet in the act of composing these lines in retrospect. Memory is thus a mode of organization for the mind's images, collapsing time in order to shape these images into the significant relationships that constitute what Wordsworth calls their 'power'. This function of memory conquers randomness and arbitrariness through making an aesthetic form in which these 'spots of time' can exist in consciousness. The other, and related, function concerns the nature of this 'power'. Renovation, repair, nourishment are the terms in which Wordsworth describes the 'efficacious . . . spirit of the Past' as it works to achieve the 'future restoration' of spirit that only memory can effect. Memory is conceived as having an ameliorative function because it is the source of the individual's affective identity: in William Carlos Williams's words, 'Memory is a kind / of accomplishment / a sort of renewal . . . '.[44] Thus, memory, for both these poets, has a developmental role to play in the moral education of the feelings.

Images and Words

A closer look at the implications of writing about what is 'in the mind's eye' entails a consideration of the relationship between words and mental imagery. The vocabulary to describe imaginative activity is notoriously confusing, firstly, in the uncomfortable way in which the words 'imaging' and 'picturing', terms drawn from the language of seeing, have come to represent the experience of other sensory forms of imaging for which we do not possess any appropriate generic verbs; and, secondly, in the arbitrary and imprecise way such terms are used. Wordsworth again is helpful. Writing of the power of deep feelings that impressed his childhood memories, such that they 'lay / Upon his mind like substances', he continues

> He had received
> A precious gift; for, as he grew in years,
> With these impressions would he still compare
> All his remembrances, thoughts, shapes and forms;
> And, being still unsatisfied with aught
> Of dimmer character, he thence attained
> An active power to fasten images
> Upon his brain; and on their pictured lines
> Intensely brooded, even till they acquired
> The liveliness of dreams.[45]

The power of the poet's 'concentrating imagination' is the quality that transmutes impressions into images and images into mental pictures.

Wordsworth's language fills out the three-fold relationship that Langer (1951) has described:[46] *impressions* have a 'dimmer character' than images; *images* can be 'fastened' upon the brain, they are comparatively stable in form and their 'pictured lines' suggest an outline drawing or schema; *pictures* acquire kinaesthetic and other sensory qualities associated with 'the liveliness of dreams'.

The three-fold relationship is one that clearly involves a sharper definition, a more permanent imprint and a clearer focus as the mind shifts from one to the other. They may be regarded as successive stages in the formation of mental pictures.

How then do the writer's images or pictures relate to his story-making? We have asserted already that, when Sassoon spoke of his thinking as 'a series of mental pictures', he spoke for many writers. What follows will help not only to justify the assertion but also serve to discriminate amongst three linked aspects of the relationship between images and stories: the first is to do with the writer's 'envisagement' of his theme (to use Langer's term),[47] the second with his development of plot, and the third with his apprehension of a 'virtual world'.

In the earlier discussion of the work of John Fowles we noted how a strong image may act as inspiration for a story. The 'envisagement' of the whole theme of a work, however, may well have more pervasive effects on its nature, as Henry James implies. At the end of his 'Preface' to *The Wings of A Dove*, James comments on one feature connected with the centre of interest of the novel which, he speculates, is perhaps true of all novels; that is, the reflecting mirror of language that constantly throws up images of the controlling 'centre'. James says: ' . . . what I find striking, charming and curious [is] the author's instinct everywhere for the *indirect* presentation of his main image.[48] An image may encapsulate a theme by permeating all aspects of the form in which the story is cast from the turn of a phrase to the structure of the whole. Examples of this quality are legion. It is fundamental to the aesthetics of fiction; indeed, the central image of a novel, whether *The Rainbow* or *Red Shift*, is often signalled in its title as well as reflected in the elements of its composition.

Another example appears to stress the assistance imaging gives in the development of plot. C.S. Lewis, in an essay about writing for children, notes the reflective state of mind and the multi-sensory nature of his mental pictures before going on to suggest that such pictures possess an inherent generative quality to combine into the linear sequence of a story. He comments:

> . . . I have never exactly 'made' a story. With me the process is much more like bird-watching than like either talking or building. I see pictures. Some of these pictures have a common flavour, almost a common smell, which groups them together. Keep quiet and watch and they will begin joining themselves up. If you were

very lucky (I have never been as lucky as all that), a whole set might join themselves so consistently that there you had a complete story without doing anything yourself. But more often (in my experience always) there are gaps. Then at last you have to do some deliberate inventing, have to contrive reasons why these characters should be in these various places doing these various things. I have no idea whether this is the usual way of writing stories, still less whether it is the best. It is the only one I know: images always come first.[49]

The respective roles of the conscious and unconscious mind that Lewis mentions are discussed more fully below. For the moment, we need to note simply that the processes connected with the incidence and growth of mental imagery appear to be similar to those that psychologists have told us occur in the development of language. Images flash upon the 'inward eye', just as words perform a silent 'inner speech'. Both images and words have the innate power to group themselves together into sense and to join themselves up into sequences. The sequences may develop such an internal consistency and direction that they virtually comprise a story in themselves. The author's plot, on such occasions, is a 'given'.

Other writers go further and describe experiences of imaging that provide them with a full, sensory picturing of their story world. Nor is this facility the monopoly of visionaries like Blake who, according to Gilchrist, 'could summon up before his abstracted gaze' any of the familiar forms and faces he was asked for and proceed to draw them.[50] This sort of vivid, eidetic imaging is rather more widespread amongst writers than has generally been acknowledged: it was Herbert Read who pointed out that Rosamond Harding had cited many examples of it in *The Anatomy of Inspiration* without realizing that she had done so![51] The nature of such imagery, in particular its multi-sensory quality, is caught in two accounts that share the same metaphor. Shelley's biographer, Medwin, describes how the poet

> could throw a veil over his eyes and find himself in a *camera obscura*, where all the features of a scene were reproduced in a form more pure and perfect than they had been originally presented to his external senses.[52]

And, in a letter to Peter McKellar, Enid Blyton up-dates the same notion to the twentieth century when she likens her story-images to watching a film. Clearly, although her imaging is of the same style as C.S. Lewis', it is a much fuller fantasy and, from her own account, places her in the role of recorder rather than inventor of the story world. Miss Blyton says of her hypnagogic imagery:

> My night 'images' were always more than merely 'images'—they were a coherent line of events in the form of a narrative. My simile of a 'private cinema screen' is the best I can think of. But

it's a 3-dimensional screen, complete with sound, smell and taste—
and feeling! This is why I can describe things so realistically in
my stories, 'as if I had been there'. I have been there—but only
in my imagination![53]

Blake and Blyton make curious bedfellows in their experience of eidetic
imagery. While their juxtaposition lends strength to the view that writers
operate with the images and stories that are everyone's mental currency,
it also indicates that the special quality of the creative imagination lies in
the writer's use of his medium.

To understand how memory images relate to words, to investigate the
transmutation from image to the form of story or poem, the prime literary
source is Coleridge, with whom we must include the book that the poet's
work provoked a century later, John Livingstone Lowes' *The Road to
Xanadu*. No comparable study of the ways of the imagination exists in
the history of fiction, perhaps because no novelist has shown Coleridge's
fascination with the creative processes undergone during writing.

Lowes coins the phrase 'sleeping words' to put alongside the notion of
'sleeping images' in order to suggest the idea that both words and images
exist (sometimes separately, sometimes in close correspondence with each
other) in similar states in the preconscious imagination, both available for
recall and use in the conscious activity of writing. In Chapter 17, 'A Sea-
Change', Lowes hints at several qualities of words and images in relation
to the immanent design of *The Ancient Mariner*.

> Images do not stream up to consciousness in utter nakedness.
> They clothe themselves as they come—now neatly and precisely,
> now with the precipitate sketchiness of belated schoolboys tum-
> bling out of bed—they clothe themselves, as they waken to
> consciousness, with *words*. For sleeping words share with the
> sleeping images 'that shadowy half-being' (it is once more Coleridge
> whom I am quoting), 'that state of nascent existence in the twilight
> of imagination and just on the vestibule of consciousness,' . . . [54]

Thus words and images reside in 'mysterious interdependence' in the poet's
memory. Both provide the raw material for art in that they can be stored
in the memory and made available to the writer, through chance or choice,
in the preconscious mind. Words retain their essential identities, yet
attract other associations; images are less substantial in memory, less
definite and more likely to merge into new forms. Both 'sleeping words'
and 'sleeping images' are conceived as mental substances whose very
nature is one of constant change, combining, splitting, dissolving, re-
combining in a state of permanent psychic activity. Yet imagination is
clearly more than simply bringing these images and words into consciousness; that would produce imagery, delirium, hallucination at most. The
creative imagination must involve, as an integral component, mental

action that achieves two ends that we associate with art: the sense of directed thinking that produces appropriate form, and the expression of a new idea or insight. These two criteria, of course, are the ones that Coleridge expounded in the celebrated thirteenth chapter of *Biographia Literaria*.

In the exercise of creative imagination, then, the writer draws upon raw materials existing in varying states of readiness to be incorporated into poem or story. Some images and words arrive unbidden from the mental storehouse of memory and are lodged in art immediately in their finished form. Most words are not 'given', however, but require labour and skill either to will them into existence or to fashion them into sense. Our concern is not with the niceties of Coleridgean definitions but with the one clear principle that he and Lowes together demonstrate, namely, that the workings of the creative imagination involve the constant psychic interplay of the conscious and the unconscious mind. Accordingly, we must now consider the literary evidence for this aspect of composition.

Conscious and Unconscious Thinking

What Lowes did for Coleridge's major poetry, Kathleen Coburn has done for his *Notebooks*. In a series of lectures given while she was still at work on the *Notebooks*, Coburn demonstrates Coleridge's remarkable gift for psychological insight and self-analysis, faculties that enabled him 'to be aware that there are areas of the self outside or "below his own consciousness", and that these are, creatively, not the least important and valuable sources of . . . poetic energy'. She goes on to quote a remarkable entry of 1807 in which Coleridge strives to express the idea of varying levels of consciousness. The Notebook reads:

> I fall asleep night after night watching that perpetual feeling, to which Imagination . . . has given a place and seat of manifestation a shechinah in the heart.—Shall I try to image it to myself, as an animant self-conscious pendulum, continuing for ever its arc of motion by the for ever anticipation of it?—or like some fairer Blossom-life in the centre of the Flower-polypus, a life within Life, and constituting a part of the Life that includes it? A consciousness within a Consciousness, yet mutually penetrated, each possessing both itself and the other—distinct tho' indivisible!
>
> [CNII 2999][55]

'Life within Life', 'consciousness within a Consciousness', Coleridge's phrases describe autonomous mental experiences that are simultaneously both integrated wholes, yet components of his total consciousness. The life of the mind is conceived in corporeal terms: images relate to the mind as cells to the body, 'distinct tho' indivisible'. This cellular nature of the creatures of his consciousness is, as Lowes had implied and Coburn demonstrates, a pervading awareness of Coleridge. It is therefore not surprising to find that it was Coleridge who, so far as we know, invented the word 'subconsciousness'[56] in an attempt to describe his sense of a layered mental life, especially as he experienced it in dreams. The account of Coleridge's dream experiences in relation to *Kubla Khan* is too well-known to need comment and, in any case, too idiosyncratic for our purposes. Yet, the vivid, multi-sensory imagery of the poet's mind in producing the poem and the interplay of conscious and unconscious elements, though unusual in their intensity, are not as extraordinary in their occurrence as tradition would imply.

This interplay of conscious and unconscious thinking is constantly remarked upon by writers, usually in the form of metaphor. E.M. Forster speaks of letting down a bucket into the well of the unconscious;[57] Housman refers to an 'abyss';[58] Amy Lowell expresses her shifting states of mind in terms of dropping a 'letter into the mail-box';[59] whereas Ted Hughes prefers the role of psychic fisherman.[60] Joan Aiken adopts a culinary metaphor and likens story-making, in its combining of primary process thinking and the secondary process of verbalization, to the mixing of a *roux* in cookery.[61] Philippa Pearce is only a little less domestic when she describes her thinking in the language of horticulture and woodwork. Her distinction between 'growing' and 'making' during composition is worth dwelling upon, since it does give a sense of the development of a story which is lacking in most other accounts. She says:

> A book that is worth writing—that the writer really cares about—is only partly *made*. One may be able to make all the parts hold neatly and strongly together, as a carpenter does a good job on a box; but, before that, from the very beginning—perhaps before there is any conscious intention of writing a story—the story must grow. An idea grows in the mind, as a tree grows from a seed; it develops with the slowness of natural growth.
> ... My concern will be mostly with growth and the encouragement of growth—the cultivation, as a gardener would say: but there will also be something about making, as a carpenter makes. Growth and making can go on together, as long as the second is never allowed to interfere with the first.[62]

There is a clear distinction here between two types of mental activity: one which is 'slow' and 'natural', akin to the instinctive sensitivity of the gardener in tending his plants, whereas the other is more precise and practical, more like the skill of the craftsman in making things fit. Moreover, it is made explicit that the practical skills support the natural growth.

This combination of two distinct types of mental activity argues for a different concept of 'thinking' from the conventional one. Conventionally, by the word 'thinking' we mean something that must 'make sense', that is characterized, if not by reasoning and logic, then at least by a fairly ordered and focused activity. But what Philippa Pearce suggests is that within her creative processes her mind is one that lets things happen as well as make things happen; that it is, in the terms we have already borrowed from Piaget, both 'autistic' as well as 'directed' in its thinking.

A Rationale for Classroom Work

In terms of assembling evidence, this is about as far as I am able to go in the space available. Let us ask the final question, therefore, about what implications does all this have for creative writing in schools, for, as Bullock reminded us, our knowledge of the process we set going when we ask children to write a story or a poem is very slight. Essentially, what I want to suggest is that, in the four-phase process I have outlined together with the interaction of the two types of 'thinking' I have discussed, there exists the beginning of a coherent rationale for developing imaginative writing in schools. 'Creative writing' is not only an uncomfortable phrase and an easy victim; it is also young in the formulation of its theoretical background. It follows that we need to resist the pressure towards merely fashionable criticism, while maintaining a sympathetic rigour towards those parts of the theory which will help to illuminate the nature of the writing process.

Finding an adequate vocabulary with which to discuss the matter is again the initial problem. The conventional labels, 'creative', 'expressive', 'personal' are vague and imprecise; 'free expression' is a tautology. The first part of Robert Witkin's book[63] attempts to meet this difficulty but, unfortunately, perhaps inevitably, this leads him to discuss a complex subject at a high level of abstraction in language that yields its meaning with reluctance. What an English teacher might describe (inventing a composite term from the labels above) as creative self-expression, Witkin terms 'subject-reflexive action'. He arrives at this phrase, as a more accurate, if less palatable, description of creative writing, by making two crucial distinctions. Firstly, he discriminates between subject and object knowing, between expressive and impressive action. Expressive action is the way in which an individual comes to know the world of his own feelings, 'a world that exists only because he exists'. Impressive action is the opposite, the means with which a person comes to know the world of objects, 'the world that exists whether or not he exists'. The second distinction Witkin makes is between reflexive and reactive behaviour. In reactive expression the emotional impulse is simply released: in throwing a tantrum or committing an act of vandalism the concern is with the immediate situation and the emotional response it provokes. By contrast, reflexive expression involves not a discharge of 'unruly squads of emotion' (in Wordsworth's vivid phrase) but the retention of, and engagement with, the feelings. This 'holding on' to the intelligence of one's feelings is gained through the power of memory allowing us to work them through an expressive medium found in the world of objects. This, of course, is what every writer does. He chooses, in Susanne Langer's terms, the appropriate form to embody his feeling. The process he undergoes involves the 'producing mind' of the writer oscillating constantly between his own expressive impulse and the expressive effects of his medium. If we put these two distinctions together, it becomes apparent that the nature of 'creative writing' involves the writer in coming to know the world of his own feelings, in the reflexive mode that allows him to recall sensate experience within himself and to express it in the act of composition. 'Subject-reflexive action' is meant to encapsulate all these notions.

It follows from the above that the two fundamental elements of subject-reflexive action are the writer's feelings and his chosen medium of expression. What is the process by which feeling is embodied in form? In the final part of his book, Witkin outlines his answer in the course of describing what he means 'by the phases of the creative process when used within a teaching context'. We shall find in the description of these phases a similar pattern to the one we have illustrated and discussed earlier.

The last chapter of *The Intelligence of Feeling* outlines what Witkin considers to be the three 'invariant' phases of the creative process and gives some guidance to the teacher about how to enter the expressive act of the child and help its development 'from within'. The first phase he calls, *'The setting of the sensate problem'*, and it is made clear that

> the teacher needs to enter the creative process from the outset
> from its very inception. He needs to initiate the sensate experience
> in the child that is to be the motive power of the expression that
> follows.[64]

To some, this might seem tantamount to indecent interference with the intimate feelings of young people! Witkin's rebuttal of this objection is a particularly interesting one, for he makes it clear that this first phase of setting the sensate problem has two distinct parts, one that is very much the responsibility of the teacher, the other that is unique to the individual child. This is what he says:

> In the first place, sensate experience makes demands upon the
> individual to structure it. This structuring can be described in
> terms of the relationships between sensory elements that are an
> invariant aspect of the functioning of all human beings . . . . This
> part of the sensate problem can be conceived of as *generality*. It
> concerns the structuring or ordering of sensate experience, and
> this makes use of the same basic relationships from one individual
> to another. The second aspect, however, concerns the stuff or
> content of the sensate experience in which these relationships
> occur. While the principles of ordering sensate experience are the

same from one individual to another, the content of the sensate experience is not. Each individual's experience is unique to him, it is his *particularity*.[65]

Witkin goes on to stress that the first aspect of the creative process in school (his notion of 'generality') is the teacher's job of selecting the general area in which the creative work of the class will take place. The teacher defines the boundaries, provides the focus, stimulates the sensate problem, motivates the class towards expressive action. If we re-use the term 'preparation' for this first phase, we not only give an added dimension to the lesson preparation that is part of the teacher's daily lot, but link it directly to the four-phase process described earlier. Similarly, the second aspect that Witkin describes as setting 'the sensate problem . . . in the consciousness of the pupil',[66] can reasonably be described as the period of 'incubation', for again it is clear that, by his word 'particularity', Witkin implies that this next phase is achieved when the child relates to the stimulus, when he makes it his own, when his particular consciousness assimilates what his teacher has prepared so that it becomes unique to him as an individual.

Moreover, if we examine the nature of Witkin's last two 'invariant' phases of the creative process, we find again a distinct correspondence between them and the earlier sequence we derived from the literary and psychological perspectives. Even his metaphors have echoes. He describes the next phase, '*The making of a holding form*', as 'the seed of which the full expressive form is the flower', reminding us that the process has moved on from the teacher preparing the ground, through the sowing (perhaps 'setting' is better) of images and ideas in the child's mind, to the point where, in the metaphor he shares with Philippa Pearce, the growth needs tending. The terms in which this phase is described are significant. It is spoken of as encapsulating 'the essential sensate impulse, . . . a form that captures the structural characteristics (of the impulse) in their barest essentials'. The child's mind does more than merely own images and ideas as dead possessions, for images and ideas are compounded with words and the excitement of words lies in their generative quality. To describe this, the quieter metaphor of tending is mixed with the more vivid one of a flash of light or an electric charge, this time echoing Alan Garner. This is what Robert Witkin says.

> Because the holding form is often instantaneously produced and contains the vitality, the inspiration of the full expression, the latter being as the oak in the acorn, so creativity itself is often spoken of as instantaneous, a 'flash of inspiration'.[67]

We would seem justified in calling up our earlier label, 'inspiration', to describe both what Alan Garner means by his 'instantaneous . . . moment of very clear vision . . . when the spark flies' and what Witkin means by 'the making of a holding form'.

The final phase of the creative process is given the cumbersome heading *'The movement through successive approximations to a resolution'*.[68] Earlier we settled for the idea of 'making' to indicate the business of actually composing a poem or story. But despite its awkwardness, Witkin's heading does stress a crucial and often neglected part of the writer's making: the painstaking work of drafting, rephrasing, correcting, editing, polishing, re-writing . . . all in the pursuit of clarity. As we have seen, there are many examples from poets and novelists which testify to the importance of what Witkin describes as the task of 'establishing control over the medium'.

Here, then, in *The Intelligence of Feeling*, we have a rationale for imaginative writing in school which coincides remarkably closely both with the experiences of established authors and with creativity theory in general. It is a coincidence that has so far been ignored in educational literature. This is a pity since, if as much time and energy had been expended on understanding children's writing as has been on understanding their speech and reading, we should possess a much clearer idea of what occurs during the process of 'creative writing' and be able to counter The Bullock Report's criticisms. As it is, while there is the satisfaction of finding a coherent pedagogical theory that echoes those from literature and psychology, there is the corresponding dissatisfaction of knowing that pedagogical practice lags far behind Witkin's formulations. Of course, there are large gaps remaining in our knowledge. Clearly, we need to know a lot more about autistic thinking than we do and we need more research into the ways in which the subconscious and the conscious mind interact in the process of writing. But we know enough already to be able to lay down certain guidelines for the practice of creative writing in schools which, even where they seem self-evident, derive greater authenticity and force in having been substantiated from all the three perspectives we have taken. It is with seven practical implications, therefore, that I wish to conclude.

Some Practical Implications

Firstly, we must strive to give children plenty of 'mental space' in which to operate. If the period of incubation and the role of autistic thinking are as crucial to creativity as the evidence suggests, then the very last place in which poems and stories are best going to be written is in a 20′ × 20′ classroom box, with thirty other people, in a forty-minute period. In fact, the classroom is not quite as inimical to creative work as that sentence suggests, as my last two points will make clear, but I overstate deliberately in order to draw attention to the teacher's role in setting up an environment and an atmosphere conducive to the growth of images and ideas in thirty individual imaginations. We have seen already the importance of creative mood. An early concern of the teacher, therefore, must be to provide the conditions in which this mood can develop. Given these, there are all sorts of devices which create more mental space. It may mean deliberately setting out to break habitual patterns by trying 'intensive writing' as Margaret Langdon suggests.[69] It ·may be, in Ted Hughes' words, 'productive to give out at the beginning of term some of the subjects that are going to be written about during the next weeks. The pupils would then watch the intervening lessons more purposefully, and we cannot prevent ourselves from preparing for a demand that we know is going to be made.'[70] Or again, it may mean deliberately using strategies that make the process of writing individual and personal—looking for the growth points in each child, identifying those who function introspectively and encouraging them to devise a notebook or journal of their own or, conversely, identifying those who need to talk out their responses and providing them, through playlets, dialogues, interviews and the like, with the approaches to expressive activity that temperamentally appeal to them. Take every opportunity to provide the stimulus of experiences outside the inhibiting influence of the classroom, but, equally, be aware that the child's mental space may be as well served by regular, rigorous practice in the more technical aspects of writing.

Secondly, we must try to be conscious of the individual's timetable of creative activity. As we have heard from the authors I have quoted, there is an immense variation in the times taken to finish a piece of work. Some poems or stories come quickly, others need to be struggled at, an 'intolerable wrestle / With words and meanings', in Eliot's vivid phrase and, if 'each venture / Is a new beginning, a raid on the inarticulate',[71] then, to make insistent demands such as 'this work must be finished and handed in by tomorrow morning' is nonsense.

Thirdly, in Philippa Pearce's terms, we must nourish the 'growth', while giving pupils the tools to be 'makers'. What this means in the classroom is a balancing act, maintaining a balance between the teaching of technical skills and the exploring of personal experience. I began by hinting that, in pursuing our rightful concern for the child's responses to experience, we are sometimes too easily satisfied with receiving *any* response. At its worst, this can lead to unfelt writing uncritically accepted. The corrective is clear: the discussion of the children's responses to a subject—their feelings about it, their ideas, their ways of looking, sensing, interpreting, all the ways in which they come to *know* it—must be balanced by practice in the means of expressing that personal knowledge. And a concern with 'means' will lead to work on how to handle language, how to make this tool work *for* you rather than *against* you. I am not advocating a series of dreary exercises but rather lessons where children can play around with word sounds, nonsense poems, riddles, 'concrete' poetry; where they try out different forms to see if they can manage the 'carpentry' —inventing limericks and parodies, writing in couplets and blank verse, making ballads, haiku, even sonnets. One book that may be of interest here is Brian Powell's *English through Poetry Writing*[72] since he takes a line on the creative process which stresses form, an unfashionable but nonetheless crucial emphasis.

Fourthly, we should take up the clues that authors give us about the importance of memory. The demand to 'be imaginative' can induce panic, blankness or just mute incomprehension from pupils. After all, what *do* we mean when we use this formula? A more fruitful invitation might be 'can you remember . . . ?' where we direct the child's attention towards points of significance in his personal history. Imagination, as Stephen Spender reminds us, is itself an exercise of memory. He continues:

> There is nothing we imagine which we do not already know. And our ability to imagine is our ability to remember what we have already once experienced and to apply it to some different situation.[73]

In encouraging children to remember we are not merely inviting a potted history of an individual. Remembering involves a child in selecting, shaping, ordering and evaluating past experiences in relation to his present self all of which, as Wordsworth indicates, contribute powerfully to an individual's concept of self and to the moral education of the feelings.

Fifthly, we can afford to be more overt than we are about the process of writing. If, as teachers, we show an interest in where ideas come from, what past experiences are being explored, and how these can best be converted into poem or story (what, in mathematics, is called the 'working') then children are likely to feel that writing is of greater importance and use to them than if we simply concern ourselves with the end products. One way to encourage an interest in writing, therefore, is to talk with children about their own mental imagery and to suggest that this is a vital part of their raw material. 'Image-making', Langer says, 'is . . . the mode of our untutored thinking, and stories are its earliest product . . . . Pictures and stories are the mind's stock-in-trade.'[74] If this is so, then to talk about this coinage of the brain is a good starting-point for creative writing. It has the dual advantage, too, of indicating to children that the stuff of writing is both idiosyncratic and commonplace. The invitation to articulate what is in the mind's eye—impressions, images or pictures—can strengthen the focus of a piece of writing and help a child to translate image into language.

My last two points can best be framed as questions. Given the nature of the four-phase creative process and the nature of modern classrooms, when does the individual child need to share and when does he need to be private? As a rough guide, he needs to share during the first and last phases of writing, during the periods of 'preparation' and 'making'. So, my sixth point is simply that, as part of the preparation for writing, teacher and pupils should engage in the collaborative act of generating words, images and ideas publicly, on the blackboard. Words that are simultaneously *from* the class and *for* the class are words that are alive with personal meaning for that particular group of children. The more exchange that goes on in sharing words, the more ideas and images are being created, and the more chance the individual child has of gaining control over the medium. Just as the establishment of this control is prepared for jointly, so it is resolved jointly. Hence, at the final stage of the process (a series of 'successive approximations' as Robert Witkin reminds us), it is equally important for the individual to share in his efforts to make his meaning clear and coherent. This sharing may be the overt, practical business of providing a known outlet for poems and stories through magazines, displays, taped anthologies, readings and the like, bearing in mind the work of the Writing Research Unit which has alerted us to the ways that a sense of audience influences the process of composition. But, equally, the sharing here might take the form of sensitive comment from the teacher to the individual child about the details of his writing. The teacher's role is a tricky one for he is aiming at intervention without interference. He is trying to help the child towards verbal precision and order, *not* to interfere with the nature of his 'sensate impulse'. Whereas the teacher's concern in the period of preparation has been with the 'what' questions, with the broad area of what the class was going to write about, now, in this final stage of resolution, his concern will be primarily with 'how' questions, how to assist the individual mind to say what it wants to say.

Finally, we must acknowledge that imaginative writing needs privacy and separateness. None of the sources I have quoted refers to the nature of the activity in any other way than to suggest it is a very private, individual, unique act. And it derives its uniqueness from the middle phases of the creative process where ideas are incubated in the sub-conscious. Providing the right conditions for this individual introspection is the single biggest practical problem, for we all know that in most contemporary classrooms these conditions of privacy and separateness have to be fought for. But we can help ourselves by thinking more clearly about the teaching strategies to adopt. We have few doubts about the conditions that will best serve our needs in drama. We go and book the hall, or the drama studio, or an open space, because we acknowledge that drama is a particular sort of activity which needs talk, movement, noise, space. Therefore, we have a special room for it. But we have this other very special area of activity which is just the opposite of all those things, one which needs privacy, quiet, and individual concentration. We rarely think of organizing our rooms to facilitate these qualities. A classroom lay-out which has desks round the perimeter with chairs facing the walls, thus giving each child his own vertical and horizontal surface rather like a library carrel, seems to me to go some way towards meeting these needs without precluding an easy transition to other activities as the occasion demands. Whatever solutions we take individually to meet this problem, it is certainly timely, given the current emphasis on the role of talking in small groups, to stress the importance of the private imagination. Perhaps, in due course, the slogan 'talking to learn' will give way to another: 'silence to think'.

These seven implications for teaching clearly not only overlap but also contain the seeds of contradiction when we try to put them into practice. Creative activity is compounded of paradoxes and antitheses: sharing and privacy; introspection and expression; encouraging growth yet making things fit; playing with words within the discipline of form. The demands of freedom and the need for constraint are in permanent tension within the creative process. We need to live with these apparent contradictions and acknowledge, as Bruner does, that

> As soon as one turns to a consideration of the conditions of creativity, one is immediately met by paradox and antinomy. A 'determinant' suggests itself, and in the next pulse its opposite is suggested.[75]

My hope is that I have been able to suggest the outline of a rationale while maintaining a due respect for the paradox.

Notes

1 Adapted from DICKENS, CHARLES *Hard Times*, Ch 1.
2 WITKIN, R. (1975) *The Intelligence of Feeling*, Heinemann Educational Books, especially Part III 'From Within the Expressive Act', pp. 169–89.
3 BRITTON, JAMES, *et al.* (1976) *The Development of Writing Abilities (11–18)*, Macmillan Education for the Schools Council; ROSS, MALCOLM (1975) *Arts and the Adolescent*, Schools Council Working Paper 54, Evans/Methuen Educational.
4 *A Language for Life* (Bullock Report) (1976) HMSO, p. 164.
5 HARDING, ROSAMOND (1948) *The Anatomy of Inspiration*, Heffer and Sons, 3rd ed.
6 JUNG, CARL (1933) 'Psychology and Literature', in *Modern Man in Search of a Soul*, Routledge and Kegan Paul.
7 JAMES, HENRY (1934) *The Art of the Novel*, Charles Scribner's and Sons, New York.
8 MONTAGUE, C.E. (1930) *A Writer's Notes on His Trade*, Chatto and Windus, p. 180.
9 JAMES, H., *op. cit.*, p. 119.
10 HARDING, R., *op. cit.*, Ch. 2.
11 FOWLES, JOHN 'Notes on an Unfinished Novel', in BRADBURY, M. (1977) *The Novel Today*, Fontana, Collins, p. 137.
12 JAMES, H., *op. cit.*, p. 120.
13 SASSOON, SIEGFRIED (1939) *On Poetry*, Arthur Skemp Memorial Lecture, University Press, Bristol, pp. 19 and 25.
14 HARDING, R., *op. cit.*, p. 144.
15 FOWLES, J., *op. cit.*, p. 136.
16 SPENDER, STEPHEN 'The Making of a Poem', in GHISELIN B. (ed.) (1952) *The Creative Process*, Mentor Books, p. 118.

17 GARNER, ALAN, 'A bit more practice', in MEEK M. *et al.* (eds.) (1977) *The Cool Web*, The Bodley Head, p. 198.

18 LUBBOCK, PERCY (1921) *The Craft of Fiction*, J. Cape, p. 62.

19 MICHELANGELO (trans. Elizabeth Jennings), *The Sonnets of Michelangelo*, The Folio Society, 1961, p. 43.

20 HARDING, R., *op. cit.*, p. 144.

21 *ibid.*, p. 127.

22 *ibid.*, pp. 132–4.

23 WORDSWORTH, WILLIAM *Preface to the Lyrical Ballads, 1978*, Clarendon Press, 1921, p. 171.

24 WALLACE, IRVING (1968) *The Writing of One Novel*, Simon and Schuster, New York.

25 WALLAS, GRAHAM (1926) *The Art of Thought*, J. Cape.

26 WALLACE, I., *op. cit.*, p. 21.

27 *ibid.*, pp. 82–3.

28 FOWLES, J., *op. cit.*, pp. 136–8.

29 FOWLES, J. (1977) *The French Lieutenant's Woman*, Panther edition, p. 86.

30 FOWLES, J. (1977) *Daniel Martin*, J. Cape, p. 304.

31 HOUSMAN, A.E. 'The Name and Nature of Poetry', in GHISELIN, B., *op. cit.*, pp. 86–91.

32 LOWELL, AMY, 'The Process of Making Poetry', in GHISELIN, B., *op. cit.*, p. 111.

33 GARNER, A., *op. cit.*, p. 198.

34 PEARCE, PHILIPPA 'Writing a Book: A Dog So Small', in BLISHEN E. (ed.) (1975) *The Thorny Paradise*, Kestrel, pp. 140–5.

35 HARDING, R., *op. cit.*, p. 8.

36 WALLAS, G., *op. cit.*, pp. 79 ff.

37 PATRICK, CATHARINE 'Creative Thought in Poets', in *Archives of Psychology*, XXVI, 1935; GHISELIN, B., *op. cit.*; RUGG, H. (1963) *Imagination*, Harper and Row, New York.

38 HARDY, BARBARA (1975) *Tellers and Listeners*, The Athlone Press.

39 STEVENSON, R.L. *Essays on Travel*, quoted in HARDING, R., *op. cit.*, p. 51.

40 SPENDER, S., *op. cit.*, pp. 120–1.

41 *ibid.*

42 FOWLES, J., *Daniel Martin*, p. 269.

43 WORDSWORTH, WILLIAM (1932) *The Prelude*, Bk. XII, lines 208–25, Golden Treasury edn., Macmillan, p. 181.

44 WILLIAMS, WILLIAM CARLOS *Paterson*, Bk. II, 3, quoted in HARDY, B., *op. cit.*, p. 56.

45 WORDSWORTH, WILLIAM (1913) *The Excursion*, Bk. I, lines 139–48, The World's Classics edn., OUP, p. 463.

46 LANGER, S. (1951) *Philosophy in a New Key*, Harvard University Press, Cambridge, Mass., pp. 144–6.

47 *ibid.*

48 JAMES, H., *op. cit.*, p. 306.

49 LEWIS, C.S. 'On Three Ways of Writing for Children', in EGOFF, S., *et al.* (eds.) (1969) *Only Connect: Readings on Children's Literature*, OUP, Toronto, pp. 217–18.

50 GILCHRIST, A. (1942) *Life of William Blake*, Dent.

51 READ, HERBERT (1943) *Education Through Art*, Faber, pp. 42–3.

52 *ibid.*, p. 43.
53 BLYTON, ENID, 'Letter to Peter McKellar, February 26th 1953', in STONEY, B. (1974) *Enid Blyton: A Biography*, Hodder and Stoughton, p. 210.
54 LOWES, J. LIVINGSTONE (1978) *The Road to Xanadu*, Pan Books edn., p. 282.
55 COBURN, KATHLEEN (1974) *The Self-Conscious Imagination*, OUP, p. 22.
56 *ibid.*, p. 21.
57 FORSTER, E.M. 'The raison d'être of Criticism in the Arts', in *Two Cheers for Democracy*, (1965), Penguin edn., p. 121.
58 HOUSMAN, A.E., *op. cit.*, p. 86.
59 LOWELL, A., *op. cit.*, p. 110.
60 HUGHES, TED (1967) *Poetry in the Making*, Faber, pp. 60–1.
61 AIKEN, JOAN 'Purely for Love', in HAVILAND, V. (1973) *Children and Literature: Views and Reviews*, The Bodley Head, p. 152.
62 PEARCE, P., *op. cit.*, pp. 140–1.
63 WITKIN, R., *op. cit.*, pp. 1–29.
64 *ibid.*, p. 169.
65 *ibid.*, pp. 169–70.
66 *ibid.*, p. 180.
67 *ibid.*, p. 181.
68 *ibid.*, p. 183.
69 LANGDON, M. (1961) *Let the Children Write: An Explanation of Intensive Writing*, Longmans.
70 HUGHES, T. *op. cit.*, p. 23. Ted Hughes advocates a 'brainstorming' approach similar to that of Margaret Langdon: 'When the time comes to write, it should be regarded as a hundred-yards' dash'.
71 ELIOT, T.S. (1944) 'East Coker', in *Four Quartets*, Faber.
72 POWELL, B. (1968) *English through Poetry Writing*, Heinemann.
73 SPENDER, S., *op. cit.*, p. 121.
74 LANGER, S., *op. cit.*, pp. 144–6.
75 BRUNER, J.S. (1962) 'The Conditions of Creativity', in *On Knowing: Essays for the Left Hand*, Harvard University Press.

'I Have Therefore an Axe to Grind'

Eric Hadley
Lecturer, Department of Education, University of Cambridge

In our sessions I thought at a level I haven't reached since I left
University twelve years ago. When does a practising teacher have
time for prolonged disputation of a text with his colleagues? I
learned to trust and value my own opinion again . . .

Every teacher needs some indication from his students as to the effect of
his teaching. Without a response, a sense that our energy and interest are
reciprocated, the effort seems wasted—it feels like thrusting into nothing-
ness. Without confirmation (which includes disagreement) our understanding is undermined and our expression of that understanding seems
eccentric.

What am I to make of these reflections sent to me by a teacher and which
are her response to the work she did with me recently on an in-service
course for English teachers? They deserve a context—especially as I'm
trying to work out how this response came about and what part I might
have had in it. I say in-service course but not the 'tips for teachers' or
'organization and management' type (I've been on those too and don't
care for them, but more of that later). Rather, I was teaching a mixed group
of teachers—school teachers, FE teachers, training college teachers, a
Dutch teacher and an Austrian teacher—in a study of Brecht's *Galileo*.
Over a week we read it together, acted parts of it, read some of Brecht's
poems and I introduced some of his short stories. At other times during
the week we listened to lectures by eminent speakers—critics and writers,
watched Kotynzev's harrowing version of *King Lear*, etc.

At another point in her letter my correspondent writes, 'whether you
hit the right note through luck or judgement we'll never know, but I'm
perfectly prepared to pay you the compliment of believing that it was
judgement!' For the purposes of this course, I did re-read the play twice
in all its versions and all that I could find by Brecht in English about it.
I skipped through some dreadful biographies, read his own marvellous
early journals, re-read most of his poems and his essays on poetry, re-read
the short stories, more plays, the *Short Organum*, the *Messingkauf Dialogues*.
Isn't this what any group of intelligent adults should expect from their

teacher—don't adults whose business is learning have a right to expect *learning*, the best we can manage, from their teachers? Besides, it was a pleasure—I didn't do it because I had to. And at the same time I was reading Shostakovich's *Testimony*, reading about the crisis in Poland, thinking about learning and thought and what they had to offer in the context of Brixton and Toxteth, thinking about Galileo the teacher and his marvellous exposition of the accessibility of learning and its power in the hands of ordinary people.

'Luck or judgement?' That seems to me like a good definition of preparing for your class. But I'll take the compliment and call it 'judgement'—a term we use retrospectively in teaching when things go well and to shore up our self-confidence when we know very well that there are absolutely no guarantees. I like Brecht but I can't *make* anyone else like him, no matter how long I engaged in 'disputation'. But I know reading 'The Doubter' and 'On Doubt' transformed the atmosphere within that group and affected everything else we did afterwards. How do you record that moment of change in teaching? Do you judge it by the quality of silence at the end of a reading or by people rushing out at the end to buy the poems as if they'd discovered a new country on the map which they just had to go to? And what teaching did I do while reading these poems and stories—how complicated a simple choice is in teaching—this rather than that, now rather than then—mood, atmosphere, time of day, weather, laziness—judgement or luck—they're all there somewhere.

I'm still worried about that word 'disputation'—it's both too arid and not serious enough to convey the note of our discussions and the way they were governed by text. Brecht puts it better: 'It's only when confronted by such characters that they will practise true thinking; that is to say thinking that is conditioned by self interest, and introduced and accompanied by feelings, a kind of thinking that displays every stage of awareness, clarity and effectiveness.'

The text taught us some hard lessons in that respect, pulled us up short. There was our attempt to read the First Scene and our difficulty in sustaining its energy and activity—Galileo fills the stage, moving about, washing, eating, explaining, testing. He is everywhere—except in that room we worked in. Feeling diminished at our own incapacity to convey his stature, we learn again. Pleasurable recreation imposes its own disciplines on the learner—preparation, practice, attention—so the next day we rehearsed at 8.55 in the morning.

I'm grateful for the response I got and I've tried to convey a little of what I hope my correspondent took back into school with her. But I'm depressed by it too, even more so when she continues: 'pupils take what we say as such gospel truth that I often get the feeling that I wouldn't know if I was feeding them rubbish.' The fact is that these remarks and the ones I quoted earlier are such a familiar refrain that I'm no longer shocked by them. Nevertheless, their implications are disconcerting and they deserve disentangling because I believe them to be deeply bound up in the attitudes of English teachers and demonstrably affect their practice. I say attitudes even though there is usually an attempt to seek their causes in circumstances—'When does a practising teacher have time . . . ?' In making this distinction I don't wish to dismiss the very real demands made upon English teachers and the appalling conditions many of them work under—but they can make that analysis themselves.

If I can return to my correspondent's remarks, three questions occur to me. Firstly, what are we to make of the gap implied between intellectual life fondly remembered at university and intellectual life in school? Secondly, is it quite impossible to think of school as a place which sustained varied opportunities for a collaborative development of that life with colleagues and pupils? Thirdly, is it possible that the argument which has raged for almost a decade about the 'standards' of pupil's work has been an even more cynical diversion than we had supposed. In other words, that not pupil performance but the poverty of teacher self-expectations and therefore their expectations of their pupils, should have been the main concern. The argument I want to advance is that the engagement and associated activity I tried to convey in my opening is essential to the formation and development of the English teacher and not some little holiday from the daily grind.

The person we most consistently ignore when speaking of education is the teacher. We ignore, that is, the personal and intellectual development of the teacher both at the training stage and when he or she has become a full member of the profession. It ought to be clear enough from what I've said so far that concentrating my attention on the teacher doesn't preclude an interest in the child. In fact, my precise intention is to suggest some of the places English teachers might go in order to clarify their thinking about children and the way children learn. To put it another way, I am interested in what resources English teachers have to call upon in their teaching. It's a fine word 'resources', related, I discovered when looking it up in the dictionary, to 'resurge'—to rise or come back again. In using the word I have something very different in mind from its singular form so beloved of educationists in phrases such as 'teachers as resource', 'resource-based learning', 'resource centre'. Here the brisk administration and transmission of inert matter has replaced any sense of an active and resilient principle within the individual to which one has recourse and out of which one grows.

Here, perhaps, I shall be accused of being insufficiently interested in organization. I certainly find myself in disagreement with those that argue that 'videotapes, guides and packs of discussion materials may prove the best way of helping teachers to help themselves, develop their art and thus help pupils develop their language for life.' This model seems to me the logical extension of the 'narrow practicism' which dominates teacher training and which I've dealt with at length elsewhere. Knowing 'Twenty-

Four Things to Do with a Book' not only simply satisfies the short-term exigencies of 'keeping them occupied' it also confirms the view shared by many teachers that developing expertise has to do with collecting new approaches. Equally, the text-book publishers and resources bank producers promote the view that there is an 'answer' to teachers' problems— witness the thoughtless mass administration of packages like SRA reading labs.

The organization I am interested in only has reality as the organization of the processes of feeling and thought within the individual—individual teacher and pupil. If English teachers really wish to 'develop their art' then their recourse will not be to 'strategies' but to that art which embodies the finest impression of human organization. They may be able to 'help their pupils develop their language for life', by taking into the classroom with them a more rigorously articulated expression of the processes of their own learning and response. The teacher only begins to teach when he or she is capable of laying bare these processes within the classroom just as a 'language for life' (if that phrase means anything) begins to find expression when we dwell in the presence of someone who can give us their 'living expression'. The responsibility which this view of teaching imposes finds a fine expression in these words of Coleridge: 'It requires no ordinary skill and address to fix the attention of men on the world within them, to induce them to study the processes and superintend the works which they are themselves carrying on in their own minds.'

'No ordinary skill and address . . . ' conveys to me the sense of difficulty and possibility we ought to have as we contemplate teaching. It has the virtue too of not beginning in the defeat implied by the phrase 'good enough' teacher on which the authors of the working paper on the future of English teaching I quoted from earlier place so much emphasis: 'less-able child, sired by "good enough" teacher, out of discussion material'.

The degree of self-consciousness on the part of the teacher that Coleridge is alluding to is essential if we are not to succumb to the deadening 'common sense' which dominates thinking in schools. One witnesses this sharply in the experience of students as it corrodes the convictions (naturally in the process of formulation) with which they begin teaching—'I don't think that will work'; 'You can try it if you like but . . . '; 'Our kids won't make anything out of that . . . '. Of course, students need experience and they need the expertise of fellow practitioners but they (like all teachers) need recourse to something else than the 'school common sense' compounded of proverbial lore and routine and characterized by protective scepticism.

I shall return to the needs of students later but for the moment I'll develop further some thoughts on the resilient self-consciousness which English teachers need to display. I referred earlier to the recourse that English teachers would have to art but as a reference it's in danger of remaining simply a gesture—something that in the 'common-sense' world we can all accede to and then quietly leave to take care of itself. When it isn't 'servicing' the other subject areas, English ('spent the afternoon reading stories again, have you?') finds itself associated with the other 'holiday' or 'safety-valve' subjects on the timetable—art, music, and drama. That the English teacher's recourse to art is more than a gesture I tried to suggest when formulating our task as 'bringing into the classroom those participating voices in the conversation of mankind, that, ironically, we call *works* of literature.' This inevitably means that we are involved *critically* in our teaching with our language and our history (which includes the world we live in now). Here I have in mind Coleridge's dictum: 'What a magnificent History of acts of individual minds, sanctioned by the collective Mind of the country, a language is.' So when I speak of art I am not speaking of something 'otherworldly' anymore than when I use the term 'critically' I have in mind the self-contained games that are played with texts. The critical consciousness I'm attempting to define does not belong to that hermetically sealed world. L.C. Knights expresses it in the following way: 'As a teacher—as someone, that is, whose main function is to keep alive the masterpieces, great and small, that help us to find our humanity—I have therefore an axe to grind: I want to bring out the value of my own pursuits in relation to the field of public affairs.'

There is no shortage of targets near to hand upon which the English teacher—axe sharpened and alert—might practise his skill. Statements such as the following which deny responsibility and purpose appear with regularity: 'In an increasingly complex society, language too becomes more complex, and for full and adequate participation in that society, people need to assimilate roles and uses of language that did not exist a few generations ago. Yet they still need to be able to express ideas and feelings very simply, and to feel that their ability to do so will be valued.'

I think this is what Lawrence meant—he had headmasters, inspectors and Whitehall in mind—by 'stunting a bit sometimes about the high ideals of human existence'. It lacks the directness of school common sense but like it is essentially static. As John Berger remarks of a related example: 'It belongs to the ideology of those who are socially passive, never understanding what or who has made their situation as it is.' In the face of such an ideology—and it is all pervasive—it perhaps won't seem so surprising that I stressed the need for a resilient critical sense. To put it bluntly, never more urgently as their contribution to contemporary rationality have English teachers needed to confront the appropriation of our history and language with those living voices I mentioned earlier, letting their stories, their embodiment of the complexity of individual and communal life energize our own language and stories. What this creative task means for teachers of English is exercising the fullness of our judgement, listening alertly for the authentic voice of reason and humanity, voices which are not simplifying, vague or bent only on asserting themselves but which cut through the slippery accommodations of so much contemporary discourse.

I've alluded to the needs of students training to be English teachers and I now want to deal with them in detail. My colleague, Tony Adams, and myself have written at length about the way in which we attempt to satisfy some of those needs, so I presume in what I say a systematic preparation for practice and a properly supervised school experience. There is however, an issue concerning the professional preparation of students which needs to be taken further in the light of the above: 'In its concentration upon "vocationally oriented practicism" (Simon, 1976) professional education comes to exclude any notion of "general education" or that an important aspect of the PGCE year will be continuing education of the students in their own discipline and opening up of other fields at their own (postgraduate) level.' The separation of the intellectual and personal development of the individual from his or her development as a 'teacher' has its beginning where such views prevail. The student who has his learning devalued and who is discouraged from looking to that learning for the clues and principles upon which he might give some coherence to his experience and thought about the learning of others risks this only too familiar fate described by Coleridge:

> Are not all masters, all those who are held in estimation, not scholars, but always masters, even in their sports; and are not the female teachers always *teaching* and *setting right*? Whilst both not only lose the freshness of youth both in mind and body, but seem as though they never had been young. They who have to teach, can *never afford* to learn; hence their improgression.

To quote Coleridge again: 'If we hope to instruct others, we should familiarize our own minds to some fixed and determined principles of action.' Coleridge speaks of 'principles of action' and not a theory of instruction to which we should have recourse. In seeking out these principles, literature has a central part to play. To have it as the focus for our reflection seems to be the best guarantee that our sense of the 'individual' will be maintained and that the process will be thoughtful in the fullest sense. The importance of literature lies for me in its capacity for engaging the self in reflection whilst at the same time demanding and developing a response to what in human terms lies beyond the self in others. But there is something missing in this account—the very ground without which nothing I have said has any foundation—and that is the spirit of that engagement and the way in which it will affect the kind of English teachers these students become:

> Teachers of youth are . . . either unsound or uncongenial. If they possess that buoyancy of spirit, which *best fits them* for communicating to those under their charge, the knowledge it is held useful for them to acquire, they are deemed unsound. If they possess a subdued sobriety of disposition the result of a process compared to

which the course of a horse in a mill is positive enjoyment, they of *necessity become ungenial.*

What my teacher-correspondent to whom I referred earlier has had confirmed or rediscovered in her engagement with literature was the 'unsound' principle of pleasure. This is what surprising numbers of my own students (most of them with English degrees) have to rediscover if they are not to perpetuate the vicious circle of ungeniality. Coleridge is touching here on very similar ground to his great contemporary, Wordsworth, who declared:

> We have no sympathy but what is propagated by pleasure; I would not be misunderstood, but whenever we sympathize with pain it will be found that this sympathy is produced and carried on by subtle combinations with pleasure. We have no knowledge, that is, no general principles drawn from the contemplation of particular facts, but what has been built up by pleasure and exists in us by pleasure alone.

In constructing any course of reading and study one is inevitably forced into making a selection and it is perhaps worth laying out the constraints which govern the 'Child in Literature' course which I offer in my own department. The course began its life as part of an option system available to students in their third term (the term following block teaching practice) and initially it was open to students of all subject disciplines. This had two disadvantages—firstly, non-'English' students were over-awed (quite unjustifiably) by the presence of large numbers of 'expert' English students; secondly, because of a limit on numbers, many English students were excluded from the course. In order to try and overcome these problems I shall in future continue to offer the course within the option system to non-specialists while including it in the English programme for the third term. Time, too, is a constraint for as a maximum we can hope for seven three-hour sessions in that third term. However, every institution will have its own organizational problems and what I'm more concerned about is insisting upon the place of literature in teacher education—for all English students and for as many other students as can be accommodated. Nor is there any great novelty in making such a suggestion; both David Holbrook and Peter Abbs, for example, have, with their own particular emphasis, described their work with students.

The title of the course, 'The Child in Literature', indicates a particular emphasis in the choice of texts. I mentioned in my introductory remarks that although my primary concern would be the formation of English teachers I wanted to suggest some of the places they might go in order to clarify their thinking about children and the way children learn. It seems natural therefore that we should attend to texts which have at their centre an endeavour to search out what makes for and thwarts growth in the individual, particularly during childhood and the process of education. So a list of texts we have attended to would include: selections from Coleridge: Books, 1, 2, and 5 of *The Prelude*; Blake's *Songs of Innocence and Experience*; *Jane Eyre*; *Huckleberry Finn*; *Hard Times* and *Great Expectations*; Carroll's *The Alice Books*; Tolstoy's *Childhood, Boyhood and Youth* and selected educational writings; Lawrence's *The Rainbow* and *Fantasia of the Unconscious*. In addition, I should mention films which have added their own perspective on the emergent concerns of the course, notably Truffaut's *L'Enfant Sauvage*; Hertzog's *The Enigma of Kaspar Hauser* and the Taviani Brothers' *Padre Padrone*.

The participants in this course are all teachers full (and one of the first surprises is how as an activity it fills your thoughts) of that classroom experience. They will be full too of that school common sense I mentioned earlier, and the descriptive categories which replace thought they will have picked up elsewhere in their course and at school—'roles and relationships', 'pastoral functions', 'underachieving children', 'autonomous learning'. What they have is a lot of bits—including a bit of Piaget, a bit of Hirst and so on. What a relief first of all then to come back and think about yourself after the first real shock of having your time filled by thinking about others. So one of the first things that I would hope the course offers is something quite opposed to the fragmentation I've just described—that the texts enforce concentration and a sense of continuity. I stress the sense of concentration and continuity *in the reader* and I'd put with it that developing continuity of feeling and thought within a group which has its common centre in a text. The organization of the course does not lie external to its members as a theme—The Child in Literature—nor are the connections made by individuals and the group the 'lines', 'traditions' or 'relationships' of conventional literary criticism. English teaching is bedevilled by endless reduction of the 'text' to 'pre-text' disguised as relevance. Naturally, we come to the texts and read them with our educational experience and 'issues' in the front of our minds but the 'connections' we make are the result of allowing the text to work upon us. This involves us in an act of imagination which we carry into our thinking, and which changes our thoughts and their expression. The text is not something which confirms or illustrates the thoughts we had.

To give some body to the 'connections' I've talked about I shall indicate an account of a piece by Tolstoy—*Schoolboys and Art*—which I've drawn to the attention of my students and a number of teachers. It is an account of an incident which took place while Tolstoy was walking home from school at Yasnaya Polyána with three of his pupils. It opens with the boys pouring out of school at the end of the day with the sense of release that we all recognize—shouting, squealing, tumbling in the snow. As Tolstoy wryly remarks, 'In the open air, out of school (*for all its freedom*)'—school is still school in the most progressive of establishments—and he senses too a new freedom of relationship with the three boys who tag along with him, a lack of restraint which seems artificial within an institution. Nevertheless, there is no false note in his account of that relationship—if he enters into the world of these children it is out of his firm recognition of the independence of that world and their individuality. There is no attempt to idealize the three boys—they and their circumstances are known out of a firm and adult sympathy. As they walk through the wood with him, Tolstoy conveys their unique self-possession:

> Semka, went on in front and kept calling and 'ah-ou-ing' with his ringing voice to someone at a distance. Pronka, a sickly, mild, and very gifted lad from a poor family (sickly probably chiefly from lack of food) walked by my side. Fedka . . . talking all the time . . . now relating how he had herded horses in summer, now saying there was nothing to be afraid of, and now asking, 'Suppose one should jump out?' and insisting on my giving some reply.

What establishes the relationship between Tolstoy and the three boys are the stories he tells them. In school they have been listening to Gogol's gruesome tale of Vii, an Earth spirit which 'affected them greatly and excited their imagination.' Now, with their imaginations further charged with speculations about wolves in the wood he talks to them of Caucasian robbers and the great leader Hadji Murad. At the most terrible part of the story Fedka suddenly clasps Tolstoy's hand and urges him to go on. Tolstoy now makes an important distinction between the relationship established by the power of the story and those who attempt to 'relate' to the children by imposing *themselves* upon them and forcing their sympathies. 'I've seen a lady in a peasant school, wishing to pet a boy, say: "Come, I will give you a kiss, dear!" and actually kiss him; and the boy was ashamed and offended, and could not understand why he had been so treated.'

Tolstoy ends his story telling by telling of a 'brave' who surrounded his enemies, sang his death song before killing himself. First, there is silence and then—as so often happens—what comments there are seem to despatch the matter quickly:

> 'Why did he sing a song when he was surrounded,'
> 'Weren't you told?—he was preparing for death!'
> 'I think he said a prayer'

and then on to another story—speaking now as English teachers we might be talking of the short attention span of the children or preparing some supplementary questions! But Tolstoy himself is surprised when, before he can finish his story, Fedka suddenly asks, 'Why does one learn singing? I often think, why, really does one?' Tolstoy's speculations at this point deserve our full attention.

> What made him jump from the terror of murder to this question, heaven only knows; yet by the tone of his voice, the seriousness

with which he demanded an answer, and the attentive silence of the other two, one felt that there was some vital and legitimate connexion between this question and our preceding talk. Whether the connexion lay in some response to my suggestion that crime might be explained by lack of education ... or whether he was testing himself—transferring himself into the mind of the murderer and remembering his own favourite occupation ... or whether the connexion lay in the fact that he felt now was the time for sincere conversation, and all the problems demanding solution rose in his mind, at any rate his question surprised none of us.

From the moment of Fedka's question the whole tone of the conversation changes—questions and answers pour out from the boys about the use of things, the value of art, the different kinds of beauty. But again in his account Tolstoy exercises an uncommon tact and restraint—the boys are after all talking about matters dear to his heart. As one might easily be he is not carried away by the success of the moment, that sense which pushes us on excitedly as teachers when at last the kids are responding. What he clear-sightedly conveys is the partiality of that 'success'. Sëmka is what he is—not to be forced or manipulated—and Tolstoy responds generously but without illusion: 'Sëmka's big brain understood, but did not acknowledge, beauty apart from usefulness. He was in doubt ... feeling Art to be a force, but not feeling in his mind the need of that force.'

There is no defeat in recognizing the limits of one's influence, however much one may be persuaded of the irrefutable power of one's stories or arguments. Such a recognition is the best defence the teacher, and particularly the English teacher, has against self-indulgence. There are boundaries which to step beyond is an impertinence. At the end of his account Tolstoy leaves each boy at the threshold of his home and a life, which no matter what he thinks of it or how he would like to improve it, is independent of him. The forcing and manipulation of 'response' is the greatest danger which English teachers have to guard against—insistence upon it is more psychologically barbaric than any amount of force-feeding with facts.

To return to Tolstoy's reflections on the sudden, unexpected question Fedka asks: I like the way Tolstoy takes nothing away from the boy and doesn't try to turn him into an object of pedagogical interest, just as there's no attempt to explain the outburst as the result of some planned adult intervention: 'What made him jump ... heaven only knows ... whether the connexion lay in some response to my suggestion that crime might be explained by lack of education. ...' I'm sure we're meant to feel the flatness of that suggestion—the kiss of death to any story. It is the glib notion of cause and effect which in slack conversation we use to 'connect' matters—to explain them or tidy them up. A language of inert and tired generality compared with the art with which he gives us the precise moment of Fedka's question: 'Sëmka picked up a dry stick from the snow and began striking it against the frosty trunk of a lime tree . . . frost fell from the branches on to our caps, and the noise of the blows resounded in the stillness of the wood.' It is a wonderful moment, not stagemanaged and not repeatable, and it is right that such a question, full of wonder and wondering, should come out of it. Tolstoy's 'heaven only knows' points us to what is beyond our power to intervene in or predict where learning is concerned. Where we are perhaps less powerless is in promoting and recognizing the conditions of that learning. The boy's question is phrased abstractly but the condition of that abstraction is the excitement of the walk, his excitement at the stories he has been told and which continue to work upon his imagination, the immediate human context of his friends and his teacher. None of this has given him the words he uses but together they make the moment right for his most serious thoughts to find expression.

Tolstoy also speaks of the boy 'testing himself' and there is that sense of him trying something out, moving out beyond his 'ordinary' considerations (certainly he has been provoked beyond the boundaries of the earlier conversation the boys have). And Tolstoy interestingly speculates how the boy's question springs from feeling the story in relationship to himself ('he has a wonderful voice . . .') and not simply from an act of empathy ('transferring himself into the mind of the murderer . . . ').

The first point to dwell on is whether, as English teachers, we don't tend to make our point of departure where, in fact, we want our pupils to arrive. In reading stories, I presume we will have let them work upon us, felt their power, thought about them and allowed them to prompt new questionings within us. These questionings themselves, with the activity of imagination they imply, emerge over a period of time. At the same time, we are more experienced readers than our pupils and these questionings emerge with a certain ease which we would be mistaken in presuming on the part of those pupils. What this calls for is an act of restraint—the kind of admirable tact that Tolstoy displays—not to begin with them where *we* have arrived. The kind of question the boy asks—which we would never ask for him in advance—is where we tend to start. The conditions of that question—the time the story has needed to work upon him and in which the necessary excited act of imagination takes place—we overleap. The result is so often that puzzled blankness, that sense of 'what has this got to do with me?', which so many apparently *well prepared* English teachers will have encountered when asking for a response.

This is precisely it, of course: what has it got to do with the child? Tolstoy is at some pains to show that the child does not remain locked in the 'personal'—his response to the story isn't simply one of 'identification'. This is another fallacy English teachers are prone to when they guide response along the familiar lines. 'Now has this ever happened to you?' or 'Imagine you were in this situation.' The child enters the realm of knowledge beyond the 'personal' by recognizing a question or problem larger than himself which is nevertheless tacitly in his deepest personal concern '. . . remembering his own favourite occupation (he has a wonderful voice and immense musical talent . . .)'.

What we recognize in Tolstoy's account is the teacher bringing the fullness of his adult intelligence and sympathy to bear on his observations of the child. As I suggest earlier there is no simple minded 'identification' with the child but equally there is no sacrifice of intelligence. If anything the child clarifies Tolstoy's own thinking for him (who is giving language to whom, we might ask). 'It feels strange to repeat what we then said, but it seems to me that we said all that can be said about utility, and plastic and moral beauty.'

I have dwelt at such length with Tolstoy to demonstrate—with the necessary economy—that recourse to literature on the part of the prospective and practising teacher can involve him or her in a discipline of thought which enforces a synthesis of thought and experience as opposed to the fragmentation I spoke of earlier. It is that sense of fragmentation which leads, I believe, to that suspicion of 'theory' which teachers have and their preference for the 'practical' at the expense of a continuing scrutiny of the principles which govern their practice.

I have sketched out what I believe to be the significance of literature in the training of English teachers. I have no masterplan for a massive change of emphasis in 'in-service' provision for English teachers, though it is perhaps worth saying that the course I began by mentioning is the only one of its kind promoted by the DES. Rather than elaborating on large-scale national initiatives my real hope—slightly frayed as it is—lies in fostering the opportunity for collaboration among colleagues within a school. Here, and I speak from personal experience, the Head of Department has a crucial role to play. I remember one ex-colleague going for an interview where his prospective Head of Department's first question (she was a nationally known 'English' figure) was, 'Oh, you're from *X* School are you—all they do is read books there, don't they?' So one has to use the word 'role' carefully in the full recognition that there are English teachers who are bureaucrats, politicians, ministers of mercy, businessmen, hypnotists, etc. I have to confess that I have not been addressing myself to them but rather to those who look for confirmation that to teach others is to learn oneself.

But what of the young teacher who once remarked after listening to me rehearse some of the ideas I have expressed here, 'I don't think I have it in me to be that kind of teacher.' One's initial response is reassuring— good teachers don't spring fully armed from the ground or from PGCE courses. Again, I come back to the crucial role of the Head of Department and the powerfully formative effect one can have on young individual teachers able to understand and effect the circumstances and who are very different from the outside 'experts' who man national and local courses. This still does not quite get at the heart of the young teacher's point, which I might as well admit is unanswerable, in that no one can supply conviction or, as the organizers of training courses would sometimes have us believe, alter people's dispositions.

I don't say this out of a sense of defeat but out of a growing realization of the extent to which teachers depend in their teaching on what sustains them as individuals. A recent reading of John Berger's *A Fortunate Man* has made a deep impression on me. Berger's 'fortunate man' is a doctor, but a teacher would find the investigation of this man's working life fertile ground. Readily accessible and determinedly non-theoretical it offers a remarkably subtle analysis of 'conviction' and 'motivation'—the way they grow and change and affect a man's work—a life work, literally. I was particularly struck by Berger's comment that there are doctors who, like his subject, 'want to experience all that is possible, who are driven by curiosity. But "curiosity" is too small a word and "the spirit of enquiry" is too institutionalized. They are driven by the need to know.' What sustains the doctor is more than medical knowledge or intellectual curiosity, his appetite for experience has a human centre—in his own life and the life of his patients. What should characterize an English teacher is the same appetite for experience—'he needs to know' and he recognizes the same 'need to know' in his pupils. It may seem paradoxical to call that 'need' impersonal but there is nothing self-indulgent about it and it is related to what we call the 'impersonality' of the great artist. Thinking back to the Tolstoy we can recognize how, *rarely*, the impersonal needs of the teacher and artist are united. We recognize a man who has given himself over wholly to the experience and who attends fully to its implications. There is a mutuality of understanding—in attempting to understand his pupils he understands himself more fully. Such sympathy admits of no collusion with or patronage of its object. He is being, in other words, as serious as he can be and it is that example that he enforces in those who attend to him fully.

A Study in Method: Some Aspects of the Post-Graduate Certificate of Education

Anthony Adams and Eric Hadley
Lecturers, Department of Education, University of Cambridge

No discussion of any aspect of work in teacher education can afford to ignore the detailed statement made as the final Consultative Report by the UCET Working Party on the PGCE: *The PGCE Course and the Training of Specialist Teachers for Secondary Schools.* Although it does not detail work going on in specific subject areas, it does explore the principles by which such work might be governed and their relationship to theoretical considerations and practice, as well as discussing the organization of courses, teaching practice and the partnership between training institutions and schools. It seems worthwhile, therefore, to begin our discussion of the approach we have developed in the training of English teachers by considering certain aspects of the UCET Report. Questions of methodology and relationships with schools we shall come to later; we shall begin with questions of principle, not least of all because we feel there are severe limitations in the views expressed in the UCET Report, views that need to be challenged before they become an orthodoxy.

Like all incipient orthodoxies, the Report proceeds through a series of 'reasonable' assumptions which negate argument and disqualify dissenting voices:

> ... it can be reasonably assumed that students come to the course with sufficient mastery of the academic content and intellectual skills of the subject they will be mainly teaching, or can readily acquire these under their own personal initiative. They can therefore be prepared to teach one major subject without the need for any explicit attention to the students' own personal study of the academic content of that subject ... the PGCE course can be directed almost exclusively to questions of professional education and training as such.

We dissent from this view on the following grounds:

1. It presumes a homogeneous group of students within any 'methods' group discounting the fact that each student brings a different

educational case history; widely differing experiences and routes through higher education; widely different aptitudes and abilities.

2. Characteristic of the report as a whole, 'knowledge' is treated as if it were a package which the student brought along, neatly parcelled, to the course.

3. In its concentration upon 'vocationally oriented practicism' (Simon, 1976) professional education comes to exclude any notion of 'general education' or that an important aspect of the PGCE year will be the continuing education of the students in their own discipline and the opening up of other fields at their own (post-graduate) level.

We shall return to the implications of these remarks for the way we organize our own course in detail later but there is a second area of principle which the UCET Report deals with and which demands preliminary comment. The Report does not fail to recognize the need for the personal development of students, that training involves more than the assimilation and manipulation of skills and techniques:

> . . . beyond the achievement of skills are needed dispositions and other personal qualities that motivate the teacher to act according to his or her best judgement in difficult circumstances and that provide appropriate immediate responses in circumstances where premeditated action is often impossible . . . . If we want skills of judgement we must train for them. If we want dispositions and other personal qualities we must produce circumstances in which they can develop.

In one sense it is curious that in a document which devotes so much time to the art of the possible, off-loading whole areas of enquiry as inappropriate to a one-year course, this most complex aspect of teaching is unquestioningly regarded as 'trainable'. We are not alone in feeling that the Report is disturbingly silent on the question of what precisely these 'dispositions' consist and how the necessary personal-judgemental skills will be trained. Instead we are offered an account which at best is distinguished by its circularity:

> (d) *The understanding, skills and personal qualities necessary to teaching the subject to secondary school pupils.*
> This involves (i) an understanding of the different methods of teaching the different elements of the subject in (a); it includes understanding what is involved in planning, carrying out the task and evaluating the achievement in each case; (ii) the understanding and skills to judge what ought to be done in different particular situations in the light of (i); (iii) the skills and personal qualities to carry out effectively what is judged under (ii).

What does this amount to other than a refusal to describe?

We recognize along with the authors of this Report that 'training in the desired skills and personal qualities will be abortive if it fails to provide the circumstances for sustained practice in the light of developing, informed self-criticism' *but* we remember too Coleridge's remarks that 'it requires no ordinary skill and address to fix the attentions of men on the world within them, to induce them to study the processes and superintend the works which they are themselves carrying on in their own minds.'

The generalized and over-schematic account of classroom practice given above is related to the simplified assertion of the 'mastery' students bring with them in 'academic' terms. Just as it is imagined that they arrive with a 'finished' package, so they go into classrooms 'knowing' (in apartness from the children) what they are going to do. They 'plan the lesson' but they do not 'plan for' the children. It is an account completely lacking in any notion of relationship in learning.

All teacher training suffers from this kind of generalizing and it is self-defeating because you cannot 'train' for what for every teacher is the 'unknown', and however specific we seem to be making our pre-teaching 'simulations' and 'situations' they still remain generalizations—to the student they always happened to someone else.

What was involved, just to take one example, in training the appropriate 'dispositions' in one of our students a couple of years back? *X* was a man in his mid-forties who had given up his job in the police force, taken 'A' levels and read English at university. He came to us full of 'dispositions' and 'attitudes' towards children and discipline which were well trained by his years with the police. In the staffroom he was brisk and assertive— he had a disposition to 'lay the law down' and not listen to advice. In the classroom he had a disposition to regard 'response' as 'cheek' and to resort to the kind of English teaching he had experienced as a boy thirty years before. Yet with smaller, informal groups (the sort that only exist on teaching practice) he was warm and approachable—yet even here with an inclination to be condescending particularly to the black kids who form a substantial proportion of this school's population. The man, much to our surprise, got a job. Neither of us could put our hands on our hearts and say we changed this man's disposition, particularly as the description we have offered of him caricatures the complexities of his case history. We should be careful even of saying that experience changes the disposition of students. How many of us have encountered students who retain their disposition to teach even when they have been defeated over and over again in the classroom and who neither respond to the reaction they engender in children nor accept the advice to end this self-imposed torture?

We have dwelt on this matter not out of a sense of defeat but because before we attempt to describe how we go about trying to create the 'circumstances in which dispositions and personal qualities can develop' we have to assert that it is a complex matter and an area in which there are no guarantees. Not to recognize this is to resort to the crudest behaviourism.

Moreover, the authors of the Report can only talk with such disingenuous confidence and simplification of training dispositions by glossing at the same time the innumerable complexities of classrooms and the infinite differences between schools: as if students were being trained for some monolithic, generalized 'school'. This leads to some interesting contradictions: 'Students must be trained for schools as they really are and not for idealized conditions . . . . It would be unfortunate if a desire for a more direct practical effectiveness in PGCE courses resulted in narrow uncritical conservatism.' Again, we look for further guidance and find none, not even any recognition of the inevitable disparity which students perceive (and are frightened by—this is one disposition we train) between the generalized picture we present of teaching possibilities, child potential and school constraint and the reality of the schools they encounter. Like it or not we are in the business of idealizing—how else could we begin to inspire dispositions like 'spontaneity', 'courage' and 'flair' which breathe life into the inert, schematic model of classroom activity this Report presents us with? How else could we try to change the 'narrow uncritical conservatism' that characterizes so much English teaching in schools and which neither of us has any disposition to endorse?

Any teacher educator seeing 'personal development' as part of the training he will offer his students must recognize that the training itself will create fears, conflict and tension within the persons he is training. He will recognize, too, that these need to be articulated and reflected upon. He needs, moreover, the co-operation of his students—a factor always taken for granted in this Report. For without the disposition to change, all other dispositions are useless. No teacher trainer can create dispositions unless they are being conceived in the most narrow behaviourist terms. In this he shares the same problem as his colleagues in school who, unlike the teachers beloved of the instructional and learning process model makers, are not working in adequately resourced classrooms full of paragons with minds like mini-computers and whose behaviour can be manipulated like Skinner's pigeons. As David McNamara remarks:

> All designers of models of the instructional process [and this would include the authors of this report] should have a notice above their desk which reads, 'There are thirty-five periods in a week, there are fifteen weeks in a term, there are forty different children in a class, and teachers get headaches and sore throats' (McNamara, 1976).

It is now worth attempting a profile of the more than thirty students who make up our English Methods group each year. We shall concentrate first of all on what we have learned of what they bring with them to the course.

It is important to stress this because the way we now organize our work with students has as its starting point our reflections upon their needs and qualities. If we have learned anything, we have learned to take nothing for granted—least of all 'mastery of academic content'. Moreover, if we are going to encourage students to 'start where the kids are', to recognize that they are not so many *tabulae rasae* waiting for an injection of knowledge, then we ought at least to be consistent ourselves and 'start where the students are'.

We still interview all our students, unlike a number of colleagues in other UDEs. Partly this is because it is our deliberate intention to create as varied a group as possible with at least a token representation of more 'mature' students with experience outside the school-university-school route. Pragmatically, we need to find out as much as we can about our students because we are making the preliminary allocations to teaching practice before they reappear in the October of the training year.

What we end up with typically is a group of young men and women in their early twenties from a wide range of universities, polytechnics and colleges of higher education with a handful of older students who have included women who have done a degree after bringing up a family, an ex-policeman, an ex-butcher, an ex-opencast miner, an ex-businessman, an ex-actor and so on. Not all of our students will have English degrees— psychology, philosophy and sociology have all been represented—some of them have further degrees and are highly qualified academically. There are enormous differences in the courses, content and style of teaching that our students will have followed at degree level—single honours English, joint honours with every combination, set book courses, period courses, modular courses, etc.

Much less disparity of experience is evident when we consider the school experience of most of our students. A large proportion will have come through the independent sector or through the direct grant system. Even those who have received their education in the maintained system either began it in grammar schools which were then reorganized and were largely unaffected or have been in comprehensive schools where they remained in the Express, A stream, or A band divisions. We could from our interview notes construct an interesting paper on pupil perception of comprehensive reorganization nationally. Equally interesting is the fact that only one black student has applied for the English course—proportionately we have had more Americans, Italians and Poles.

This, then, provides some generalized information about the body of students who arrive with us in October after their two week's observation in a primary school. But before we go on to discuss that first term's programme in detail, we need to draw out the implications of that generalized picture because one of its basic principles is that the first term must include an element of reorientation on the part of the students. In the simplest terms, our students are at the beginning of that transition stage during which they will cease to see themselves as educational consumers and come to see themselves as teachers responsible for the education of others. The view of dispositions we were discussing earlier underestimates the crisis this produces in many students—the questions it raises: how can I make the knowledge I have acquired accessible to pupils? What knowledge have I acquired—what use is it to me or them? Will I be able to do it? What are these people going to do to me? For the first time, in many cases, they will be asking questions about themselves and their learning. This growth of self-consciousness is the ground for any development of dispositions.

And what of their own learning and education? The first thing to stress is that in conventional academic terms they have been a success. Most of them have only known success throughout their whole schooling which is not quite the same as saying that along the way some of them have not had intimations about what that success amounts to or, sometimes, been desperately unhappy at school. We are stressing their own school experience because particularly at the beginning it is the most powerful educational experience they have had. They judge what is said and what they see from that standpoint—the most powerful models of practice they have are their own teachers. ('I'm reading English because we had this really good English teacher in the sixth form. He made it really interesting.') Within a few days of the course starting, we are asking these students to contemplate teaching English in a comprehensive school. Their own schooling and university experience have often distanced them culturally from the children they will be teaching. As for children's learning difficulties—these are people who have 'made it'. They have rarely known (or find it difficult to admit) failure in themselves—let along in others. Nor do they find it easy to understand that there are many children who do not share their belief in the intrinsic merits of education (for its own sake or personal satisfaction) or its instrumental merits (getting a good job). Meeting this challenge in the classroom is the most disconcerting one that a student has to face— for how many of them have begun to think *why* they are doing this particular subject. And the challenge of 'what use is this?' easily drifts into 'What use am I?'

The next reality we have learned to face with our students is that their degree studies themselves have often been largely passive, private, competitive rather than collaborative learning experiences. There are important implications here for attitudes towards talk, discussion and sharing of experience in learning, the construction of knowledge through conversation in the classroom, the whole nature of education as a collective endeavour. The mode of discourse in which these studies have been pursued is often severely limited (usually the essay) and specialized in its associated vocabulary. It will be rare for the students to have been encouraged to express themselves subjectively or had those self-expressive interests validated. There are implications here for 'subject' language inside the classroom— both teacher language (the language of his own discourse) and pupil language (what varieties of expression he will consider appropriate from his pupils).

It would be no exaggeration to say that for a number of our students each year their studies have left them feeling like Ursula in *The Rainbow*:

> To what warehouse of dead unreality was she herself confined? What good was this place, this College? What good was Anglo-Saxon, when one learned it only to answer examination questions, in order that one should have a higher commercial value later on? She was sick with this long service at the inner commercial shrine.

(Lawrence, we remember, trained to be a teacher and did teach. His depiction of Ursula's teaching experience in *The Rainbow* stands as a central text upon which any prospective teacher could valuably reflect. His educational writings, partially collected in *Lawrence on Education* (edited by Raymond Williams, Penguin) are endlessly provocative and relevant.)

To return to an earlier point, many students do arrive with us heavily dissatisfied with the 'knowing in apartness' which has characterized their most recent educational experience. Ironically, at the same time, many of them are talented young people—poets, playwrights, actors, directors, musicians, illustrators. These activities they have nurtured whatever their 'education' has amounted to. Part of our responsibility is to encourage them to see that these are the very talents which we desperately need in our classrooms and that with varying degrees of intelligence and expertise they are a common possession. 'I didn't know I had it in me.' How often we have heard that remark at the end of the first term; how often our students have demonstrated to us that self-discovery can take the most unexpected of expressions.

As with all Post-Graduate Certificate of Education courses the main constraint on the Cambridge course is time. The problem of having to place many of our students in schools a considerable distance from Cambridge, which will be discussed later, means that one of the three terms of the course has to be used exclusively for teaching practice and, inevitably and rightly, this term assumes the major significance in the eyes of the students. A main concern therefore has to be the development of a course which can be perceived as having a unity in the experience of the student rather than one which consists of a slab of teaching practice placed in the centre of two loosely related terms of theory.

The same applies to the treatment of educational theory itself in the course. Some time ago the decision was made to abandon the teaching of the foundations area subjects of educational philosophy, psychology and sociology by means of separate lecture courses. Instead we have evolved a largely seminar-based course under the title 'Situations and Themes' that tries to explore areas of educational theory through a series of incidents in a school-based simulation exercise. The details of this do not concern us here except in so far as it has had an effect on some aspects of the Methods work, but it is important to recognize that the main thrust of developments in the Department's work as a whole has been towards presenting the course as a unified whole and not allowing it to become segmented as traditional PGCE courses frequently did. Our aim throughout is to produce a series of related experiences for the students which will lead to their growth and development as people and, through this, to their eventual classroom success and professionalism.

At the start of the autumn term then (known in Cambridge as the Michaelmas Term) some thirty very varied students assemble as that year's English Methods group. We have already stressed the diversity of this group which is a potential strength to be drawn on in the learning that will take place during the year. Most of them will come with high ideals. They want to communicate their own enjoyment of literature to others (the most frequent answer one receives at interview when they are asked what attracts them to teaching); at interview also most will have said that they would like to do their teaching practice in a comprehensive school. They have very little idea what this means, however, and, for most of them, 'teaching' is a rather nebulous concept which is most clearly related to the kind of work that they did in the sixth form and university. A very generalized idea of 'the comprehensive school' lies at the back of most of their minds, drawn largely from what they have read in the press and heard on television. All comprehensive schools are the same: large (though this term would itself be variously defined depending upon the size of the school from which they themselves came), potentially full of trouble-makers and violence, containing some able children (the potential elite with whom the enjoyment of literature can be shared), and essentially unknown territory.

To say this is in no way to be dismissive of the students we meet for the first time as a group at the beginning of the Michaelmas Term. To recognize this quality of innocence in their perception at this stage is the first step towards providing them with the experience they need if they are to make anything of their teaching practice at all. And somehow all that needs to be done in the way of preparing them for the practice term has to be done in the eight weeks that are available in the Michaelmas Term.

For them it is already, of course, the teaching practice that looms largest in their minds. We have made a provisional allocation of them to the available teaching practice schools. At interview we do ask about their preferences for kind of school and area. There are constraints in the case of those who are married as we feel that they ought to have a local school if at all possible but for the majority we have made very careful decisions about which school we feel will be best for them. Our practice of ranging over a wide area means that we are able to choose schools which we feel to be good, that is, with a style of English teaching not totally at odds with our own ideas and with a Head of Department who will prove to be an effective in-school supervisor for the teaching practice term. But in allocating each student to a particular school from those available to us we try to select the one that has for that student the greatest possibility of growth and development during the practice. For some it will be the large urban comprehensive; for others it may be a smaller Home Counties ex-grammar school turned comprehensive. Our own ideology does mean that nearly all the students will go to a comprehensive school of some kind but, within this limitation, we have a large number of varied schools to choose from and to which we try to fit the various students beginning the course. The first thing they receive when they begin the course on their arrival in Cambridge and at the Departments is a letter of welcome which gives some necessary administrative information and tells them which school they have been allocated to for teaching practice. The letter, incidentally, is signed personally— we want from the first to suggest a collaborative relationship rather than one of teacher and taught so far as they are concerned. This is not always easy. Many of them have been conditioned to expect a more authoritarian structure than we are willing to provide and some continue to call us by our surnames throughout the course.

The first day of the term (before formal teaching begins) we sit in one of our offices awaiting the inevitable stream of students who will call on us to discuss their teaching practice allocation and to see if it can be changed. The reasons for these requests for change are themselves of a varied nature and some of them are quite justifiable and we are able to accede to them. Many of the others are, however, simply an indication of the lack of confidence the students have when they are faced by the realization that they are going to be doing their practice in a real school and their primary need is for reassurance. During the first week we are likely to have met all the students individually and to have confirmed by the end of that time in our own minds the judgements that we had already made about the teaching practice school. Any adjustments that are needed can then be made before the term really gets under way. The important point to establish is that in the end we retain not only the right but the duty to make the decision about the nature of the practice school because only we have the necessary professional knowledge to make this decision. It is an unescapable part of our duty as lecturers on the course. Some of the students, especially those who have come from universities where they have had (quite rightly) a large say in the planning of their courses, feel that this is undemocratic and that it belies all that we are beginning to tell them about student autonomy and ways of working in an open classroom. We feel that this is, in itself, an important lesson. There are some decisions that people can make for themselves and they should be encouraged to do so. There are others where professional knowledge and expertise is required and in their case the role of the teacher means making decisions on behalf of other people. It is the first of many lessons they have to learn during the eight weeks of what is meant by 'the role of the teacher'.

The fears and anxieties about teaching practice having been at least allayed for the time being (they crop up again dramatically later in the term), the course as a whole can begin. English Methods work occupies about half the total teaching time for the week, roughly two and a half days. Along with this the students follow courses in general educational theory (the Situations and Themes course mentioned above), one or more subsidiary subjects ranging from classical studies to the teaching of games, and (in many cases) an afternoon a week devoted to the teaching of the humanities and associated film study. In addition we encourage all English students to join the drama course run by a talented and experienced local teacher and open to *all* students of the Department. All of these elements are important in the total package provided for the students but in this account we shall be concentrating upon the largest element, the English Methods work, more or less exclusively. It is, however, important to recognize the total work load that a student carries. There are some reasons for regretting this: we feel strongly that there is insufficient time for reading and reflection, for example, and we have put into the English work additional elements that encourage reflection yet which increase the student loading still further. But we make the point to them at interview that the pace will be hard, it is not like following a more leisurely undergraduate course. There are advantages as well as disadvantages in this loading of the students' time—they are beginning to learn what it is to work a professional day, to understand just how hard teachers work and how demanding it will be when they are in their practice schools. In the programme of school visits that we arrange in the Michaelmas Term some of them will have to catch buses to school at 8.30 in the morning and this, too, comes as a shock after the undergraduate life style they have enjoyed.

We can divide the English Methods work into two complementary areas: that which is officially timetabled and that which we add to the timetable unofficially. Both are of equal importance and the 'unofficial' element may be the one where the most real growth of the students takes place. Central to this is the keeping by the students of a journal—an idea adapted from the way we worked with pupils in schools. The journal is intended as a private diary in which they reflect upon their own experience as they are undergoing the course and try to relate this and their developing thinking to their own experience when they were at school themselves. For many of them, too, this is the first time they have done any personal writing since they were in the lower secondary school. They have a job to make the journal honest and reflective and to escape from the more familiar formal essay format. They are told from the outset that the journal is a confidential document which no one will read except themselves—they can share it with us or with each other if they wish but there is no pressure to do so. The notion that one can write for oneself as the audience and that writing can be a way of working out one's ideas and making sense of new experience, integrating it into oneself, is new for many of them. Like most of what we try to do with them in the term it combines a teaching point about what one might do with pupils in school with a new kind of experience for them as students. They develop their teaching expertise as they develop themselves as people. The writing of the journal is fundamental to this development and growth.

The journal serves other purposes also. As part of the Situations and Themes course all the students are required to do one piece of written work. (There have been voices raised saying that they should do more but we have resisted this on the grounds that there would not be time for the work to receive a proper and considered response by the Department's staff. As in all things we feel that we should teach by example as well as precept and that it would be counter-productive to demand written work from students to which we could not respond adequately.) The written work grows out of philosophical and sociological exploration of the curriculum, the justification for the subjects that we teach, and the students are asked to hand in to their Methods lecturers a piece of written work justifying their own specialist subject and its place in the curriculum. Before we began the journal writing the outcome of this exercise was drearily predictable, commonplaces and clichés telling us what they thought we wanted them to say, ideas and material drawn out of books and totally unrelated to experience. The work was always in essay form and made up in technique for what it lacked of any sense of real content—the kind of essays that they had been writing for most of their undergraduate years, in fact. Again we felt that to encourage this regurgitation of the thoughts of others was a positively harmful lesson for intending teachers. The different mode of writing that they had practised in the journal paid dividends here and the exercise took on a new meaning. What we now ask them is to hand in some edited extracts from their journals (edited so as to preserve the confidential nature of the original writing) which seem to them to have a particular relevance to their thinking about why they are training to be teachers of English. This also provides us with an unobtrusive opportunity of checking that the journals are actually being kept. At the end of the term we return these journal extracts and use them as the starting point for an individual counselling session with each student in which we discuss the experience of the Michaelmas Term and their orientation towards the teaching practice term. The journal thus comes to play a vital integrative function in the structure of the course as a whole.

This function continues into the teaching practice term. The students are encouraged to keep writing their journals and to use them as the advance planning for their lessons and as a place in which they can reflect upon the experiences of the classes that they teach. Not all of them do this, of course, but there is no doubt that the majority who continue with their journal writing find that it is the most productive way in which they can develop their own understanding of what is happening to them while on the practice, a means of talking to oneself and reflecting in tranquility upon their experiences. Later, further extracts from their teaching practice journal can grow into the piece of written work that is required as part of the formal assessment of their progress on the course (Section II of the examination, as it is known, and which will be discussed later).

(It will be recognized that the journal concept owes a good deal to books on English teaching such as Dan Fader's *Hooked on Books* (Pergamon, 1966); its other important source is Peter Abbs' *Autobiography in Education*. Although both of us would have reservations about the later direction of Abbs' work we would fully accept and welcome his insistence upon the importance of placing the new experience within an autobiographical context and reappraising the past experience in the light of the new. It was also Wordsworth's method in *The Prelude*, possibly the best book on teacher training ever written.)

Journal writing begins in the first week of the Michaelmas Term alongside the more formal aspects of the Methods work which are divided on the timetable into two whole days, one of which is in the Department and advertized as a series of 'lectures' on the teaching of English. The other is spent in school in 'school experience'. The third element in the Methods work consists of two one-and-a-half-hour seminars, each student working in a group with about fifteen others and meeting each of the two lecturers once a week. In our pre-planning we try to link all three of these elements into an integrated whole.

But the students themselves arrive for the first of the timetabled Methods sessions expecting a lecture on how to teach English. They arrive with their notebooks at the ready, willing and eager to take down the words of wisdom that they imagine we can hand over to them. So much of their education up to now has been of this kind. It has taken for granted a view of knowledge which we have already criticized in our comments on the UCET consultative document, the view of knowledge as commodity that can be packaged and transmitted ready made from those who possess it to those who do not. Our major task during the first half of the Michaelmas Term is to destroy this notion and to substitute a different view of knowledge, one that will stand them in better stead as teachers. But to change this view is a major undertaking. It is not only an attack upon the kind of formal education in which they have been successful throughout their lives up till now but it is also an attack upon what they have already defined for themselves as their role as a teacher. It is the biggest piece of disposition change in which we, and they, are engaged throughout the course.

Our intention, too, is to avoid the conflicts which bedevil all education courses over the place of 'theory', 'practice' and 'teaching techniques'. The 'what to do' of 'technique' and the 'how to do' of 'practice' have to be grounded in the 'why we do ... and what happens when we do'. This is the area in which 'theory' has its beginning—as an activity of thought which deepens and stimulates 'technique' and 'practice'. Theory ought to operate as an organizing principle, a clue which might give some coherence to experience and thought and not, in Coleridge's words, as 'specific information that can be conveyed from without, storing the passive mind with the various sorts of knowledge most in request, using the human soul as a mere repository'. This is why we have placed such a stress on the need for reflection on the part of the prospective teacher—not some sort of woolly, self-indulgent day dreaming but the profoundest self-assessment and evaluation of experience.

Although we do commend books on the theory of education and English teaching to our students, to place the stress there, in the first term, would be worse than useless. It would only confirm their powerful desire (another source of friction) for 'answers'. As Robert Witkin wisely remarked in a recent lecture: 'Learning involves a sense of your own existence in relation to the "problem" ... education has to feel as if it grows out of your own experience.' To put the emphasis here seems to us the very opposite of an anti-theoretical stance. We are giving the student, we believe, a way of developing his theoretical perceptions throughout his teaching life-time. The failure to recognize that this process is rooted in the 'personal'—a failure endorsed by the UCET document—is why so many teachers emerge from PGCE courses contemptuous of what they perceive as 'theory'. It is an issue, too, that we shall return to in our concluding remarks.

The books we find most valuable for student discussion at this stage are John Holt's *How Children Fail* and Herbert Kohl's *36 Children, The Open Classroom, Reading, How To*, all books with deep 'theoretical' implications but mercifully jargon free and with the smell of the classroom about them.

When the students arrive at the first advertized lecture hungry for the knowledge they think we can provide for them they discover a lecture room without any chairs but a pleasant and comfortable carpeted floor. They are told to sit down and after some initial hesitation they do so on the floor itself. This has two purposes behind it. It helps to break down the initial assumptions they have brought with them about the nature of university classes and the role of lectures; it also creates the atmosphere of informality that is going to be essential for the workshop elements of the course. It would be easy to dismiss some of the matters on which we have spent time so far in this article as merely trivial, not germane to the real business of teacher training. As we write this in March 1980, however, we are also considering the reports from schools on school practice of the current year's intake of students. It is not just a coincidence that of the three possible failures this year one was the only student who firmly resisted the notion of sitting down on the floor in this opening session; one of the others was the only student who failed to keep a journal in the Michaelmas Term. It is in such trivia perhaps that true dispositions are both shown and developed.

Once they are sitting down we read to them. Again this has several purposes. One of the things we feel they all need to learn to do well if they are to be English teachers is to read aloud well to others; they need to learn how to perform in public. We seek to give them an example of this is action;

we read well and with genuine and obvious enjoyment. Above all we enjoy each other's performance. We follow a similar programme from year to year but each year there will be some new material from each of us reflecting our own reading and development during the year. The fact that it is fresh for us is important. The notion of enjoyment is central to this first 'formal' teaching session of the course.

What do we read to them? In fact what we do is to introduce them to some sampling of the range of children's literature. The material ranges from picture books (some of which we can present with slides) such as *Rosie's Walk*, simple stories for young children (*The Elephant and the Bad Baby*), books that we have found successful with younger secondary school pupils (*The Shrinking of Treehorn*), comic books (Briggs' *Fungus the Bogey-man*), and more demanding English and American works of children's literature (*Where the Lilies Bloom*; *The Machine Gunners*). This is partly to give them some resources that may be useful in the classroom (we are always astonished to see how many of these make their appearance on teaching practice) and we distribute a list of children's books to help guide their own reading; it is also to introduce them to an important literary genre that will have been totally neglected in most of their degree courses.

But the underlying purpose is much more important than either of the above. It is to give them, possibly for the first time since they became students of English literature, the sheer pleasure of being read to and enjoying books for their own sake. No one is going to ask them to write essays on these books, to contrast and compare them, to isolate the themes with which they deal—to do anything with them at all except to listen and to respond. At first they find this very strange. This was not what they came to the University of Cambridge for. There must be some catch. Just enjoying something is not in itself a sufficient intellectual activity. When it becomes clear as it does by the end of the session that there is no catch and this is in fact just what it is all about another lesson has been learned about the nature of the teaching process and the nature of the classroom engagement.

(In reading this year's journals we were struck by the number of students who remembered and wrote about this experience of being read to—it tends to live vividly in their memories after the course is over and this is some indication of the shock which it represents to their expectations of what a university does. Most of them comment favourably upon the experience; some add that they find sitting on the floor for an hour or so very tiring. This is in itself quite illuminating. Their bodies as well as their minds have got accustomed to certain forms of behaviour as appropriate to a university!)

The other 'formal' elements of the course can be dealt with more con-cisely. As already explained, one day a week (about six in all as some weeks get taken up with other things) takes the form of a workshop. Typically a day each will be devoted to examining children's own writing, to poetry, short stories and drama, to planning and organization of lessons, and to the teaching of 'the basics'. (We deliberately postpone this session until after the first visit to the teaching practice school. In the present climate, it is important they have some discriminating advice and suggestions about spelling, punctuation, 'grammar' and the teaching of reading.) The normal pattern for this work is to use the morning to set up a series of experiences for the students to explore usually leading to some work being done in groups which can be presented to the rest of the students and us in the earlier part of the afternoon. We then use the last hour of the day to try to draw out some of the theoretical implications for classroom work of the experiences they have gone through during the day. As with the children's literature session this provides them with a good deal more in the way of resources they will be able to use on school experience in the Michaelmas Term or on teaching practice and, most importantly, it gives them the opportunity to practise themselves some of the techniques they will want to use when teaching children in the classroom. During the drama day, for example, many as we suggested earlier discover strengths in themselves they had never realized that they possessed. They find that they can participate in or lead a group, that they can perform to others with confidence, that they can work out a play production (and even learn the lines) in the course of a few hours. Learning to work under pressure and learning to work as part of a group are all experiences which contain some of the most important learning for these students at this stage. In the process, too, they learn certain techniques and skills—how to use a tape recorder effectively, how to make masks and use lights, how to work a spirit duplicator. The Department, like most others, provides a course in educational technology for students in which these techniques are taught. Unless they are taught within a real context in which they have to be employed in the kind of workshop session we have described there is again the danger of them being merely external learning, not taken into and explored in a context in which the learning will 'take'. (The implicit analogy with an injection for smallpox is deliberate.)

The material used in all of these workshops is especially selected to extend their awareness of what is available: sound poetry by Edwin Morgan in the poetry workshop; plays by Arden and Brecht in the drama session; Caribbean short stories in the short story workshop. As with the introductory session on children's literature, we try to extend their experience intellectually, emotionally, socially and even physically and provide them with a model for the ways in which they can help their pupils to make experiences for themselves.

Albert Hunt's *Hopes for Great Happenings* (Eyre Methuen, 1975) describes a very similar way of working with art college students and Hunt's work has been influential on our thinking. We believe that it has important implications for work in higher education generally. (See also David Craig's *Experiments in English Teaching*, Edward Arnold, 1976, to which

Hunt contributes a chapter.) His book was originally to have been entitled, *The Making of Experience*, and that title neatly sums up what we have in mind in our workshop sessions.

There is not time in the workshops themselves adequately to follow up all the theoretical issues that are raised and the seminars that each of us conducts with the students in two groups concurrently with the workshops give an opportunity to go into the theoretical considerations in more detail. There is always an attempt to continue to relate these seminars to experience in the shape of materials and illustrations that are used to support them but matters such as attitudes towards language variety, models of language and composition, the teaching of poetry, teaching the novel in the lower and upper secondary school find their place here. The seminars are regularly supported by a series of handouts which further extend the range of resources available to the students and which are also intended to guide their further reading after as well as during the course itself.

The real value of the workshops, which are experiential, and the seminars, which are theoretical, is that taken together they provide opportunities for personal growth and discovery by the students and the opportunity to fit these discoveries into an intellectual framework. The writing of the journal in which they reflect upon these experiences and the learning that has gone on and relate it to their previous experience is the means whereby all that happens in the course is integrated in the students' own perceptions. There is one major departure from the pattern of working described so far and that is the session devoted early in the term to micro-teaching. For this session, the students are divided into three groups and set the task of 'teaching' the group whatever they choose and at their own level for a ten-minute period. The sessions are recorded on videotape and the following day we talk the groups through our perceptions of the teaching points raised by each session.

The students themselves view these sessions with an interesting mixture of nervousness and self-interest—nervousness at expressing themselves and interest in 'what I must look like'. We feel that group viewing is imperative. In the first place it defuses the sense of the sessions being some kind of inquisition while at the same time enabling us to stress that observation of the 'class' reaction is as important as the 'teacher's' style and approach. For example, we regularly observe (as in 'real' classrooms) that some student has not been 'taught' throughout the whole session—never looked at, asked a question, etc. All kinds of small, generalizable lessons emerge about use of voice, eye contact, change of pace, physical positioning, gesture, 'vision' in the classroom, use of blackboard and other technical aids, teacher 'presence', and so on.

We ourselves find the sessions immensely valuable as the first real indications of potential strengths and weaknesses. The sessions have to be planned and we regularly discover one or two students who do not know where to start (or cannot be bothered). Some students are brilliant performers but dominate the group and allow no learning to take place. Others show remarkable flair when things go wrong—like a girl this year who, teaching the group how to make bread, found herself literally 'stuck' in the dough mixture, and conducted the rest of the lesson rooted to the spot.

The crucial point in the group sessions is to reinforce the good teaching points. Students who are obviously in need of help we follow up with an individual session where we give further advice. This is particularly true when students' voices lack clarity or variation when reading or explaining.

In conclusion, we also distribute to the students an observation guide which we encourage them to use when privately viewing their own portion of videotape and doing a self-appraisal and which will guide their observation while on school experience.

The final element in the Methods work of the Michaelmas Term is provided by school experience. As with so much else this has both a formal element which is timetabled for one day a week and an informal element which we have ourselves constructed and which takes up about an hour and a half one afternoon a week after the schoolday is over. We have an arrangement with a local comprehensive school for our students to go there one day a week to work with a group of first-year children who volunteer to stay on for an hour after school in what has become known as an 'English Club'. Here the students work informally with a small number of pupils, almost on a one-to-one basis so that a group of about four students will work with about six or eight pupils. Both the student groupings and the pupil groupings are very largely self-selected and based upon friendship groups. The pupils are all necessarily volunteers although they will include some who are very able and need some extra work by way of 'enrichment'; others will be less able and need 'extra English' to help them with their general progress.

Apart from increasing their contact with children this scheme has several advantages from the students' point of view. First of all, those who take part in it from the student end are also, technically, volunteers, although in practice most of the course volunteer to take part. We stress to them that this means a regular commitment, that children will be expecting them to turn up and that, once undertaken, nothing except the most serious illness will excuse their absence. We do feel very strongly that one of the things we ought to train is a quality of professionalism, a sense of responsibility in what they are doing, even at the mundane level of being punctual and conscientious in attendance. We know of no other way of training these qualities except through direct experience of what responsibility means in a scheme such as this. Secondly, it leads to the students again learning to work in groups, this time with the specific purpose of planning and preparing small pieces of teaching for their pupils. This leads to a good deal of discussion during the week (all of which has to be done outside regular class time) and to searching through the available resources for teaching materials. What do we do with them? is the first level at which they are engaged. They learn not only to work together in preparation but also to work together in front of children in the classroom and this seems important in developing the sense of corporateness within the group that is one of our aims at this stage of the course. Finally they come to realize very quickly that what do we do with them is not the fundamental question, that how we relate to each other and to the schoolchildren is the question at the heart of the teaching experience. Even in the six weeks the scheme is able to run it proves to be a useful preparation for teaching practice and a way in which the students can become more at ease, more essentially themselves in the classroom. During these sessions one of us is always 'on call'. We take the initial 'ice-breaking' session and remain during the following weeks to offer advice and monitor progress.

The final week of the scheme generally ends in a presentation by the children and the students of a selection of the work that they have been doing to parents and other friends of the school—drama work—improvized and scripted, reading of stories, tapes of poems, work around themes. We feel that this, too, is important. It gives the pupils a sense of achievement and it provides a shop window for the school which helps their pupil relationships. It gives the students a clear-cut aim at which to level themselves and some sense of the public role of education. Parents, and their perceptions, do matter as well as the children. If we had more of this kind of thing in teacher education, we might have to worry less about accountability; certainly we feel this kind of direct accountability is likely to prove more profitable than the expenditure of public funds and energy on the Assessment of Performance Unit.

There is also the formal school experience element in the course of the one day a week spent in school. How does this differ from the scheme already described? As so often, the two things complement each other. What has been described has a special quality because both children and students are volunteers—that anyone could volunteer to do more school-work itself comes as something of a revelation. It entails a different kind of relationship than that which exists in the more formal world of the average schoolday; it even leads to the students being nicer to the children, otherwise they will not come back for more. Also, because it is one school and because the school gives us a free hand with the children, it is a situation which we are able to control, something we cannot easily do to the same extent on teaching practice or even on the whole day school experience visits. With thirty students on the course we need to use a number of different schools for school experience purposes. Ideally we like them to be as few as possible so that we can exercise more judgement and control over what goes in but it is the exceptional school which will feel able to take some ten or twelve students once a week for six weeks. We do have one of this kind but the rest of the students have to be split between a number of schools taking anything from six to two. As a matter of deliberate policy we do not send single students to schools at this stage;

the stress is always upon the *shared* experience. We debated for some time whether to follow the practice of some of our colleagues in sending the students to a variety of schools so that they see a range of educational establishments or whether to concentrate their experience in the one school and eventually decided upon the latter so as to maximize their contact with individual groups of children whom they can really get to know.

It must be emphasized that this is not seen by us, the schools or the students as a preliminary stab at teaching practice. It is rather part of a deliberately phased, gradual induction into the teaching practice experience. We encourage them to take responsibility for small groups of pupils in a variety of ways, sometimes splitting classes between them and teaching together, sometimes working with a remedial pupil having problems over reading, and so on. Ideally we would like them to observe some lessons other than English, to discover about practical work in a science or craft lesson for example, to learn something about the pastoral structure of the school, and (when the schools can be persuaded to make this possible) to follow a class around for a whole day so as to discover what a school day looks like from a pupil's point of view. As in so much of our relationship with schools it is a matter of delicate negotiation and adjustment between what we would ideally like to happen and what the school feels it can provide and, since the students are only there for one day a week, it means that we are dependent upon reasonably local schools for co-operation. We can therefore exercise less freedom of choice and control over this element of the course than the rest which we have described but we organize regular conferences between ourselves and the local schools at which the role and nature of Michaelmas Term school experience is discussed in detail.

A few principles guide our allocation of the students to the schools for this school experience. All of the schools are ones in which we shall be placing students for teaching practice and we make a point of sending any student who will do his teaching practice in one of them to the same school for school experience. This limits the range of institutions he becomes familiar with but we feel that the greater familiarity that is built up with the particular school, its staff and pupils is a superior gain. The majority of the students will, necessarily, do their teaching practice in other schools and here our policy is to try to send them to a school as similar as possible to that in which they will do teaching practice. This means that we like to have available a middle school, an 11–16 school, and an upper school to choose from in selecting the appropriate school for school experience by the pupils. When we ourselves were trained the 11–18 secondary school could be taken as the norm; now with the patterns of secondary education so varied throughout the country and with the necessity of preparing students for these the game has become more complex. There is no longer a single constituency that can be taken for granted. One of the important things that the students learn through the school experience and the discussion with each other that results both inside and outside seminars is the range and variety of provision that exists within the system.

Two developments of very different kinds point the way forward. In the middle school six of our students are attached to they find themselves working with class teachers and have to abandon all notions of themselves as 'subject teachers'—helping as they will be with reading, mathematics, art, cookery, science. This is an experience we would like to give all our students—raising as it does fundamental questions about the organization of the curriculum, particularly how children construct meaning through language across the curriculum.

In one very co-operative 11–18 school another valuable pattern has emerged. Here one of us together with twelve students works with anything from forty to a hundred children from a different year group each week. The work has involved a fifth-year drama workshop on their 'set' play, a fourth-year Brecht workshop, a first-year Shakespeare day. Most interesting was the visit by a party of third-year pupils to the Department for a day resulting in the production (printed by off-set by the students) of a booklet containing all the work produced by the pupils during the day.

We do not need to spell out the very real lessons in preparation, planning, organization of resources this teaches the students. Equally, it is the most valuable way we have found of breaking down the barrier between work in the Department and work in the school. We offer it, too, as one model of the potential co-operation between school and training institution which the UCET document endorses. If for no other reason than it attempts to answer the perfectly reasonable question all schools must ask: 'You send us your students, but what is in it for us?'

The final element in the Michaelmas Term course is another of the things that takes place outside the formal timetable and probably one of the most important of all the learning experiences that the students pass through. A few weeks after term begins we set up working groups (self-chosen by the students who have begun to get to know each other by now) with the specific purpose of preparing a production to take round the local primary schools at the end of our term, just before Christmas. Such productions might take the form of a play (we have had a version of the Second Shepherds Play paraphrased and scripted by the students themselves, and a melodrama that they have written themselves as a parody of a Victorian melodrama, for example) or a looser variety show of some kind (one group produced a Monster Show based, very loosely indeed, on *Where the Wild Things Are*, one of the picture books we had introduced them to in the initial Methods session. Another group produced a pantomime based on 'Chantecleer and Pertelote', words and music written by the students).

Each year the decision about what they are going to do is left to the students concerned and each year there are more interesting variations upon the basic idea. But they do learn in the process how to reach a decision as a group, how to work together and get a production that actually works in reality, how to stand up and hold an audience (no mean task with sixty excited infants in front of you), and how to work to a deadline. The schools have been told when the productions will be taken to them and the students recognize this as a real responsibility. In the midst of all the other things that are being demanded of them in the course this is a lot extra for them to take on; nonetheless they always do it and they always do it very well once an initial and inevitable phase of chaos has been passed through. They are learning, amongst other things, that if you make demands upon people which stretch them to the limits of their capabilities it is amazing how much they can manage to meet the challenge that is presented.

The primary school productions grow naturally out of the workshop sessions we have already described, they enable the students to put into action some of the techniques that they have learned and to discover again strengths of which they did not know they were possessed. They also discover to their delight before they actually go on teaching practice that they can hold an audience and keep the kids quiet when they want to.

It would be wrong to give the impression in the course that we have described for the Michaelmas Term that all is plain sailing throughout. In spite of our attempts to describe it to them at interview many of the students find it harder work than they were expecting and begin to rebel at the demands made upon them, they find the emotional demands as well as the personal commitment that such a course entails more than they were ready for. A few may drop out in consequence; our experience suggests that this is no bad thing, they would have had a difficult time on teaching practice anyway. They have not yet grown to the point when they can translate their educational role from consumer to provider. But the majority survive and, even if they grumble, they succeed magnificently in meeting the demands made upon them. This is itself a valuable learning experience: they discover just what you can do when you are up against it; and, of course, when they do succeed in all the elements of the course they are elated and buoyed up by the results. There are also the things that do not work so well, there are disappointments as well as successes. It is no bad thing to discover that the teacher has to live with failures as well as successes in the daily life of the classroom. We believe that in schools as well as in the way we work in the Department such ability to live with the failures as well as the successes is made much more possible through the support that one's colleagues can give, hence the emphasis that we place on the students working in groups.

It has to be emphasized that a major source of inspiration for the students comes from the sense of commitment that we, the lecturers, are able to invest in it through our own participation and example. We are both fully stretched and engaged in teaching other courses besides the PGCE but one, or more commonly both, of us will be in some way engaged in all the student activity that we have described. We try to show by example what enthusiasm and commitment to a teaching programme entails. Although we by no means agree about every aspect of English teaching we do a lot of joint teaching, most of the week in fact. This means that we are able to provide mutual support. If one of us has to be away at a meeting the other can cover for him; we try to show in action what a teaching team, or partnership, might look like. Above all we argue with each other eloquently and passionately in front of the students, making it clear that there are no absolute answers and that these are things about which people can care deeply and still remain friends and colleagues working closely together. Over four years we have gradually built up a very close working relationship, one based upon a mutuality of trust; we try not to let each other down, and this seems to us the best possible source of instruction for our students.

The crucial time in the term always comes the week after the students have paid a whole day preliminary visit to their teaching practice schools. We know that it is at this stage that the course will begin to seem to fall apart around us. The primary school productions will look as if they will never reach maturity, the seminars and the workshops will produce bad temper rather than collaborative work. The real source of this is of course the surfacing of the anxieties that have underlain all the term's work by the students, the uncertainty about what it will be like on teaching practice. Will I be able to survive? is the question uppermost in all their minds. For most of the term this question has been unspoken, the visits to schools bring it home most urgently to their minds. It is a period that has to be lived through with difficulty by both them and us but the productions in the primary schools, and the party that generally follows, end the term on an up note and the students go home for Christmas preparing themselves emotionally as well as intellectually for what they will experience in the teaching practice term.

We have already made clear some of the principles on which we chose teaching practice schools. The peculiar circumstances of Cambridge with its collegiate organization mean that we have had to adopt a whole term practice rather than a split practice as the basic pattern. Even if it were not a constraint we would favour this. We feel that in a subject such as English where knowledge of the pupils is the primary consideration behind effective classroom performance there is insufficient time for this to be acquired in a split practice. But, beyond this, the whole term in school gives much greater flexibility in the pacing of the practice; it enables the student gradually to be inducted into the teaching role and ensures that there is time for the necessary learning and adjustments of attitudes and dispositions to take place. The last benefit is the sense of actually belonging to a school and feeling, as well as observing, what the natural rhythm of a school term is like, having some awareness, even on a part-timetable, of just how tired one becomes at the end of a long practice.

The fact that the Department has some 225 students to place and that the Homerton College of Higher Education also has four years of students on a variety of courses to place in the area restricts the number of Cambridge schools available to us. We have already explained why in any case we prefer to have a wider range of schools than those provided by rural Cambridgeshire and the city to draw upon and our first consideration in selecting a school is the quality of in-school supervision the student will receive. This means that the schools are explicitly selected in our case for English students and that we make the placements of the students in schools. We most emphatically do not believe that this should ever be done by an administrator who is not engaged in the teaching process. Just as a Head of Department in a secondary school must be involved in staff selection if he is to run his Department effectively, so a lecturer in an Education Department must have the final responsibility for practice placement and there must be some fruitful relationship between his view of the teaching process in English and that taken in the school selected for practice. Given the wide range of our students we need a wide range of schools to select from when we are considering individual placements but they all need certain things in common. These will include some sympathy with the way in which we work with students in the Department and a full and genuine commitment on the part of the school supervisor to be a partner with us in the training process. We agree with the tenor of the UCET document that training must be a joint enterprise between school and training institution and that, so far as possible, the students' work should be jointly planned and we would want this partnership to be as fully developed and as equal as possible. There is currently a need for more understanding of those things that can best be pursued in Departments and Colleges of Education and, currently, the Cambridge Department is seeking funding for a research proposal which will look closely at the role of the school supervisor and ways in which this partnership can best be developed.

As with so much else in teaching, however, the real source of development lies in terms of personal relationships. Most of our teaching practice schools will get used year after year, though a change of school supervisor (usually, though not always, the Head of Department) because of a move to another job means also that every year a few schools move into the list as a few move out. Roughly two-thirds remain the same, however, from any one year to the next. Over the years we have built up a close and personal relationship with many of our supervisors. They are friends as well as colleagues; when we go on a teaching practice visit we find a welcome that is personal as well as professional. In some of the smaller schools this is also true of the pupils. They get used to our visits year by year and there is sometimes the opportunity to visit the schools less formally outside the teaching practice period and to engage in work with pupils and staff in various ways. We welcome these contacts and would like circumstances to permit more work of this kind to take place. It is only within such a context that the areas of mutual trust and respect can be developed that will genuinely bring about the joint training the UCET document recommends.

There are, in addition, more formal structures that help to cement our relationship with the practice schools. Although it is a ridiculously small sum, we have a tradition of paying our supervisors for the work they do with students and, because they are intimately involved in the assessment of students, we pay them an assessor's fee also. These sums are very limited indeed but they are a token of the value and importance we place upon the school's role in the training process; it helps to make the supervisors feel, with every justification, that they are a part of the Department's professional organization and part-time members of staff. It implies a different kind of relationship from that which usually exists between training institution and school. Much more important than the money payment is the series of supervisors' conferences that we hold. These take place at least once a year; sometimes we organize a smaller local conference in addition for those who have looked after students for the Michaelmas Term school experience when we explicitly discuss that and the way in which it can be developed.

The main conference is a vital event in the life of the Department. We invite either at the end of the summer or the beginning of the autumn term the supervisors who have had English students in their schools in the previous spring term or those who will be doing so in the coming year. Sometimes it is a mixture of both. The conference lasts for a day and, given the widely flung nature of the schools, supervisors can travel a considerable distance to attend. We pay all the expenses involved and offer overnight accommodation, if needed. We also ensure that there is a social element to the conference: we provide a very good buffet lunch with wines, for example. Over the years the supervisors have come to establish not only friendly personal relationships with ourselves but with each other. They come to the conference looking forward to seeing again old friends with whom they can exchange experiences. It is all part of the fundamental task of establishing a team with whom we can work and within which a real partnership can develop.

So far as the business side of the conference is concerned it provides the opportunity to tell the supervisors of changing patterns in the work of the Department, in the general educational theory part of the course as well as on the Methods side, in the Michaelmas and Easter Terms so that they can see how the practice can develop a continuity with the other experiences the student is having. We explore in detail what we do in Methods work and seek the school supervisors' comments and advice on this. We offer and receive comments upon the effectiveness of the previous year's practice and explore ways in which this can be improved. Where we have found a school that has developed a particularly valuable approach to working with students, we invite the supervisor concerned to talk about this. The conference is not just an information imparting occasion (though it is an essential element within our communications network); it is the primary source of the future planning for the following year's work and the main source of new ideas about how teaching practice can be improved. It provides the blueprint on which we, as lecturers on the Department staff, work in the provision of detail for the following year's programme. Generally a written record is kept of the conference proceedings and discussion and this will be forwarded to all the following year's supervisors so that there is a starting point in common.

It will be seen, therefore, that, in spite of the diversity of institutions with which we work, there is a good deal of coherence of philosophy about how we should work with students and the development of this is an essential part of our pattern of work as a whole.

One reason for seeking this is the absolutely central role of the school supervisor within our system. With students anything up to 120 miles from the Cambridge base we cannot, as we could if they were more locally placed, drop in for the odd visit on numerous occasions in the practice term, seeing one or two lessons on each occasion. Even if we could do this we would not want to. Our teaching practice visits commonly last a whole day in the one school and we will work with a student throughout their teaching practice day. Most students will receive two such whole day visits during their practice although arrangements can be made for more direct contact of this kind where there are students with serious difficulties. We believe that there is far more to be gained by this whole day visit than by a great number of shorter visits such as are the norm in most training institutions. Like anything else in teaching there has to be time for relationships to grow. However well we have got to know students in the pre-practice term the relationship with them when we go into the schools is essentially a very different one. They have to get to know and to trust us in a very different context; we have to have time to talk with them and to explore their teaching in detail. A whole day is in fact often not long enough and we will frequently work with students for one or two hours at the end of the day as well as having lengthy discussions with the school supervisor. Particularly where students are based a long way from Cambridge we like to have two or more in one area. In Swindon, for example, we generally have four students, paired in two schools. Not only does this mean that they can be mutually supportive during the term (often to the extent of finding lodgings together) but it also means that, when their timetables fit, we can spend two or three days in the area, staying overnight. In such circumstances we would normally meet with the students as a group, often with their school supervisors as well, informally in a pub one of the evenings and use this occasion for a more relaxed but very important discussion of the practice. We value this kind of personal contact with the students on the teaching practice very much and, whatever its cost in travelling time and expenses, it is a major source of growth for the student during the practice term. By contrast, it is the students based in Cambridge, where it is much more difficult to find the opportunity for working in this way, that tend, if anything, to be neglected.

It should be added that it is also the Department's policy to place students in groups in large towns such as Norwich and Bedford and to organize seminars for these groups during the practice term. The seminars have in part a pastoral function and are intended also to provide a link between the work of the Michaelmas Term and that of teaching practice to prevent too stark a dichotomy between theory and practice. In theory they provide an opportunity in the teaching practice term for further discussion of theoretical issues illuminated by the student school experience. Our experience of running such seminars suggests that their main value lies in the pastoral side and the benefits to the students of meeting each other and talking over mutual problems while on their practice. They do provide, however, a further point of contact between a lecturer from the Department and the students on teaching practice and this, together with the two more formal teaching practice visits, means that each student will have about five visits of some kind or another from the Department during the teaching practice term. The seminars are of course conducted by all members of the Department's staff so that the English students in, say, the Norwich area, will be looked after for the area group seminars by someone of a different discipline, as well as being seen by us. The extra contact has a particular value in that it may provide a further means of communication; we often receive an early warning of a student with problems through the information gleaned or offered at the area group seminar. The English students are on the whole even more widely deployed than the rest of the students on the course since we place such a high priority on the quality of the school supervision and this makes it the more important to place them in groups so that our extended visits can play the role played in the other areas by the group seminars. We are only just experimenting with pairs of students in the same school and it is still difficult to persuade some of the schools to take on the extra load of two students. We are convinced that there is much to be gained from this where we have been able to identify two mutually supportive students and we would welcome further experiment in joint timetabling and the sharing of some classes in common. But all this remains in the future.

One thing we would welcome, and hope to develop, is providing the students with some perspective on the total pattern of education in their area, not just the school where they are on practice. For example, there is some advantage in placing students in a middle and an upper school which received pupils from the middle school concerned. This enables mutual visiting, possible exchanges of classes, and some awareness of the process of continuity within the educational system as well as extending the age-range of pupils the students meet. Again developments of this kind are as yet in embryo but further experiment along these lines will be developed as a result of discussion at the supervisors' conference.

While on practice the students will teach a one-half to a two-thirds timetable, and also engage in some observation of classes. Ideally, although even with the most co-operative of schools timetables do not always allow the ideal to take place, we would like to see the student gradually inducted into the teaching process, observing and working with the regular teacher of a class for some time and then taking over more responsibility for the planning and management of the class until he is doing the bulk of the teaching, though still with the regular class teacher participating from time to time. As with all else that we have been exploring, the keynote here is *collaboration*; the collaborative teaching of classes between student and student and between student and supervisor is very much the pattern we seek to develop. In the same way we would like the student's timetable at the beginning of the practice to be relatively light but to increase as he is ready for it and becomes more confident until at around half-term about a half timetable is the norm.

Observation of other classes is also something on which we would place considerable stress, though we hope that 'observation' will generally mean participating and helping with the class as well. But the advantages to English students of observing lessons in other curriculum areas, such as science and craft, are enormous and we feel that they can learn a lot both by seeing a good practical lesson and by watching teaching in a discipline with which they are relatively unfamiliar. All of this of course makes a large demand on the practice school and is not always under the direct control of the supervisor; we are dependent upon the Head and the other Heads of Department as well so that building up the total relationship between ourselves and the practice schools is a long-term objective made possible only through regular and long-term involvement with particular schools.

The final general point concerns the role and status of the student within the school itself. Naturally we hope that all the schools we use are welcoming places and that the student will be accepted into the community of the staff as a whole. This, for the most part, is the case. But we also think it important that the school does not try to pretend to its pupils that the student is anything other than a student. Quite apart from the fact that such pretences hardly ever work we believe that there are other issues at stake. In principle we believe in honesty with pupils and we find that they too can be exceedingly supportive when they know what the role of the student is and why he is teaching them as well as, or instead of, their regular teacher. Class loyalties to their normal teacher can run deep and the student can be at a disadvantage if they feel that he has supplanted the situation they are familiar with. If pupils, class teacher, school supervisor, and student can all be openly involved in a collaborative activity of training this seems to us the most fruitful setting for the student's work.

We have also found that pupils can be surprisingly helpful, and even protective, so far as 'their' student is concerned. Curiously enough in some ways, though symptomatic of their own role uncertainty, this is often the most difficult thing for the students to accept. They want to be accepted as 'real' teachers; they always want to plunge into full class teaching before they are ready for it. Discussing the nature of practice with supervisors who help them to resist the temptation to fall in with the students' importunate demands in this respect is vital. It is not insignificant that students who are able to accept their role as being that of student are nearly always those who do well on their practice. They have the necessary inner strength to be honest with themselves and their pupils about the role they are playing in the school. The way they introduce us when we visit them in the classroom is usually the first indicator of this. They vary from ignoring the fact we are there and not introducing us at all to the class, which seems to us the worst of all possible things, to explaining that we are there as their tutors in the university Department of Education, which we find much the best way. The student who can do this easily and simply is generally already on his way to developing the strengths that he will need in the classroom.

Our own visits are slightly curious occasions and vary greatly from student to student in the impact that they make. We are very anxious to impress upon the students that we are not there in the role of visiting examiners but essentially to help and advise in the progress of the practice. In fact the teaching practice assessment is done by the school itself which is another reason for placing a high premium on the quality of the supervisors we select. We certainly do not believe that it is possible to judge a student on the basis of a few visits and seeing a few lessons torn out of a total context and we argue that only the school which works daily with the student throughout the practice term is any real position to make this judgement. We do, of course, have the advantage that the school supervisor lacks of seeing a good many students and forming more of an overall picture but we are judging the performance of a particular student in a particular school and we feel that the school is in the best, in fact in many ways the only, place where this judgement can be made. Above all, what one ought to be looking for is the student who is making progress throughout the practice—there may be still a good deal to be done even at the end but one is looking always for potential and this means having the total picture. We would be concerned about a student who appeared to have stayed still and not made much, or any, progress between our two visits, for example. We have already said that the school supervisor is paid a fee as an assessor and, under normal circumstances, his judgement is the one that the examiners would accept. We would offer to the examiners a statement on behalf of the student if we felt from our own observation that the student had been badly treated by the school assessment but we would never intervene in order to urge the failure of someone whom the school wished to pass. Our role as moderator therefore could only serve to urge an upgrading of a student, never one in the reverse direction. (Of course in many cases the final grade will be arrived at by an agreed award reached after discussion between ourselves and the school, ideally taking into account all the teachers who have come into contact with the student, and sometimes the views of the student himself. Nonetheless, whatever procedure is adopted to arrive at the final grade, the responsibility for awarding it is clearly that of the school practice supervisor.)

This is so different from the kind of relationship that students have previously experienced with university teachers that it is very difficult to persuade them of the truth of the facts outlined above. There are some every year who insist on treating us as visiting examiners and who try to put on what they feel to be an appropriate show when we are visiting them and who frequently make themselves absurdly nervous about the visit in consequence. This is one reason why we tend to get more out of the second visit than the first. A major part of our job on a teaching practice visit is to put the student at ease, to allow us to play the part of collaborative consultant rather than assessor in the practice situation. The assessment of teaching practice is always a difficult matter and there is a danger of being too anxious to get the student through at all costs; this is in our view not always in the student's own best interest—and certainly not in the best interests of the profession and their future classes. If anything, training institutions ought probably to fail more students. But we are convinced that such decisions ought to be arrived at by a mutuality of agreement between school, ourselves, and the student concerned. To enable this requires great honesty on all sides, and considerable maturity on the part of the student. It also runs counter to the tradition in a profession where the writing of confidential references by one member of the profession on another is very common. Trying to develop this tradition of assessment in the schools we use is still not easy but where it works it provides the fairest and least fraught method we have been able to evolve. Where things go wrong, as with some student they will do every year, we are glad to have fail-safe devices such as the opportunity to write extra supportive reports to the examiners and, in more extreme cases, the opportunity for extra teaching practice at the end of the university summer term. Our work in the classroom on teaching practice observation is probably no different from that of any other experienced colleague in this field. We have recently, however, adopted the policy of making duplicate copies of any notes that we write and giving a copy of these to the student and to his school supervisor. This means that everyone is fully in the picture and the future development of the student can be a truly collaborative activity. It also gets rid of the disconcerting effect of having someone write notes upon you in a classroom without your ever seeing what they have written. In our view if this degree of openness could be adopted in teaching generally and there were less secrecy and confidential reporting on teachers only benefit would result. Commenting upon and being commented upon by other practitioners in the field would seem to be the hallmark of professions other than teaching. But the fact that we are there for a whole day and that we see the student in a social as well as in a professional capacity does build up the time for the creation of those conditions of trust in which effective advice in so personally and emotionally taut a situation as teaching practice can be offered.

It ought to be re-emphasized that the main source of commentary upon the students' teaching practice experience must be himself and that the journal, which he keeps during practice, is the main instrument whereby this honest and personal commentary is made possible. Used properly, the journal is the place where the advance planning and thinking through of how lessons may develop takes place; it is also the repository of frank (because private) comments on the student's own performance and his responses, of agreement or otherwise, to the advice given by ourselves and by his school supervisor. The journal is the heart of the thinking through of the practice.

We occasionally see teaching practice journals though this is rare. At their best they are very personal and very private documents indeed. But they are a major source of the personal development of the student on teaching practice as they are during the Michaelmas Term. They are also linked with another very important element in the assessment of the student. We have long ago abolished the examination paper that the Department used to set on the Methods work, on the teaching of the Special Subject. It has been replaced by what is known in the jargon of our examination system as Section II. (The formal means of assessment in the Department entails that the Certificate in Education is awarded provided students succeed in three sections. Section I consists of two papers, each of three hours, on aspects of educational theory; Section II, discussed above, relates to the teaching of the main subject; Section III is the assessment of teaching practice. A student must pass in all three sections for the award of the Certificate.) Although there is a number of modes under which the work for this section can be presented it is in essence a piece of submitted work which relates to some aspect of the teaching of one's subject, in this case English. Unfortunately the bureaucratic jargon in which university examination regulations have to be written means that the students all too often feel that they have to write in a style more suited to a Master's thesis than a field report of classroom experience, but it is the latter we are essentially looking for. The students have to submit a title for their piece of work for approval in advance though there is ample opportunity to change the title as teaching practice develops. The approval committee that has to agree the titles with the students tries to give as much of a direct classroom focus as possible by insisting upon titles specifying as precisely as they can the age-range and ability of children to whom the title is intended to relate. The kind of thing that would be ideal would be on the lines of 'The teaching of two contrasting short stories to third year pupils in a comprehensive school mixed ability class'.

The submission takes the form of an extended essay (7000 to 10,000 words) although it can be shorter and accompanied by appropriate teaching materials. From our point of view the ideal Section II grows out of the student's journal; as with the essay they write in the Michaelmas Term if they can present their submission in the form of edited extracts from their journals together with a reflective commentary this is exactly the kind of thing that we are looking for. The essence is the account of a sequence of lessons with a commentary upon them and some attempt at evaluation of what has gone on. Although part of an examination submission, the Section II work at its best is also a learning experience; the kind of reflection upon one's classroom experience that all teachers need to engage in. To transform an examination into an instrument for personal growth and learning is no mean achievement and the flexibility of Section II is a useful means to this end. For the English students it is intended as a further opportunity for personal writing and the reflection that grows out of it. Over recent years the quality of the work submitted, as confirmed by the judgement of the external examiner, suggests that the examination need be no bar to the development of the students.

We emphasized in our discussion of the programme for the Michaelmas Term that its present form had evolved in response to our perception of student needs and the same principle holds true for the Easter Term, when our students return from teaching practice. It would be an understatement to say that they came back to us as very different people—some are brimming over with the excitement and confidence of a successful term's teaching, others have grave doubts about whether teaching is for them, yet others have had their confidence undermined and face the final term knowing that a period of further practice awaits them. The problem for us is how do we hold the whole thing together when the forces which make for disintegration and a sense of anti-climax are so strong. It would be only honest to say that we feel dissatisfied with how the Easter Term has gone in past years and that only within the last year have we begun to find a pattern which meets student needs.

Initially, the majority of students are glad to be back. They have seen little of each other during the teaching practice term, and there is gossip to catch up on and a multitude of teacher horror stories to recount. But this initial feeling can be quickly dissipated. Understandably, many of them feel that they can 'do it' now and, after the activity of teaching practice, 'talking about' soon begins to wear thin. For some of them, school experience has confirmed all their doubts about us, fresh from 'the chalk face' the note is often, 'Well, it's all very well you talking about these approaches but the reality I've had to face . . . ', 'Mixed-ability teaching, group work, reading aloud are all very well in theory but . . . .' So there are new tensions within the group.

If the horizon in the first term was limited by 'getting through teaching practice' the new bogey has become 'getting a job'. Very few students have jobs when they return and understandably they are deeply concerned about job prospects especially when in the present circumstances they may have written thirty applications and drawn a blank each time.

In the past Section II work was still being completed in the opening weeks of term and as the deadline approached classes disintegrated. Looming at the end of term is the written examination about which we both have very strong reservations but which for some students takes on the form which their finals had and stricken with misplaced anxiety their impulse is to bury themselves in the library.

Finally, Cambridge in late spring is a very pleasant place to be in and the temptations to retire to the river have a logic not mentioned in *The Logic of Education* (even if you carry it with you under the guise of 'revision'). Time allocation for Methods work remains roughly the same as in the Michaelmas Term and the subsidiary, drama, humanities and film courses recommence. Situations and Themes are replaced by a variety of Options courses offered by each member of staff. The students choose two from a list which ranges through Language in Education, Victorian Education, The Child in Literature, Communist Education, Games and Simulations in the Classroom, and many more. The intention of these (examined) courses is to deepen theoretical understanding—sessions take three hours a week. At the moment, there is heated discussion within the Department as to whether we should abandon the two option system and move to one option plus a 'common core' structure which all students would follow. It is not within our brief to elaborate upon this argument except to say that it centres on the place of 'theory' and the extent to which we, as a department, are 'simply' preparing students for the demands of their first appointment.

With these background considerations in mind we can now return to our own students. Within a few days of their return we will hope to have interviewed each student individually. This is a crucial meeting during which we will discuss the supervisor's report with the student and their progress on teaching practice. The final report is, of course, a confidential document but we feel it only fair to intimate to students what has been said about them. This is always made easier where supervision has been conducted in the open manner we discussed above. This is particularly true when we are engaged in the tricky, personal negotiation over further practice. We should not underestimate the shock of 'failure' for students and the self-justification and rationalization it often leads to and which hampers honest recognition of strengths and weaknesses. This is frequently accompanied by a strong sense of injustice which projects itself on to the 'unsympathetic supervisor' as disgruntlement over 'inadequate direction and support'.

This initial meeting is also the forum for discussion of progress in job applications. We brief the students carefully in the first term about practical matters like letter writing, curriculum vitae, etc., and also explain to them the pressures and intricacies of the job market—the policy on applications of the various LEAs, areas of shortage, nature of appointments. This invariably needs to be gone over again with individuals who now have a much more specific idea of the kind of school and department they want to work in. Equally, students seek advice on patterns of interview, their own interview technique and how to make the crucial judgement of accepting or rejecting an offer on the minimal information that can be gathered on the day. Here our own experience of interviewing and our contacts with schools throughout the country are of great value. We make a point, too, of explaining what we are likely to say in support of applications they make as well as giving them guidance on the kinds of institutions we feel they would be best suited to—advice, again, which sometimes runs counter to their own views.

After these initial interviews, our immediate concern is to maximize on the wealth of experience and material which the students have brought with them from teaching practice—while it is still fresh in their minds and while they still want to talk about it and share it. In a way, too, this is our means of reasserting our aim in the first term of getting them to see that they have a good deal to learn from each other. Central to this procedure is the use we make of Section II. In the past it was handed in for assessment to the Methods tutor two or three weeks into the term. It was assessed and then, after moderation by an external examiner, handed back without comment to the student. This seems to us a fundamental waste of student endeavour and anti-educational in that the work has no prospective audience other than the examiner (like so much written work in English). Instead we now insist that for our own students Section II work be completed by the beginning of term and that they bring it and any associated material along to the first Methods session where they will be able to share it with us and their contemporaries. In that first session, the students are divided into three groups—each group chaired either by ourselves or by colleagues we have brought in to help with teaching practice—Section II work forms the basis for a detailed exchange of views firmly rooted in the teaching experience. We decide the make-up of the groups in advance and there is a number of factors at work here. We feel strongly that the third term should be a time when the experience and expertise of the students is widened. In each group, therefore, we ensure that the whole spectrum of schools and English teaching is represented. The student who has worked in a small Fenland comprehensive has a great deal to learn from the student who has worked in an ILEA school—and vice versa. Equally, the student who has worked in a mixed-ability context has something to offer to the student who has experienced English teaching in a 'banded' or 'streamed' context. There are many other considerations—different patterns of examining, organization of resources, whole class teaching, individualized learning, and so on. All of these considerations take on meaning and are de-sloganized when you talk to the person with experience who has the children's work and his own resources, lesson notes, etc. to back up that experience. Students who might say to us 'mixed-ability teaching doesn't work' at least have to think their position through when it is challenged by the first-hand experience of a fellow student. They may not be convinced but, as we have stressed elsewhere, even providing circumstances does not guarantee change.

In the afternoon, we follow up the discussions with a plenary session in which there is a more general sharing and discussion of the implications of what has been said. These sessions have a practical aim, too, because we will be expecting the students to tell us what their priorities are for the seminar programme. Again, in previous years, we have decided this in advance, but we feel that the students by now should have a say in the course design and may, in fact, wish in some cases to lead the seminars themselves. This leaves us much freer to use the seminars as places where we can now begin to introduce 'theory' which will illuminate and develop thought in the areas they have chosen to discuss.

How to keep the impetus going? We are both agreed now that this can only be achieved by further school experience. In past years we have rung the changes on visiting speakers, 'projects', but all to no avail. Moreover, none of our previous attempts—however well intentioned—answered the need for further experience and development of expertise. As one of last year's students put it: 'I've been on teaching practice, but I want my *practice* improved.'

In co-operation, therefore, with a small number of local schools we arrange for our students to work on four occasions at least for a whole day in school. This time they go out as large groups (fifteen students) accompanied by one of us. In deciding on the personnel of each group we try to ensure that they will gain experience by a different sort of school and with an age group with which they will have had little previous contact. So those students who have worked in Upper schools we try to place in Middle or Junior schools; those who have worked in Middle schools we try to place with examination classes. Another of our aims is to enable students to try out ideas which were too ambitious within the context of teaching practice. Now they have the time, the manpower and the resources. Many students, for example, have had little chance to do any drama work.

We could do nothing without the co-operation of the schools for they are, in effect, saying, 'Here are 30–100 children. They are yours for the day.' But it is not a one-sided arrangement because what we are offering is a massive input of manpower and resources, which enables us to offer activities they would like to provide themselves but which they are hard pressed to do. We have, for example, been able to work with pupils on their examination texts—particularly in drama—bringing the texts to life through our own performances and providing workshop activities for the pupils. For a group studying *Henry IV, Part I*, for example, the students produced a memorable, two-hour adaptation of *Henry IV, Part II* and *Henry V* followed by rehearsal sessions and discussion. With Middle School pupils they have worked on dramatization of stories leading to performance, illustrating stories, poetry-writing sessions, etc.

Ideally, we like the school to give us a specific brief, as, for example, one local comprehensive school has done for next term—'Come and work with our Fourth Year on *Julius Caesar*. It is their set play and by the time you arrive they will have had one read through of the play.' Week by week, then, the students are faced by a new scenario which involves a great deal of planning and organization on their part, which involves them working together again and which gives them the chance of using the technical resources at their disposal. One half-day a week is set aside for the initial planning of these sessions and for a debriefing on the previous week's work.

Both of us are convinced that the students learn more in this way than through any amount of lecture or seminar teaching. Not that there isn't furious discussion and disagreement but at least we have moved beyond the posturing from fixed positions that used to beset discussion in the Summer Term. The discussion you have about 'Teaching Shakespeare as an Examination Text' is very different when you are planning how you will make the play accessible to a group of fourth formers *tomorrow*.

It may be argued (students themselves argue this way sometimes) that there is something 'unreal' even about this further 'experience'. We would remind our readers of what we said earlier about the 'narrow uncritical conservatism' of so much English teaching and ask, 'Isn't it our responsibility to show our students what is possible?' That it is possible for Shakespeare to be something other than a dreary reading round the class; that children are not naturally antipathetic to literature; that children (like students) respond to being told '*Yes*, you can do that', instead of 'No, that's a good idea but we haven't the time.' The students we are training are the best guarantee of change that we have—more significant than any number of government directives, theoretical curriculum innovations, or increased allocation of resources. There is no resource more important than human resourcefulness.

Further school experience, then, is the centre-piece of our work in this term. Although the general pace of the term is more leisurely, some students will no doubt complain again about the work load (memories will soon fade)—if so, we both have a sheaf of letters to hand from ex-students in their first years of teaching.

Earlier, we remarked on the lack of success of previous programmes centred on visiting speakers. There were notable exceptions—Albert Hunt, for example, whose influence on our own methodology we noted. We do believe it is important that our students have other perspectives on English teaching than our own and this year (now that we are happier about the central thrust of the programme) we are again experimenting with visiting speakers. Amongst them will be Ken Weber, the Canadian educationist whose work with the 'less able' deserves to be better known in this country (see *Yes, They Can!*, Open University Press); David Holbrook who will be leading two seminars on children and poetry; Robert Witkin whose work on the nature of response (*The Intelligence of Feeling*, Heinemann) has strongly influenced both of us. In addition, we have planned a session with an experienced public examiner. These sessions, we hope, will complement both the practical and theoretical considerations we shall be encouraging in our students.

'It is hoped that this report will encourage further experiment and evaluation in the PGCE courses with which it is concerned' (UCET Report). We hope that what we have written will be seen as making some contribution to this 'further experiment and evaluation'. How far the account we have given is generalizable is another matter. As we have stressed throughout, the method of working which we have evolved is limited by our particular circumstances. If, for example, our Easter Term were longer than six teaching weeks a different pattern would have emerged. If, like our colleagues in London or Bristol, we had large urban areas on our doorstep and our students were near at hand the pattern of teaching practice visits would be different and we would bring our students back more regularly into the Department during their practice. Nevertheless we would wish to emphasize (in contradiction to the general drift of the UCET Report) that we are not in the business of providing 'systems operators' to enter an educational 'system' whose stability is guaranteed and can therefore be taken for granted. Nor can we conceive of 'knowledge' as something which is stable and unchanging and where theories of its exchange will be of the 'transmission' variety—the stress for the learner being on 'storing' (a view that finds its classic expression—self-defeating in the end—in *Hard Times*). We believe that in our society the teachers we are training have to be 'systems innovators' and the view of 'knowledge' implied in all that we have said stresses the replacement of 'transmission' by 'construction'—an active, personal construction for teacher and learner alike. In his contribution to the 1976 Kings College conference on the PGCE, Professor Simon struck a similar note:

> It is the acceptance of the *existing* social structure as the natural environment of the human animal, by some schools of psychology and sociology (behaviourist and function respectively) that promotes determinist and a-humanist ideas, directly at odds with the educationist's intention of equipping human beings to think and to act in and upon society (Simon, 1976).

—a note which we feel has become muted in the final UCET Report.

At a time when the formal provision for probationer induction and in-service training in general is at risk the view which we have expressed seems the best guarantee for the future. Rather than casting our minds back to the major externally funded research projects of the past we need to encourage the notion of the teacher as 'researcher' in his own classroom. This we believe has its roots in the self-reflection and observation which we have stressed in the training of our own students. As Peter Abbs remarks, 'If we are to achieve a genuinely human education we must return again and again to the person before us, the child, the adolescent, the adult, the individual'. 'Before us' and '*within us*' we would add to Abbs' statement.

The account we have given of our work is itself conceived in this spirit. In a significant way it is our 'journal' of the years 1976–80. We have deliberately not 'theorized about', for as Robert Witkin warned in a lecture we have already referred to, 'theorizing about and observing oneself doing are not the same thing,' not least of all because the very language in which that theory is couched so often disables those people whom one most wishes to reach—in this case, our colleagues in teacher training, our colleagues in schools, and our students.

References

Except where otherwise specified in the text, references are to a series of papers in *British Journal of Teacher Education*, Vol. 2, No. 1, 1976.

5
Suggestions for Practice

Introduction

I hope that the majority of the articles in this collection have clear implications for classroom action. It has been compiled from the fundamental position that one cannot separate theory from practice in the classroom. All teaching implies some kind of theoretical position whether or not the theory is understood or acknowledged. It seemed helpful, however, to conclude with a number of very specific suggestions for classroom practice, all of which are in line with the general perspectives explored in the earlier part of the book.

Twenty-Four Things to Do with a Book*

Geoff Fox
Senior Lecturer in Education, University of Exeter

Reading is normally a private activity: a transaction between reader and writer in which the experience and sensitivities of the reader fuse with the printed text. Shared reading in school classrooms is a more public matter. At worst, fiction is used as a superfluous preface to other work: a novel about the relationship between a grandfather and his grandson becomes the stark demand on a worksheet, 'What can we do to help old people?' A recent study carried out by student teachers at Exeter University involving conversations with one hundred children in twenty different schools revealed that only one out of every ten readers said that any books 'done in class' were amongst their five favourite titles.

If a teacher is concerned to foster the unique response of his pupils, he may well provide much time in which his children are 'just reading', ideally amongst an abundant and various supply of books. He may further provide space through exploratory writing and talk for a reader to define and examine his own response to a book.

However, the sharing of a book in a public fashion—with a partner, in small groups, or as a class—can have its value. Some activities may lead to a closer reading and a deeper relishing of a book, a refinement of the individual's own response. The ideas which follow are drawn from the practical experience of a group of Canadian teachers in a workshop course who were concerned to develop a climate in which books were shared and exchanged as a central and regular practice of the class.

Time was limited, and their ideas reflect a sustained 'brainstorming' session rather than an attempt to produce a definitive list. More idiosyncratic ideas which depended upon the peculiar skills of individual teachers have been omitted, as have highly specific suggestions relating to particular books. An all-class dance drama version of *Watership Down*, for example, was not seen as a readily transferable classroom activity. Many of the ideas will be familiar to experienced teachers, but perhaps a checklist may be useful when memory or inspiration fails.

*This article was first published in *Children's Literature in Education*, Vol. 8, No. 3, 1977. It has been modified slightly by the author for this collection.

Suggestions for Individual Readers

1. A 'reading log'—possibly in a special notebook printed by a school's resources centre. The record might include: title, author, when and where the story takes place, notes on favourite characters, the part which was most enjoyed. For more established readers, the 'log' might become a journal in which a reader reflects freely upon the feelings and thoughts provoked by his reading.

2. A written description of one of the characters in the book 'as if he or she were coming through the door now', or at a particular moment in the story. A drawing or painting that is consistent with the text to set alongside the writing.

3. A letter to a friend about a book which is especially liked. This activity is most successful (and justifiable) if there is a real recipient of the letter in another school. The scheme might best be run therefore by two teachers in different schools, perhaps as part of a wider exchange of letters, information tapes, etc.

4. A letter to the author of a book (via the publisher) containing questions, criticism, expressions of enjoyment, etc. The general experience of this activity is that children's writers are not merely long-suffering, but welcome the contact with their elusive audience.

5. A poster for the 'film-of-the-book'; stars, what-the-critics-say, etc.

6. The manufacture of a cover (including front, spine and back) for a new edition of the book, incorporating title, author, publisher's blurb.

Suggestions for Pairs, Small Groups or the Whole Class

7. Each lesson begins with a three-minute (maximum) reading, *prepared beforehand*, by a member of the class. Initially, the extracts are chosen simply from a book the reader has enjoyed. Sometimes the class may talk about the reading, sometimes not. If the daily ritual is popular, and continues for several weeks, it may be useful to give the topics of the reading a focus; for example, the reading could be 'exciting', 'about an event in the past', 'funny', 'about someone you admire or envy', 'about a family', 'about someone alone'.

8. A local author is invited to come to the class and talk about his books; ideally, at least some members of the class should have read some of them.

9. With a book where a journey is important (as is the case in many books for young readers), one or several large wall maps on which the movements of the characters are plotted and perhaps illustrated by groups in the class may draw a reader more closely into the text.

10. Another journey idea is a long collage or painted background on which the class places characters, pictures of episodes, etc., as the story develops.

11. For historical fiction or novels with complex relationships, family trees either in two dimensions or as mobiles can help understanding.

12. A corner of the classroom, or even the whole room, is set aside in order to recreate aspects of the book there; maps, collages, models or writing about the book. In a neighbourhood school with younger children, it may be possible to aim for a 'display day' after school for parents and brothers and sisters.

13. A series of pictures mounted on a long sheet of paper (e.g. wall-paper) so that a 'strip-cartoon' of episodes can be put on a roller and displayed.

14. A taped 'Book Programme' in which a group discusses one book or members contribute short reviews of different titles.

15. A short extract from the story is re-told as a radio-play onto tape (sound effects, introductory music, etc.). The tape might be played back to the rest of the class or to other, younger classes.

16. A sound track without words based on a very short extract from a novel. Action-packed pieces are most fruitful and enjoyable for this work (or strongly emotive passages). Close reading of the text should be necessary.

17. Groups are assigned to work either on the same book or on different books. The task is to promote the book to the readers of their own age—the group is, as it were, hired as an advertizing agency by the publishers. Their promotions can be written, spoken or taped. The effectiveness of the groups is evaluated by another class to whom their efforts are offered.

18. A simulated 'phone-in' programme with calls either to characters in a book, asking about their motives, attitudes, action, etc. or to the author. A character or the author might be represented by a group of about four, any one of whom can reply.

19. A set of 'opening-out' questions about a book (*not* mere factual checks) for the use of individuals and groups in younger classes.

20. A fairly short extract from the story re-told with puppets (short

because it seems better to become immersed in a close and thorough reading rather than spreading energies too thinly).

21. The group is employed by a movie tycoon to 'vet' possible sources for scripts. Would the book under consideration make a good film? Has it box office appeal, and for what kind of audience? Is the subject likely to be interesting *to look at*? Will the dialogue as it stands in the book sound like 'real speech' or will it have to be rewritten? Do any stars immediately seem appropriate for any of the roles?

22. Some major incidents from a book are selected. From these episodes, a page from a newspaper is composed that could have been printed where the story takes place. Appropriate headlines, news stories, interviews, pictures (or possibly polaroid photographs, though these are very expensive), advertizements, etc.

23. Pupils work in pairs—*A* is a librarian, *B* is a borrower who likes to know what a book is about before taking it home. *B* cross-questions *A* about plot, characters, setting, and 'the way it's written'. A useful exercise to introduce books to potential readers.

24. A post mortem, in which members of a class discuss *in role as characters in a novel*, the parts they have played. This activity fosters close examination of motivation. For example, a character who has been a 'victim' in the plot now has the opportunity to challenge the actions of more powerful characters. Discussion should be consistent with the text. A variation of this activity is to place one character (perhaps represented by several pupils) on a witness-stand for cross-examination.

Thirty-Six Things to Do with a Poem*

Geoff Fox and Brian Merrick
University of Exeter

The premisses which lie behind the suggestions in this article are:

(a) Poetry is to be experienced before it is to be analyzed.

(b) The enjoyment of a poem *is* often deepened by analysis, though such close study can be carried out obliquely through various classroom activities, not only through line-by-line study.

(c) We need to discourage any message, implicit or explicit, that poems are really puzzles to which the teacher has the 'correct' solutions.

(d) A poem rarely 'belongs' to its reader on one or two readings, particularly when such readings are immediately followed by an all-class discussion of an evaluative kind; in fact, 'Do you like it?' questions about the whole poem or its diction, rhythm, rhyme, etc. are best deferred as long as possible or not asked at all.

(e) Whether a poem is finally valued or rejected, we need to provide means for reflection upon it, bringing readers or listeners and text closer together.

The contributors to the list make no claims for originality. The suggestions are all 'classroom-tested' and may well have been borrowed from other teachers. Our hope is that a checklist may provide a range of possibilities for the inexperienced, a few new ideas for the experienced and an aide memoire for the overworked.

Ideas are offered not as developed schemes of work but as starting points, intended to be useful in making poems more accessible to pupils in the circumstances of most schools. In this rather skeletal form, some suggestions may seem banal or even philistine; but we hope that many of the ideas could be developed and refined for pupils of virtually any school age. Inevitably, some of the ideas would be inappropriate to some poems,

*Graham Baldwin, Barbara Bleiman, Ro3 Charlish, Dave Klemm, Colin Padgett and Andrew Stibbs also contributed to this article, which was first published in *The Times Educational Supplement*, 20 February 1981 and arose from a teachers' workshop course at the 1980 NATE Conference at Warwick University.

and we accept that the best teaching of a poem will almost certainly arise uniquely from that individual text; just as we accept that very often the best thing to do with a poem will be simply to read it, and let it be.

The group at Warwick felt strongly, however, that poetry often needs to have its way prepared. Sometimes, the mood of a class may be such that a particular poem is an appropriate response to the moment. More frequently, the constraints of a school timetable, especially at secondary level, mean that some kind of preliminary activity is necessary before a poem is introduced. Talk around and about a topic is perhaps the most common approach.

It may be that improvization is useful: turning the classroom from the moment the children come into it that day into a busy railway terminal for Spender's *The Express*, setting up the bar of 'The Red Dragon' as a context for the anecdote of Graves's *Welsh Incident*. For some poems the pupils' store of personal memories can be explored through concentration exercises and 'opening out' questions in the silence of their own minds or in a few minutes of private writing. For others, very simply, groups could be given only the title of a poem and asked to speculate about the poem's content.

Some of the Warwick group's more idiosyncratic suggestions have been excluded ('Prepare and deliver a sample of poets' work to houses in streets named after them ... Keats Way, Chaucer Green, Tennyson Avenue, Betjeman Mews'). We have also deliberately omitted some of the most valuable approaches to teaching poetry which stem from pupils writing their own poems. We presuppose that the ideas on the checklist will work most usefully in a climate where children are writing and talking about their own work; to have gone more fully into this area would have doubled the length of the list.

Many of the suggestions imply that children choose poems to work on for themselves. They would need time to browse amongst a range of poetry books—individual copies or small sets—in the classroom. The amount of help they need in this tends to decrease as it becomes a familiar practice.

First Encounters

1. The pupils listen to a couple of readings of a poem or read it silently, and then jot for five minutes of 'instant reaction' to hold, discover, and begin to develop their own responses.

2. Pupils listen to a taped reading, perhaps with the voices of other staff or pupils from other classes (see 7 below).

3. A poem is read, without discussion, every day for a week (by the teacher and/or by class members who have prepared their readings). Closer exploration of the poem may or may not follow.

4. A section of a display board in the classroom is reserved for poems

(see also 13). These are changed regularly and those that have been on display are put into a file which forms part of the stock available to the class.

Sharing and Presenting Poems

5. In pairs or groups, children work out ways of presenting different poems in dramatic form to the rest of the class.

6. Pairs or groups prepare their own readings of the same poem which are then heard and compared.

7. Groups make taped versions of poems for their own class, year, or other classes (secondary pupils make tapes for primaries and possibly vice versa) or exchange anthologies with a 'penfriend' class in another part of the country—perhaps with sound effects, music, etc. Particularly appropriate for a group of enthusiasts— e.g., Poetry Club or advanced students.

8. Teacher directs an all-class chorally-spoken version, including sound effects, if appropriate, using a tape-recorder in rehearsal to foster the class's own critical refinement.

9. Groups, with the help of specialist colleagues if possible, prepare some movement work to accompany a reading of the poem (taped or 'live').

10. Children choose photographs or slides to project during their reading of a poem.

11. Episodic poems (for example, ballads) are presented in a frieze to be displayed around the room. Each child is allocated a section of the poem and illustrates it, with the text included in the picture. Alternatively, a loose-leaf folder can be compiled.

Becoming Familiar with a Poem

12. Well-liked poems are copied out by individual pupils into an accumulating personal anthology.

13. Pupils make poem-posters, individually or in pairs, with some appropriate artwork to set off the text. Posters are then left for, say, a three-week period in classrooms or any 'safe areas' around the school.

14. Children learn poems by heart—a practice fashionably deplored, but deeply valued by many who had to do it. The choice of poem

could well be personal and lead not so much to a test as to a contribution in a group performance, perhaps around a theme.

15. Children listen to different taped versions of a poem and decide upon their preferences.

Exploring a Poem to Increase Comprehension

16. Group discussions, with or without a guiding framework, depending on how familiar the class is with such work.

17. Pupils *A* and *B* write brief 'instant reaction' papers and exchange them; add a comment on each other's responses before discussion.

18. Pairs or groups are presented with the poem with particular words omitted and asked to speculate about what might best fit in. If specific words are omitted rather than, say, every seventh word as in standard cloze procedures, groups' attention can be focused on particular aspects of the poem—its imagery, rhyme or rhythm, for example, as well as its diction.

19. A poem is given to the class untitled. In pairs, they propose titles, leading possibly to consensus. Compare with the poet's title.

20. As a way of exploring the structure of a poem, pairs or groups are presented with segments to be placed in what they judge to be the best order. This is then compared with the poem itself.

21. Some 'wrong' words are included in a version of the poem. In pairs or groups, pupils decide which they are and propose alternatives.

22. Pupils attempt parody or imitation: of a whole poem, or of specific techniques (for example, conceits) or of form (for example, concrete poetry).

23. Pupils make a picture (which may or may not incorporate the text) which illustrates or captures the essence of a poem. Abstract pictures might be feasible with older pupils and collage is also a possibility. Liaison with specialist colleagues could be helpful.

24. Invent the story behind the poem. What has happened before? What is happening 'off stage'? What might happen later?

25. Pupils play 'Chinese Whispers' (in which whispered messages are passed around the group and the original and final versions are compared). The 'messages' are sometimes prose, sometimes verse— perhaps a few lines from a ballad. The accuracy (ideally) retained

in the verse messages compared to the prose *should* open up the areas of rhyme, metre, oral tradition, etc.

26. Pupils rework a poem in a different genre (for example, as a newspaper item). What has been gained and what lost?

Asking Questions

27. Groups prepare 'factual questions' for others in the class or for younger classes, to use as a way in to the poem.

28. Groups prepare open-ended questions on matters of opinion about the poem for other groups to use.

29. Groups prepare a list of their own questions about a poem (matters of fact or of opinion) which they want to ask their teacher.

30. Pupils annotate a poem to meet the likely questions of another (possibly foreign) student.

Collecting Poems

31. Classes or groups prepare an anthology—written or to be spoken— of remembered children's rhyming games or jokes in verse.

32. Pupils 'find' poems—how many found poems are there around the school, the neighbourhood, today's papers, local graveyards?

33. Groups prepare an anthology of favourite television jingles to set alongside an anthology of most-loathed television jingles. Performed either on tape or live.

34. The English Department builds up and uses a stock of cassettes which include readings by poets, actors, teachers or children (see 7) of a variety of poems arranged in ten- or fifteen-minute programmes (cf. radio's *With Great Pleasure*). These might be grouped around a theme or a particular poet's work. The programmes can be heard, and re-heard, by individuals or groups and possible modes of response could be suggested at the end of a programme either on the tape or in an accompanying typed booklet (which might also include the text of the selection).

35. *Desert Island Poems*—a group or a pair (subject and 'Roy Plomley') prepare a list of, say, five favourite poems with readings and reasons for selection.

Demystifying

36. There still seems to be money (for example, in regional arts associations) to bring a poet into several groups to read his poems and to be asked any kinds of questions: these informal visits to manageable groups seem more useful than large poetry readings.

A Possible Thirty-Seventh

Forget It or Attack It—to persevere with a poem disliked by a class seems entirely counter-productive once it has had a fair hearing; and negative responses need to be expressed and respected.

Twenty-Two Ideas for Variety in Comprehension Work*

Mike Taylor and Bill Deller
Tutor in Charge, Essex County Language and Reading Centre,
Chelmer Institute and English Adviser, London Borough of
Waltham Forest

There is a groundswell of opinion among committed English teachers and academics against standard comprehension exercises—the sort that typically present a short passage, usually of fiction, followed by many often factual or trivial questions.

The problem, as Roger Knight (*The TES* 1 January 1981) said, is that there are strong institutional pressures which ensure that such a cut and dried, written and seemingly purposeful activity continues to be a staple diet in many schools with only cosmetic changes of vocabulary and approach.

Talented English specialists will no doubt continue to read stimulating fiction with their classes, exploring the issues and implications that sensitive reading involves, but there is clearly a need for an alternative orthodoxy which will enable hard-pressed or non-specialist English teachers to feel confident enough to escape from the passage-plus-questions model of comprehension.

The following list of suggestions was devised to enable a teacher, or better still, a department, to prepare practical ways of encouraging engaged, active reading. Several of them derive from the pioneering work of Christopher Walker and, more recently, the Schools Council 'Effective Use of Reading Project', 1979. Many of the ideas are most profitably undertaken collaboratively with pupils working in pairs or small groups. By discussing alternatives and by challenging or supporting opinions and hypotheses, pupils can progressively refine their reading responses and make explicit their developing comprehension of the text.

We do not claim that the list is particularly startling or original, and like any list of exercises it can be abused. (Cloze procedure, for example, seems, judging by some recently published material, to be developing into

*This article was first published in *The Times Educational Supplement*, 2 October 1981.

an often arid and empty exercise equally as stultifying as more traditional approaches.) All that is offered is a checklist of possibilities. The rest depends, as always, on the skill of teachers in the classroom.

1. *Cloze.* Pupils are given a copy of the text from which key words have been deleted. They have to provide replacements for the missing words. The skill is to delete various types of words or phrases from simple syntactical omissions through words, the substitution of which involves a sensitive understanding of the meaning of the text, right up to substitutions which demand stylistic or aesthetic discrimination. Where appropriate, whole chunks can be deleted and the pupils asked to speculate on what was in the original, working from their understanding of what is left. In our experience the danger of this technique is the 'right answer syndrome'. The value of the method must be in the discussion rather than simply homing in on the 'correct answer', that is, what the writer of the passage originally wrote. In many cases a group of pupils will come up with an equally valid alternative. Another variation is to give the pupils a text where bits of the original have been replaced by inferior alternatives.

2. *Prediction.* At its simplest this involves dividing a narrative into instalments and asking the pupils to speculate on what happens next, using evidence from the instalments they already have. The problem with this method is choosing a text, the outcome of which isn't blindingly obvious—most horror stories, for example—or too deeply obscure. In fact, it's better to choose a text where the development of the plot is related to the characters of the protagonists rather than to the demands of a genre (good literature in fact!). The number of instalments can be tricky too. The thing to avoid is a superficial guessing game. Pupils need to consider what a person like this would do/say next in a situation like this.

3. *Finishing Stories.* This is very similar to prediction only here pupils have to complete a story of which they are given the first part only. Their ending must be in keeping with the events, characters and style of the original.

4. *Sequencing.* This involves jumbling up the paragraphs of a piece of prose or the stanzas of a poem and asking the pupils to rearrange them in a sensible order. Pupils should be alerted to the syntactic and semantic devices writers use to order their texts. It is best to start with texts that have a clear, logical order like instructions or recipes or a strong narrative framework and then move out to texts of a more complex cohesion.

5. *Mysteries, Judgements, Problems.* The idea here is to present pupils

with a text which requires a decision of some kind. It may be a relatively simple problem—a 'whodunit' short story or a description of a mystifying event like the Marie Celeste story, where the pupils are required to choose between alternative theories. It may be a more human problem—a court case with the statements of various witnesses, or something from the problem page of a magazine. Here pupils give their verdict or advice on the evidence of the texts in front of them. Better still is a literary text which invites pupils to make judgements on the actions and behaviour of the characters involved.

6. *Compiling Questions.* After reading a short story or poem the pupils are asked to make up a few questions, the answers of which they would genuinely like to discover. If done between groups, one difficulty is that a group may ask questions competitively designed to catch another group out, or concentrate merely on asking low-level questions like the meanings of words. The idea of the exercise is that the group learns to question a text sensitively and concentrates on questions that are of real interest.

7. *Character Grid.* After reading a story or play, pupils are invited to match the central characters against a series of bi-polar personality constructs, for example, selfish/considerate; proud/meek; courageous/cowardly. This is best done using a simple grid. Animated discussion revolves around various characters' attributes and motives and likenesses and dissimilarities between them. More confident pupils can devise their own constructs and compare results with other groups.

8. *SQ and R.* Here a chapter of a book or a complete booklet is presented to pupils who rapidy *survey* it, noting as many clues to its content as possible (for example, cover, 'blurb', illustrations and sub-headings). These impressions are discussed and *questions* raised as to the likely content, relevance or bias of the extract. Pupils then *read* the complete passage closely matching content to their expectation. A particularly useful tool for developing critical reading of non-fictional material.

9. *Drawings, Diagrams, Cartoons and Illustrations.* Pupils can be asked to present a narrative in cartoon form, with a picture for each stage of the story, or they may be required to illustrate a scene or character incorporating as much information as they can from the text. For non-fiction passages they can re-assemble information in some visual form, a drawing, flow chart or table. Conversely, they may be presented with a passage with illustrations and asked to choose which most accurately represents the text.

10. *Skimming and Scanning*. Pupils should be encouraged to vary their reading strategy according to their own purposes and the nature of the passage. A passage can be presented, a time limit set and the pupils asked to jot down a one-sentence impression. Using time-tables, charts or telephone directories is a good scanning exercise. Questions may be asked before a passage is read and the pupils encouraged to read fast for the answers. The point to get across is that not all passages need be read at the same speed.

11. *Errors and Mistakes*. It is a good thing sometimes to 'de-mythologize' texts. Pupils should see that books and printed material are as open to error as any other form of communication. Errors of fact are the simplest place to start (out-of-date text-books are a good source) but it is important to alert pupils to mistakes in argument.

12. *Bias and Opinion*. This follows naturally from the previous idea. As a start pupils are given a passage and asked to underline first facts and then opinions. This can lead to a quite sophisticated discussion of bias as groups go on to consider texts in which facts may be missing or presented in a distorted way. Newspapers and magazines are a good source.

13. *The Implied Reader*. Pupils are asked to guess the intended audience of a passage from the evidence of its subject matter, style and presentation. Good sources are advertizements, text-books, magazines, official documents.

14. *Hard Words*. In groups, pupils are given a passage containing difficult vocabulary. They are encouraged to use the context to guess at the meaning and only use a dictionary as a last resort. At a more sophisticated level they can discuss the necessity and effect of such vocabulary. School text-books are a rich source. In the end they can make judgements about jargon, inflated writing and necessarily complex vocabulary.

15. *Fables and Parables*. Here pupils can comprehend a short but complete text by articulating the moral or point of the story. Aesop and the Bible are obvious sources.

16. *Multiple Choice Variations*. More interesting than the 'true or false' questions usually set, pupils can be asked to respond to statements which express opinions about the text or the writer's purpose by placing them in order of validity and importance. Listing in priority skilfully chosen statements leads to closer consideration of the meaning of a text.

17. *Different Versions*. The pupils are presented with different versions of the same prose piece or poem and asked to judge the qualities of

each. Good sources are various translations of the Bible, or other classic texts, or various drafts of poems. An interesting variation is factual and fictional treatments of the same event.

18. *Changing the Form.* Pupils are asked to use their understanding of a text in their own writing, talk or drama. The events of a story can be presented in the form of a newspaper article; characters can justify their actions to a 'jury'; key episodes can be dramatized or several characters can improvize a conversation.

19. *Open-Ended Questions.* Even if a basically traditional comprehension exercise is being set it is important to set some questions for which there is no obviously correct answer and which encourage readers to consider the text as a whole (for example, what happens to a character after the extract finishes? What sort of person do you imagine the writer of this passage is?).

20. *Texts, the Understanding of Which Results in Something Other than Writing.* The aim here is to get away from the idea that comprehension of a text always involves written or indeed oral 'answers', for example, instructions, recipes, knots or origami. The test of comprehension is whether you can do whatever the text is requiring.

21. *Logic and Philosophy.* This involves close reading of short, densely argued passages. You can start with small arguments in logic, through algorithms (logical trees) to full-scale philosophical arguments. It is best done in groups, with confident readers.

22. *Forms and Official Documents.* These are a rich source of material available from any Citizens' Advice Bureau. The aim should be not just to get pupils to fill in forms successfully but to discuss the user as implied by the content and presentation of the form and to resolve any confusions and difficulties which arise through poor design or wording. A recent publication, *Gobbledegook*, by Tom Vernon for the National Consumer Council has some useful examples.

While such activities provide a useful stimulus for developing active comprehension, we must stress that effective understanding of texts can only grow from the seed bed of a rich and varied programme of individualized silent reading through class, school and local libraries, bookshops and other activities: teachers must not feel they always have to *do* something with a text beyond encouraging children to read it!

Contributors

Anthony Adams is a University Lecturer in Education at the University of Cambridge. He has been both Secretary and Chairman of the National Association for the Teaching of English and has taught in a number of secondary schools. He is Vice-Chairman of the Schools Council English Committee. He has also written many books, articles and text-books on the teaching of English.

Gillian Barnsley is Lecturer in the Department of Curriculum and Teaching, Rusden State College of Victoria, Australia.

Michael Benton taught English for ten years in a variety of secondary schools before moving to his present post as Lecturer in Education at the University of Southampton. He has written a number of articles on aspects of literature teaching, co-edited the poetry anthologies, *Touchstones, Poetry Workshop,* and *Watchwards* (Hodder and Stoughton) and is a joint author of a forthcoming book, *Teaching Literature* (OUP).

Daniel Chandler taught English in comprehensive schools for seven years, most recently at Stantonbury Campus, an innovative community school in Milton Keynes. He is now a freelance educational consultant, spending much of his time running workshops for various educational groups on the creative use of the new technology. He believes that the microcomputer is the most powerful educational tool we have ever possessed.

Bill Deller has taught English in a variety of secondary schools and was for eight years Head of English in an 11–18 comprehensive. He is at present English adviser for the London Borough of Waltham Forest.

Geoff Fox has taught in secondary schools in England and the USA. He now lectures at the University of Exeter and has also spent several summers working with teachers in Australia, Canada and the United States. He has collaborated in books for classrooms and teachers, is a regular reviewer for *The Times Educational Supplement* and is an editor of *Children's Literature in Education.*

Eric Hadley is a Lecturer in Education in the University of Cambridge. He has taught in a number of comprehensive schools and has a particular interest in the teaching of literature. He is a member of the secondary committee of the National Association for the Teaching of English.

Peter Hanna is Principal Lecturer, Roehampton Institute of Higher Education, London.

Mike Hayhoe lectures in the School of Education in the University of East Anglia. He is interested in assessment and evaluation, has been a GCE examiner, is a member of a CSE panel, and is on the 12–16 committee of the National Association for the Teaching of English and its 16 + Examinations sub-committee.

David Jackson has taught in secondary schools and is now writing, lecturing, and teaching part-time at Toot Hill Comprehensive School, Bigham, Notts. He is also co-ordinating a local publishing project in Nottingham. He has edited various English text-books, such as *Family and School, The English Project* (Ward Lock Educational) and *Storyhouse* (OUP).

Len Masterman is Lecturer in Education at the University of Nottingham. He has taught in primary, grammar and comprehensive schools and in a College of Education. He has recently written *Teaching about Television* (Macmillan). At one time he contributed a regular television article to *The Times Educational Supplement* and was closely involved in the Schools Council Projects on General Studies and Social Education.

Brian Merrick taught in a variety of secondary schools before joining the English Department at St Luke's College, Exeter. He now lectures at the University of Exeter.

Bill Mittins retired recently after many years as a Lecturer in Education (especially the teaching of English) at the University of Newcastle. He is the author of a couple of school grammars and, with the assistance of three colleagues, of a study of attitudes to English usage. He is the present Secretary of the National Association for the Teaching of English as well as one of its past Chairmen.

Margaret Swan is Associate Professor and Principal, Nova Scotia Teachers' College, Truro, Nova Scotia, Canada.

Mike Taylor has taught in primary and secondary schools. He is currently tutor in Charge of the Essex County Language and Reading Centre, Chelmer Institute, which supports primary and secondary curriculum development in English teaching and language across the curriculum, as well as a range of award-bearing courses.

Andrew Wilkinson is Professor of Education at the University of East Anglia. He is author, or joint author, of various books, including *Spoken English* (1965), which formulated the concept of oracy, and *Assessing Language Development* (1980). He is the founder Editor of *English in Education* and *Language for Learning*. He is also an Italia prize winner.

He was formerly Director of the Language in Education Centre at Exeter University where the research described here was carried out.

Subject Index

Name Index